IS YOUR NAME LUCKY FOR YOU?

Lynne Palmer

Published by
Lynne Palmer

IS YOUR NAME LUCKY FOR YOU?

ISBN 0-9652296-7-X

Library of Congress Catalogue Number 99-093880

First Printing May 1999

Published by:

Lynne Palmer
Toll Free: 1-800-615-3352
Web Site: www.lynnepalmer.com
Email: lynnepalmer@lynnepalmer.com

Printed and bound in the United States of America

BOOKS BY LYNNE PALMER

Astrological Almanac (annual)

Do-It-Yourself Publicity Directory

Astrological Compatibility

Prosperity Signs

Signs for Success

Your Lucky Days and Numbers

Nixon's Horoscope

Horoscope of Billy Rose

ABC Chart Erection

ABC Major Progressions

ABC Basic Chart Reading

Pluto Ephermeris (1900-2000)

Money Magic

Astro-Guide to Nutrition and Vitamins

Gambling to Win

The Astrological Treasure Map

4

CONTENTS

Table: Alphabet and Astrological Correspondences to Numbers

	Vibratory Number		Vibratory Number
A...............	1=Mercury	N...............	14=Taurus
B...............	2=Virgo	O...............	16=Mars
C...............	11=Neptune	P...............	17=Gemini
D...............	4=Scorpio	Q...............	19=Leo
E...............	5=Jupiter	R...............	20=Moon
F...............	17=Gemini	S...............	21=Sun
G...............	3=Libra	T...............	22=Pluto
H...............	8=Capricorn	U...............	6=Venus
I...............	10=Uranus	V...............	6=Venus
J...............	10=Uranus	W...............	6=Venus
K...............	11=Neptune	X...............	15=Saturn
L...............	12=Pisces	Y...............	10=Uranus
M...............	13=Aries	Z...............	7=Sagittarius

Alphabet Combinations And Astrological Correspondence to Numbers

	Vibratory Number		Vibratory Number
CH...............	8=Capricorn	TH...............	9=Aquarius
PH...............	17=Gemini	TS...............	18=Cancer
SH...............	18=Cancer	TZ...............	18=Cancer

Table: Numbers And Astrological Correspondence to Alphabet

	Vibratory Number		Vibratory Number
1...............	A=Mercury	12...............	L
2...............	B=Virgo	13...............	M
3...............	G=Libra	14...............	N
4...............	D=Scorpio	15...............	X
5...............	E=Jupiter	16...............	O
6...............	U,V,W=Venus	17...............	F,P,PH
7...............	Z= Sagittarius	18...............	SH,TS,TZ
8...............	CH,H=Capricorn	19...............	Q
9...............	TH= Aquarius	20...............	R
10...............	I,J,Y=Uranus	21...............	S
11...............	C,K=Neptune	22...............	T

6

Fergie
London, England OW10 51N30
October 15, 1959 9:03 AM GMT

ASTRODYNES

PLANETS	Totals			Astrodyne Components						
	Power	%	Harmony	House	Dignity	MR	Aspects	Harmony	Discord	Neutral
MC	73.49	13.9	7.02	15.00	0.00	0.00	58.49	20.67	-13.65	44.21
Venus	60.06	11.4	13.16	14.92	-3.00	0.00	45.14	25.83	-12.67	31.47
Pluto	57.34	10.8	10.69	9.33	0.00	5.00	48.01	23.43	-12.74	31.53
MOON	47.57	9.0	-6.87	12.10	0.00	0.00	35.47	11.38	-18.25	25.10
Jupiter	43.86	8.3	11.08	14.10	2.00	0.00	29.76	26.40	-15.32	16.26
SUN	42.47	8.0	-10.36	11.32	-3.00	0.00	31.15	7.01	-17.37	22.11
Mercury	38.24	7.2	20.52	8.96	1.00	5.00	29.28	20.52	0.00	25.24
Neptune	37.27	7.0	17.21	9.09	0.00	0.00	28.18	18.02	-0.81	20.44
Saturn	36.69	6.9	1.14	8.33	2.00	5.00	28.36	24.20	-23.06	8.33
Uranus	32.98	6.2	-9.10	9.60	-2.00	0.00	23.38	6.30	-15.40	13.60
ASC	32.13	6.1	-15.85	15.00	0.00	0.00	17.13	0.00	-15.85	18.05
Mars	26.89	5.1	-3.38	11.12	-2.00	5.00	15.77	5.50	-8.88	19.97

Total   528.99 100%   35.26

HOUSES	Power	%	Harmony
Tenth	152.67	18.7	30.44
Ninth	124.71	15.3	-4.43
Eleventh	99.39	12.2	-7.16
First	97.04	11.9	-2.95
Twelfth	96.56	11.8	39.55
Fourth	67.85	8.3	0.20
Second	58.62	7.2	6.68
Sixth	30.03	3.7	6.58
Seventh	30.03	3.7	6.58
Third	27.04	3.3	-0.42
Eighth	19.12	2.3	10.26
Fifth	13.44	1.6	-1.69

SIGNS	Power	%	Harmony
Virgo	210.01	25.7	41.13
Scorpio	149.75	18.3	25.53
Libra	99.39	12.2	-7.16
Sagittarius	65.79	8.1	16.62
Aries	61.01	7.5	-8.56
Taurus	60.06	7.4	13.16
Capricorn	55.03	6.7	1.71
Leo	43.59	5.3	-11.69
Cancer	23.78	2.9	-3.43
Pisces	20.28	2.5	7.07
Gemini	19.12	2.3	10.26
Aquarius	8.70	1.1	-0.99

-SUMMARY-

Community	395.89	48.5	29.11
Private	279.26	34.2	42.86
Friendship	141.35	17.3	11.67
Success	241.32	29.6	43.70
Vitality	235.19	28.8	-9.07
Intuition	183.53	22.5	50.01
Relationship	156.46	19.2	-1.00

-SUMMARY-

Mutable	315.20	38.6	75.08
Fixed	262.10	32.1	26.01
Movable	239.21	29.3	-17.44
Earth	325.10	39.8	56.00
Water	193.81	23.7	29.17
Fire	170.39	20.9	-3.63
Air	127.21	15.6	2.11

FOREWORD

What's missing in your life that you'd like to add? Could it be a hobby, a needed career change or a love affair? Would you like to change your personality, or improve your character? Would you like to rid yourself of bad habits and adopt good ones? Do you have problems with the affections? Did you know that the preceding can be changed through having a name that is lucky for you?

The *New York Post* newspaper in the Aug. 9, 1979 edition had an article that Marisa Berenson, the actress, was going to change her name because she figured by so doing she could improve her image. The article stated, "And being a smart cookie, Marisa realizes how much publicity the former Francis Ford Coppola got himself merely by dropping the 'Ford' from his name."

The October 20, 1981 issue of *Star* newspaper had an article entitled, "Women's Names Affect how others see them." It stated that, "A women's name affects how people react to her and even influences whether they consider her attractive, a new university study reveals." A research team led by psychology Professor S. Gray Garwood of Tunlane University in New Orleans conducted a poll. Students had to choose a campus queen from photos of six equally attractive women at another school--they made up three attractive names and three unattractive names, and put them under the photos; the most votes were those with attractive names.

The *Glamour* magazine, September 1979 issue, had an article on a survey they had taken, "Changing your name when you marry." They asked, " What's in a name? A whole identity say some women who have refused to take their husband's name when they marry. They see their own name as such a basic part of themselves that under no conditions will they part with it. But others see a name as a symbol of their marriage union ---something they'd gladly change when they marry."

In their inquiry, they discovered that women are becoming more oriented toward "me" than toward being grouped as part of a group of society, "Women today want to keep their own separate identity, and we will continue to see more of this each day." From their poll it seems like the attitudes are changing, however, they found that hyphenating the maiden and spouse's surname is still shocking in various parts of the United States and that strong pressures still exist for a woman to drop her maiden name and use her husband's surname.

It has become fairly popular to keep a maiden name when married. I believe that when Farrah Fawcett married Lee Majors, and hyphenated her name, she started a trend that others have since followed in increasing numbers. After her divorce, she went back to her maiden name, like so many other women are doing on a larger scale today than they did decades ago. As women equal rights unfold more and more women will feel freer and want to express their individuality, thus they'll either use their maiden name or search for a new name that gives them a new identity. In my opinion there isn't any better way to do this than to use astrology to get a lucky name. It's a growing trend to change your name completely — more and more people are doing it daily. Through the years, I have helped hundreds of people change their names by using astrology. These people came from all walks of life: actors, actresses, models, writers, housewives, office workers, professional men and women, etc. Many wanted a name for their corporation; some wanted a good name for a marquee; and others consulted me for a good name for a newly born baby. The reasons could go on and on.

Much of my valuable time was spent adding letters to an existing name to obtain a name that would be lucky for the individual, or the nature of the business of a company or corporation in existence of about to be formed. In despair, I finally taught the interested person how to add his or her name and discover which planet or sign it vibrated to.

Many books have been written on the various systems of Numerology. With the exception of _The Sacred Tarot_ by C. C. Zain, this is the FIRST COMPLETE BOOK WHICH COMBINES BOTH ASTROLOGY AND NUMBERS. The ancient Hermetic System set forth in _The Sacred Tarot_, and my book, have not been altered as many present-day systems in Numerology have; it dates back to the Jewish Kabala, Moses, Abraham and Adam. This Hermetic System definitely works! I've seen it happen time and again. It's amazing to watch people change their personalities and attract luck just because they acquire a new name.

The September 29, 1979 _TV Guide_ had an article titled, "A Star is born (again)" and in sub-titles was, "Her once-bright career fading, Suzanne Cupito changed her name, her resume and her luck." And she did, and since that time, she has risen to star in "Moviola" on TV, playing the part of Scarlet O'Hara. In 1981 she got married---a southern wedding in a copy of the Scarlet O'Hara wedding dress---she has never been happier. She's portrayed Vivian Leigh in two films and the "Moviola"...She found her new name in a romantic novel. She decided to throw away the past and start all over again. "I was toying with keeping my first name and past and just making an easier last name. But one day I was reading an antebellum novel called 'Floodtides' and the heroine's name was Morgan Brittany. I just said to myself, 'That's it, that's perfect.' I took the last money I had, and flew to New York. I got six national commercial spots in a month. From there on, I'd hear, 'Where have you been?'"

From a lazy Venus (Suzanne Cupito) vibration she became known as Morgan Brittany, a Saturn vibration, the planet of ambition and hard work---the complete opposite of Venus! And according to the article, from the time she took her name, everything turned uphill for her.

And what about Marisa Berenson when she changed her name by adding on her famous grandmother's (French designer Elsa Schiaparelli) surname? Her former and new name both vibrate to the same number (10) and planet (Uranus), thus, this did not change her vibration— it gave her favorable publicity and because her thoughts are associated with this name, it will make her feel better and perhaps it will improve her image --that is if Uranus is a lucky vibration for her. This planet's influence is to be unique, different, original and non-conforming--thus she did use Uranus traits just by adding on the new name -- because Uranus is the planet that wants change and isn't afraid to do it regardless of what anyone else has to say about it. But she'll still have those traits with this same name vibration.

Furthermore, when Francis Ford Coppola dropped the "Ford" from his name, he didn't change his name vibration either--both names vibrate to number 7, Sagittarius. Therefore, by shortening his name, he made it appear more attractive, easier to remember and received tons of publicity--but he's still under the Sagittarian vibration--which by the way, is considered the luckiest sign in astrology. If Marisa Berenson Schiaparelli and Francis Ford knew the method as outlined in this book , they might have even fared better--only time will tell.

Through the years, various names are popular. Names become popular when associated with certain movie stars or heroine's in movies or books. In 1999, according to the Social Security Administration, the ten favorite names are: Kaitlyn, Emily, Sarah, Hannah, Ashley, Brianna, Alexis, Samantha, Taylor and Madison---all names for baby girls. The most popular names for baby boys are Michael, Jacob, Matthew, Nicholas, Joshua, Christopher, Brandon, Austin, Tyler and Zachary. And as each year passes, new favorites names will top the list.

And then there are names of a business, restaurant, company or creative works that you may take into consideration. Give a corporation a name that will make you wealthy and successful in your endeavors. Give an about-to-be-born baby a headstart on life by selecting a name that will vibrate harmoniously--a name that will give this child a positive outlook and bring happiness. Lessen your baby's heartaches or struggles that otherwise might be encountered while growing up. And why not change your own name, or add a letter, an initial or hyphen your name? That is if it hasn't brought you your desires. Attain Your Lucky Name by following the methods as outlined in this book. With the information contained in this book, you have an added tool with which to accomplish your goals and enjoy a richer, fuller future. So as you start this new journey, may I wish you bon voyage and love, happiness, wealth and prosperity with **Is Your Name Lucky For You?**

CHAPTER ONE

THE ANCIENTS: NUMBERS AND ASTROLOGY

As far back as one can remember people have been changing their names, either to please themselves or for a specific purpose in relation to their religions beliefs. Mystical activities were as popular in the past as they are today. The ancients from most cultures practiced all sorts of rites. They believed that numbers had magical powers that could help or influence others. Their children were given names that vibrated to numbers that would influence a child's lot in life and bring good health, wealth, happiness. Some numbers were meant to be good omens, others bad.

Not only did Kings and Queens change their names in the past, but so did ordinary people. Throughout all periods of life there were those who changed their name for one reason or another: many were writers, artists and actors. It is common practice for those who emigrate to change their name to a name which is easier for foreigners to spell and pronounce. The courts are filled daily with cases of this kind.

Many who changed their names in ancient Egypt, and in other times, followed some system. The Brotherhood of Luxor (Luxor is a town in central Egypt, on the Nile, where the temple of Luxor was built as a temple to Amon---the sun-God) was a select group (Akhenaton was a member) who followed certain principles and used a particular system called Hermetic. This system included spiritual areas, astrology, numerology, alchemy and magic. Only a chosen few knew the secrets it contained.

Amenohotep IV (some sources refer to him as Amenophis IV) began his reign as King of Egypt under this name (it meant "Amon--the God--is content, the god ruler of Thebes, but he changed his name to Akhenaton (some sources spell it Akhenaten) which some references say means Living in the Light, and others refer to his name as meaning, 'Service-able-to-the Aton.' The name change occurred when he instituted a complete reform to unify political, social and artistic life under the worship of one God; this worship centered about the Sun-god Aton. (Aten means 'light.') Aton represented the disk of the Sun and it means, 'It is well with Aton' and 'Aton is satisfied. (His new name joined words which expressed his religion of Life, Light and Love. Historians have recorded that, 'Such a synthesis of life and religion is unique in the world's history. Life was rich, beautiful, joyous and free, not in spite of, but because of religion. For the religion was one from which Akhenaton (Akhenaten) had banished superstition and fear and into which he had introduced sunshine and happiness.

Pharaoh Akhenaton (Akhenaten) transferred the capital of Egypt from Thebes to Amarnax, a new city which he called Akhenaton, "The horizon of the Aton." Prior to Aton the Egyptians had worshiped many other Gods, among which was Amun (some sources spell it Amen). Note the spelling of the names in both cases. Amen begins his birth name and Aton (Aten) ends his new name. Both Amen and Aton were Gods worshiped by the Egyptians and, as a ruler, he discarded one God and changed his name accordingly. This same name procedure was applied in reverse by King Tut and his wife.

Tutankhaton was born in Amarnax and at Pharaoh Akhenaton's death the
boy prince stood next in line to the throne. The prince was about nine years old when he married Ankhesenpatton, daughter of Akhenaton; this marriage secured his claim to be King of Upper and Lower Egypt.

About three years after Tutankhaton was crowned Pharaoh, and under the guidance of the priests of Amen (Bretherns of the shadow), he restored the God Amun to national importance, reopened his temples in Thebes, and polytheism once more became prevalent among the populace. Both Tutankhaton and his wife sanctioned these reforms by eliminating mention of the Aton in their personal names. He changed his name to Tutankhamun and his wife changed hers to Ankhesenamun. With the name change, both names now honored Amun, the God whom Akhenaton, during his reign, suppressed. At this time, the Hermetic system as practiced by Akhenaton was kept hidden from Tutankhamun and used by only a few that were close to Akhenaton. Through these various priests, etc., the Hermetic System was handed down, secretly, through the centuries.

During the Dark Ages, the doctrines involving the Hermetic system were kept hidden in the form of secret symbols and seals. In those days, if a person dealing in mystical areas was caught, his life was worth nothing! Eventually, the Brotherhood of Luxor (c. 1375 - c. 1358 B.C.) became the Brotherhood of Light and, in 1932 in Los Angeles, California, it became the Church of Light.

C. C. Zain, in his book The Sacred Tarot published by the Church of Light, uses the same letters, numbers, and astrological correspondents as Akhenaton used in ancient Egypt. In The Sacred Tarot he states, "The Hermetic System as determined through using numbers is quite unrelated to any system of numerology. Numerology, new systems of which are being devised each year, is a method of divination. But the vibratory science here explained, although dependent upon numbers for the determination of effects, is not numerology. It is a positive science, as precise in its results, and as independent of psychic matters, as any physical science.

Thus to use what is in this book you don't have to be psychic and you don't have to be well-versed in astrology; all you have to do is follow a few simple rules. The results will be very rewarding when your attitude and, thus, your life improves. The Hermetic system is also the only one that uses letters and numbers which vibrate to certain signs, planets, colors, gems or stones.

Just how did C. C. Zain discover this ancient system? He did historical research and found that it came from the Jewish Kabala and was used by the Jewish priests as part of their doctrine. It evidently first appeared to the outside world in the Seventh century, apparently through Neo~Platonist and Neo-Pythagorean channels (The Pythagoreans believed that the essence of all things was numbers and that all relationships could be expressed numerically. This view led them to discover the numerical relationships of tones in music and to some knowledge of lated Euclidean geometry. Their leader, Pythagoras, the Greek philosopher, had numbered the alphabet--taken from the Kabala). It wasn't until the Eighth century that part of the Kabala (that which involves numbers and astrology) put in an external appearance. Egypt, Crete, Chaldea, India, China, Mexico and Peru (the seven centers of the ancient world) also used the teaching of the Kabala. In fact, the ancient lands of Atlantis and Mu adopted it as part of the wisdom for which they became known. The main body of the Zohar part of the Kabala seems to have been unknown, except in the secret schools, until the Thirteenth century of our era.

According to C. C. Zain, the Kabala was originally passed through allegorical stories from Adam to Noah, Abraham, the Egyptians, Moses, David and Solomon. It was finally in written form at the time of the destruction of Solomon's second temple. Translators, C. C. Zain discovered, made use of the equivalent letters, but they had no knowledge of the vibratory rate it contained since they were not versed in astrology or the occult. But through the years, other systems of numerology and astrology grew out of the original one; thus, today you will find many different versions used by a wide range of people. But those who were involved in the occult used the original numbers and letters throughout the ages.

You may well wonder what numbers have to do with astrology and how it all works. "According to the Jewish Kabala," states C. C Zain in The Sacred Tarot," "... the universe sprang into differentiated existence in conformity to the law of numbers. In their interaction with one another, they form 22 astrological qualities...the 12 signs and 10 planets...22 numbers.

If you think about it, we are constantly dealing with numbers. Almost everything in life has a number attached to it: your address, telephone, model number of a TV set, radio or typewriter. a serial number if you're a member of the Armed Forces; even a dog has a number on a tag! Buildings are constructed through measurements (which are numbers); scientists use numbers in formulas. When you spend money on clothing, groceries or purchase a home, you are dealing with figures (amounts) which are numbers. It is practically impossible to escape from using a number!

C. C. Zain. in his book The Sacred Tarot, states that "The Hebrew, Chaldean and Coptic square-formed letters served not merely as letters, but also as numbers. That is, there were no separate letters for numbers, each letter being a number...And in tabulating the correspondence between the English alphabet and the ancient square-formed letters, the effort has been made, not merely to follow the precedent of translators of languages, but accurately to select the English equivalent in its thought-vibration quality of each of the 22 letters."

The Hebrew alphabet contains 22 letters; thus, there are 22 numbers (12 signs + 10 planets = 22). According to C. C. Zain, "...occult students use a true vibratory equivalent." You'll notice on the table page 5 that there is a "th" which equals number 9 and a "t" which equals number 22. As C. C. Zain says, "...the Hebrew Tau...is translated conventionally as Th; and Teth...is translated conventionally as T. But not only T in the form of the Tau cross used in many lands, but with its point down, thus represents the creative energy diverted to earthly ends, and as such it has the significance of 22 and not 9; and 9 has the vibration of Th, the serpent, the sprit of life, being the Deific number.

This translation of T and Th is the outstanding difference between conventional translators and occult students ....the real vibratory rate of a letter is the important thing in determining its correspondence in another language; and that the English equivalent of each square-formed letter has been tested out on this basis.

Furthermore, when C. C. Zain studied the Kabala, he discovered that each Hebrew letter represents an idea as well as a number. You may ask how an idea is represented by a letter as well as a number? The twelve signs of a zodiac and ten planets each govern particular types of thinking (and/or an idea) and a specific number vibrates to each sign or planet. Thus, every time you think in a particular fashion, astrological forces and numbers are set in motion.

The 12 signs and 10 planet have different characteristics which can be expressed as follows: Aries and Mars through using assertiveness, aggression and being constructive or destructive. Taurus through being patient, efficient, and stubborn. Gemini and Mercury through the use of the conscious mind to think, talk, learn and write. Cancer and the Moon through administering to the needs and wants of others, being emotional and feminine. Leo and the Sun through being kind, firm,, thinking about self-importance, being egotistical and masculine. Virgo through analysis, tending to detail and being critical. Libra and Venus through affection, love, friendship, companionship and social events. Scorpio and Pluto through sex, persistence, being compulsive, resourceful or obsessed. Sagittarius and Jupiter through religion, philosophy and optimism. Capricorn and Saturn through conservation, practicality, coldness and pessimism. Aquarius and Uranus through reform, originality and being independent, erratic and unreliable. Pieces and Neptune through promoting, dramatizing, using creative imagination or being lazy.

All thoughts radiate outward and influence, in one way or another, that which they contact. Whether the influence is harmonies or not depends upon how the energy expended is used. One person may use it and/or react in a particular way, whereas, another may express or react to it differently. One's conditioning since childhood, environment, horoscope, and name vibration (the planet or sign your name vibrates to) all play an important role in how you will be affected by your own thoughts and by those of others.

When you think about a variety of things at one time, you are using many thoughts which are representative of the planets and/or signs characteristics. If this occurs, your thought are said to be scattered--and they are!

Nearly everyone has certain characteristics that are more profound than others which are indicated by many planets being found in one sign, or by one planet which is more dominant than any other in a horoscope. If this occurs, your thoughts are said to be concentrated in one direction--and they are!

Your mind is continually working; thus, at all times you are tuned into a particular vibration which is ruled by a sign and/or planet and its corresponding number. Every time a person thinks about you, he or she consciously or unconsciously thinks of your name; thus, whatever your name vibrates to (the sign and/or planet and number) that individual is transmitting energy of that type to you. Now you can understand one of the reasons it's so important to have a name that is lucky for you!

In The Sacred Tarot, C. C. Zain mentions that, "Either a name or number, as such, is merely an abstraction, and has no energy to do anything. But when a name or number is thought, that thought is definite energy radiated toward the one then thought about. As such, it has also a specific vibratory key. Its influence is measured by the voltage of the thought; that is, by the energy supplied by the sender; and by the key to which it vibrates."

To illustrate the preceding, I will use a single name. However, normally both your Christian and Surname are taken into account, unless you, like Liberace, use a single name.

If you were to think about the name Jane, all by itself, it means nothing. However, if you know someone by that name, then you would associate the things you know about that individual with her every time her name was brought to the attention of your conscious or subconscious mind.

The name Jane vibrates to #3, which corresponds to the sign Libra (refer to Table: Alphabet and Astrological Correspondences to Numbers on page 5). J=10, a=1, n=14, e=5; thus, the numbers 10 + 1 + 14 + 5 added together equal 30, which breaks down to vibratory number of 3 (any number over 22 needs to be broken down to a final vibratory number — refer to Chapter Three for instructions.)

Thus, when anyone thinks about Jane, a Libra vibration will be directed her way. On the positive side Libra traits are expressed through being kind, charming, and lucky with socializing, friends and the affections. On the negative side Libra traits are expressed through being lazy, too sugary sweet, unlucky with socializing, friends an/or the affections.

If Libra is harmonious (according to her Astrodynes) for Jane, she will be bombarded with a high voltage of positive energy to attract good fortune in the areas which Libra represents. However, if Libra is discordant (according to her Astrodynes) for Jane, she will be bombarded with a high voltage of negative energy to attract misfortune in the areas which Libra represents.

You may ask, "What are Astrodynes?" Astrodynes measure the power, harmony and discord of the planets, houses and zodiac signs in a horoscope. For more information on Astrodynes, see Chapter Four.

Thus, you can understand that either you have a high voltage of positive or negative energy directed at you according to your name's sign or planetary vibration. Therefore it is important that you have a name that will be lucky for you. A name that, when others are thinking about you, will send harmonious vibrations in your direction rather than discordant ones. C. C. Zain believes (and

I am inclined to agree with him) that "Thoughts have the power to travel across space and bring physical changes." Therefore, by choosing a name that vibrates to a planet or sign that will benefit you, you'll be on the path toward attaining your desired goals. As your thinking changes because of the new name, so does your life. You attract what you think. Thus, find a name, use it constructively, and Lady Luck will be on your side.

CHAPTER TWO

WHAT'S IN A NAME?

The primitive tribes from the beginning of time invented titles and coined names to distinguish their members from one another. Often, after a child was born, he was given a name that seemed to fit a characteristic that he expressed continually. Or, maybe, the father wanted his son to possess a trait that would make others admire him, therefore, the boy might have been given a name that meant "admiration" in that tribe's language. Often the child's name came from one of their God's or from nature, an animal, an object they played or toiled with, or from a star, constellation, zodiacal sign, gem, stone, saint, martyr, hero, heroine, royalty, pagan ritual or religion.

In Iceland, the people are so welded to the past that they all still name themselves after their fathers, such as Olafsson and Olafsdottir (sons and daughters). It is against the law in Iceland to give a baby an untraditional name. Academic councils meet to decide the new names for concept and composites of the words of a name; they want to avoid polluting names. A farm keeps its name forever, no matter who's been tending it for the last few centuries.

Caesar was a Surname of the early Roman emperors that AFTER Hadrian (Aries name, Aries rules war, leadership) became the TITLE of the Junior Imperial colleague of the Augustus (a Taurus name; Augustus Caesar, a Neptune name---grandiose ideas; Emperor Augustus Caesar, a Capricorn name, a sign of ambition). When he used Augustus Caesar he vibrated to Uranus, a planet which represents revolutions, reform, new order).

The name Caesar by itself vibrates to Taurus, sign of beauty, the arts, and love. The words "Caesarean birth" (a caeso matris utere is Latin for "from the incised womb of his mother.") From an unhistorical tradition that the eponymous ancestor of the Roman family "Caesar". Julius Caesar was named "Caesar" because he was born by Caesarean section; also spelled "Caesarian;" Julieus Caesar vibrates to Sagittarius, a lucky sign, and "Caesarian" vibrates to Pisces, an illusive sign. Julius Gains Caesar (Neptune) was a Roman general, statesmen and writer. He introduced the Julian (Scorpio name; resourceful Scorpio) Calendar and many reforms. His Neptune name gave him grandiose thoughts. He introduced many reforms, was a dictator and was murdered.

"God" vibrates to Jupiter, the planet that rules Religion and Faith. Jesus, Christ and Jesus Christ vibrate to Aquarius, the humanitarian sign of one's fellowman. Jesus ushered (Aquarius) Christianity into the world \. He was known to be magnetic (Aquarius), intuitive (Aquarius) and a healer (Aquarius) through the touch of hand (Aquarius rules electromagnetic energy which is transformed from the hands to another's body used in ancient hands-on healing). His love of universal brotherhood (Aquarius) and the esoteric (Aquarius) has been written about. One of his teachings, "Love thy neighbor as thyself" is typical of the Aquarian philosophy.

A name that you think is English, most likely, was derived from an ancient Greek, Hebrew or Teutonic name. Names come from all corners of the globe, get changed in spelling and take on new vibrations. Most ancient names take on different meanings as they travel through the ages, due to the same method as gossip gets changed as a story is told by one person to another. Names came from the Bible, the puritans, romantic novel, poets, from the residence's of a family's ancestors or a person's forebearers had an occupation name because of the trade, business or artistic endeavor he was involved in: Baker, might have baked for a living, Cook might have been a chef, Blacksmith might have worked as a blacksmith. Names in the United States of America are more varied than anywhere in the world because of the immigrants who brought their foreign names with them; many were embarrassed by their long names that were misspelled and mispronounced thus they shortened or changed their name--or went by a nickname that an American citizen called them.

In modern times nicknames have become Christian (first) names. In many instances they have become more popular than the name they originated from. Shortened names are a growing trend, more so in the United States than elsewhere, possibly because Americans tend to be casual , informal, hurried and like to say a name quickly and spell it just as fast. Also people in the USA prefer names that are pretty, easy to remember and unusual.

People are breaking away from old tradition more and more as they become more individualistic than stereotyped. I've noticed this trend increasing. My clients who wish to change their name are more interested in inventing a name rather than going by one that someone else has. It seems like people are tired of the old and overworked names of the past. Novel names are popular and those who change to a name that is unique are enjoying the creativity that goes with thinking up a new name. Those who are not traditional nor clannish (Aries, Gemini, Libra, Sagittarius, Aquarius) with the family name are even changing their surnames (last) at a faster rate now than five years ago.

Most people have mixed vibrations because if you work with others at the office, you may have a nickname that your co-workers call you. Often people may not remember your surname, especially if it's difficult to pronounce. You may go to parties and meet people who only remember your Christian (first) name. Your parents may call you by your given name; perhaps your mother calls you by one name and your father another. Your spouse may have still another endearing name that she calls you. Thus, with all of these vibrations, you may grow up, and into, mixed vibrations. However, don't worry about it. As C. C. Zain states in his book, Imponderable Forces,"...Yet, because the people who think of him by these different names are not equal in the power with which they project their thoughts, nor do they think of him with equal frequency, these names have different importance as influences in his life."

In some cases, having more than one name vibration can be fortunate for you. There are many people who enjoy having these "multiple personalities" and wouldn't change them for anything — it's like an escape to another self.

To illustrate how two opposite types of energy can influence you, I will use William Shakespeare as an example. The name <u>William Shakespeare</u> vibrates to #15, the planet Saturn, which attracts tragedy, poverty, hard work, discipline, pessimism and a lack of confidence in one's abilities. In astrology it is considered the worst planet because is brings more misfortune than any other. The old English spelling Shakspere vibrates to #17, Gemini, the writing sign.

The name <u>Shakespeare</u> vibrates to #5, the planet Jupiter, which attracts comedy, wealth, optimism and confidence in one's abilities, and an "I don't care" attitude about a job, or an abundance of work happily performed. In astrology it is considered the best planet because it brings more fortune than any other.

Therefore, is it possible that when the public started to call him by Shakespeare (his surname) his luck changed? Did he have more confidence in himself? Is this when he started to write comedy? Did money start flowing his way more? Were better conditions attracted in his life? The answer to that lives with Shakespeare himself, or the historians; although part of his life and writings have been an unsolved mystery, calling forth many different theories.

Too many names result in mixed because they will vibrate to the different signs and planets that rule each name. By having many names you will create different and confusing vibrations. If you enjoy being a Jekyll and Hyde, several names which correspond to different signs and planets will keep you from being bored; but, success in a particular area might be hindered. By using one name, solidarity is created. If your stage or pen name is a harmonious vibration for you then this name can bring you <u>more</u> success when you legally change and use it at all times instead of using it on a temporary basis.

However, in the case of celebrities, there is an exception. <u>Every thought or action is composed of energy</u>. When actions or thought processes are put into use, you are vibrating to harmonies or inharmonious energy, depending upon how you utilize the nature of the sign or planet that is involved in the action and/or thought. Each planet or sign in astrology represents a particular mode of action or thinking.

The general populace may identify a famous person by a name other than the one the individual uses as his or her signature. When the public calls a well-known figure by only a Nickname, Pen-name, Stage name, Surname, or Christian name, the general populace transmits to the celebrity a large mass of energy which corresponds to the planet or sign to which the name vibrates. Thus, not only will the famous person vibrate to his or her own signature, but, also, to that of the public's. ("Babe Ruth, the famous baseball player," is a good example.) In some cases, this is beneficial; in others, detrimental. However, the celebrity will probably use his or her birth name more in personal matters. Thus, the <u>private life</u> will be more influenced by this name and vibration and the pseudonym will have a stronger influence on the <u>public life</u>. But either way you look at it, he or she will be bombarded with different types of thought-vibration. Hopefully, they will all be for his or her own good.

Right or wrong, people do judge others by their names as well as their personalities and personal appearance. When you're young and in school, kids call each other by nicknames. Many of these names are to make fun of a person's name. Children are impressive, and the bully type doesn't realize that these names hurt those who are being called by them. An obese person has been called "Fatso" and sometimes it sticks throughout that individual's life---unless, weight is lost. These type of nicknames are detrimental to an individual, but this game-playing of names has been going on for centuries. And until people have a better understanding of what they are creating, they will continue to call people by terrible names. It depends upon the nickname and individual involved as to what ego damage it does. ,

One individual may use a sign or planet's name vibration on the positive side, whereas someone else may use it on the negative side. As you read on, you will see how famous people have used the sign or planet that their name vibrates to, either on the positive or negative side, and what the results have been.

It's fascinating to discover just "what's in a name." For instance, the name Dolora vibrates to number 15 which is the planet Saturn. In Spanish, the word "dolor" means to have pain, grief, regret and suffer. The planet Saturn on the negative side has the same meaning.

Names can be very interesting, especially when your name vibrates to the same sign as your Sun sign, or your vocation, or character. Every name, including that of a business, city, country, animal or individual, has a vibration attached to it. This vibration corresponds to a planet or sign of the zodiac. Your name radiates certain characteristics which correspond to certain signs or planetary traits. These vibrations are brought into play subconsciously when others think about you, or when your thoughts are on yourself. The name you were christened with doesn't have much influence in your life unless you use the name constantly.

As C. C. Zain states in his book, *Imponderable Forces*, published by the Church of Light, "When people think of us by a name, whether it is a matter of reading our signature at the bottom of a letter, or merely that our name flashes into their minds, they usually, at least vaguely visualize us. Or if they do not know what we look like, the reading of a letter from us serves the similar purpose of focusing their minds so that their thoughts travel directly to us." When people think about you consciously, or subconsciously, the vibratory rate of your name is radiated from that person's mind to your own. When a person's mind is trained on you, you'll receive the vibratory rate of the name. The impact of the thoughts he sends to you can stimulate those thoughts in your physical body which have a similar vibratory key. Thus, if your name vibrates to Capricorn (the planet of stinginess), and you are involved in a financial transaction with another person, he may think of you as a tightwad even though you are generous most of the time; however, with this name vibration, your spendthrift ways, will be curtailed somewhat. Perhaps that will help bring you prosperity and happiness. But if it's a bad name vibration for you, according to your horoscope, then this Capricorn vibration could bring you losses of money due to the negative thinking that is easy to indulge in when your name vibrates to Capricorn.

The name to which you vibrate is determined by <u>how you sign your name</u>

on checks, letters, important documents, etc. According to C. C. Zain in his *Imponderable Forces* book, "...it would seem, then, that the name as thus signed probably would be more powerful as influencing him than any other designation. It would be more powerful because more thought energy of the vibratory rate of this particular signature would reach him than that of the rate of any other name."

You may say, "I sign my checks in a certain manner because that's my legal name; however, I think of myself under my nickname." This is not true because you still, subconsciously, think of yourself under this legal name; otherwise, you'd change your name and sign everything with the name you say is the one which expresses how you think of yourself. Therefore, when adding up your name so you can discover it's sign or planet vibration, keep in mind that *the name you use for signing* is how you think of yourself; and it's this name which vibrates to a particular sign or planet. This *vibration* governs *your actions and thoughts*, which are of primary importance in bringing you fortune or misfortune. But keep in mind that *your own thoughts* are much *more important* than the thoughts of others.

Did you know that, before they are finally released to the public, most movies are sent to a special research department to evaluate which title should be used? *Title testing*, as it is called, many times is performed through public questionnaires sometimes at the supermarkets, or sneak previews. Whereas others in the film industry go by their instincts when selecting a title. And yet, others go through a regular method statistical research. Many movies have flopped just because their title didn't interest the public. Thus a title, just like an individual name, is important.

Many movie, stage and television performers had already changed their names (before their names went up in lights and stardom seemed a reality) to a more impressive one to suit their show business personality. Often studio heads, an agent or producer choose their names. Methods of arriving at this theatrical name could be simple or complicated. (See Chapter Eleven). Many stars switched their last and first name or changed their Christian name, or used their Christian name as a Surname (last name). Or they dropped their middle name and used their first (Christian) and last (Surname), or used initials. He was born Herbert George Wells (Uranus; daring to be different. He changed his name to H. G. Wells which changed his vibration to Aries, also, (like Uranus) bringing Independence; however, Aries is Aggressive and brought out creativity and guts to push himself into the limelight. (For more on celebrities who changed parts of their names, see Chapter Six.)

Gloria Graham (lucky Jupiter) dropped her last birth name Hallward (Saturn; serious, and often negative vibration) and used her Christian and Middle name.

Often a manager of a potential star, changed that actors name. If you have a favorite star and want to adopt that star's Christian or Surname and combine that with your name, you can do so. Or do you have a favorite hero or heroine in literature such as "Tara" in *Gone With The Wind*? Or is there a product or name from a comic strip character such as the "Proctor" (A Jupiter name) of Proctor and Gamble (combined it is a Saturn name)? Or take a name from a comic strip character such as Superman's Clark Kent (Capricorn) or use Clark (a Uranus name by itself) or Kent (a Sagittarian name by itself) as a Christian or Surname.

Many stars adopted their mother's maiden name or their mother's first or second husband's last name. Or you can adopt a name from one of your parent's side of the family. Or take your husband's last name and hyphenate it with your maiden name, such as Farrah Fawcett did when she married Lee Majors (Scorpio: Scorpio is sex appeal with plenty of animal magnetism): she became Farrah Fawcett-Majors until she got her divorce at which time she returned to her original name.

Farrah Fawcett (Sagittarius) can't seem to get away from a Sagittarian vibration. When she used Farrah Fawcett-Majors, it vibrated to Sagittarius. The show on TV that skyrocketed her to fame, "Charlie's Angels," happens to be a Sagittarius name vibration and she starred with Kirk Douglas (also a Sagittarius name) in a movie titled "Saturn 3." She's known to be a tennis enthusiast and good player (Sagittarius rules sports).

MARRIAGE: YOUR HUSBAND'S NAME OR YOUR MAIDEN NAME?

Taking a husband's name is becoming an outdated custom more and more in our society. If you are single and plan to marry, keep in mind that your fiance's Surname will change your vibration and life. If this new Surname is more harmonious (depending upon the planet or sign to which it vibrates) than your maiden one, use it, otherwise, change it, or keep your maiden Surname. However, if your maiden name and husband's surname (when added to your first name) vibrate to the same planet/sign and this is a lucky vibration for you then it's all right to take your husband's name, if you so desire.

If you are married and your spouse's Surname is an unlucky vibration for you (depending upon the planet or sign to which it vibrates), you can either add an initial, add or drop a letter, use your maiden Surname, or change your Surname (through marriage) to a new one. Or you can hyphenate both names such as Olivia Newton-John did, that is if it is harmonious for you to do so according to your horoscope. Many people think that hyphenated names look classy, elegant, rich.

Use your married name (the one that's inharmonious for you) as little as possible--only when absolutely necessary. It would be best not to use it at all but don't let it be the cause of a divorce; if it is, then your husband's ego is in the way toward your being happy and lucky with a harmonious name. The divorce may be a solution to other deep-seated problems that may surface in the future.

Don't think that it's confusing to your children if you and your spouse have different surnames. Children are bright and this can be explained intelligently to them when they are old enough to understand it. It doesn't harm them and besides, they may brag about how modern their parents are!

There are many people who are superstitions about numbers and will wait for a certain day (number) to arrive before doing anything. Rita Hayworth is a typical example. She only signed contracts on the 17th of the month because her given name contained 17 letters, she was born on October 17, made her first acting appearance on November 17 when she was 17 years old. However, the name Rita Hayworth contains 12 letters. Her name has been identified for years with "Gilda," the role she portrayed in a movie by the same name. Isn't it ironic that "Gilda" vibrates to Libra (Rita's Sun sign) and Venus rules Libra as well as the name Rita Hayworth?

She was born Margarita Carmen Cansino (Capricorn). The "Rita" came from Marga rita. The Capricorn name vibration she was born with was not a lucky name; she was fortunate her name was changed. Libra is the sign of beauty, charm, dancing and is associated with love and marriage. How easy it is to remember her many marriages and search for happiness with a companion.

Mohammad Ali (Uranus) has always spoken out (Uranus), regardless of others. His unusual (Uranus) religion and beliefs created controversy (Uranus). His career went up, then went down, then back up again to win the title of world champion; these sudden reversals are all typical of how Uranus works. Mohammad Ali has had Parkinson's disease for a number of years. This disease is associated with the planet Uranus---his name vibration. Uranus rules high-strung nerves and tremors and twitching. Did his name attract this disease?

A celebrity can use a professional name and that name could be abbreviated in the newspapers to save space. However, the celebrity can then become known by both names. Christopher Reeves vibrates to Aquarius (sudden recognition, magnetism, anything different) and in the newspapers he was called Chris Reeves which vibrates to Mercury (newspapers). He played the part of "Superman" which vibrates to Mars (fights, physical action, nerve, guts, accidents and energy). Mercury, as well as Uranus, is involved with the nerves and its cells. Paralysis is ruled by Uranus and Uranus rules the sign Aquarius---like attracts like. Thus, as Christopher Reeves, (Uranus) did he attract paralysis (Uranus) when he had the accident (Mars) on the horse? By playing the part of Superman (Mars name) and being associated with that role did that association attract his accident?

Speaking of a film character portrayed by a movie star, one which is extremely interesting is Boris Karloff, who played Frankenstein and made himself known as a horror specialist. Both Boris Karloff and Frankenstein vibrate to Uranus (horror, shocks, the unusual and bizarre). Is it coincidence, or just fate, that he was given this role? Or did he attract the part because his name vibration was synonymous with the name vibration of Frankenstein?

He answered to "Higgins" (Saturn) until his new owner discovered him and renamed him "Benji." (Jupiter) While under the Saturn name vibration he didn't live so well; but, with his new Jupiter name vibration he started living much better. You moviegoers know this dog as "Benji". Prior to his acting career, he was living a simple (Saturn) life without too much fanfare or any delicacies (Jupiter). Since his name change, Benji has lived well (Jupiter) eating filet

Mignon steaks. It just goes to show you that even a dog who has a name change can be lucky!

The performer who used to be called "Prince" (Taurus; love and artistic vibration) was born Prince Roger Nelson (a lucky Sagittarian name). However, he changed his legal name to an Egyptian symbol. The public, and all press articles---the media---do not refer to his symbol's name, instead he is called, "The Artist Formerly Known as Prince," which is also a Taurus name---therefore, what good did changing his name do? Ironically, his Sun sign is Gemini, the dual and changeable sign that often is confused or makes others confused.

Shania Twain (an aggressive go-getter Mars name) was born Eileen Twain (a lucky Jupiter name). The name "Shania" means, in Ojibwa Indian dialect, "I'm on my way."--and she certainly is---all the way to the top.

Keanu Reeves (Cancer) is a successful movie star. His first name in Hawaiian means "cool breeze over the mountains." On his highschool hockey team, he earned the nickname "the wall" (Aquarius); unique and fast).

He was born Shaquille Rashaun O'Neal (a sensitive and creative Pisces name; also his Sun sign is Pisces). His professional name is Shaquille O'Neal, a lucky Jupiter (planet of wealth) name. When he is called Shaq O'Neal, he vibrates to Taurus, a steady and kind sign; however, when he is called by his nickname Shaq he vibrates to Neptune, the planet of acting, movies, promoting---he is an actor, rapper and basketball player. His Christian name "Shaquille" translates to "Little One."

Greta Garbo (Pisces, sign of intrigue; born Greta Gustafson, Aries, aggressive). The world at large always thought she stated, "I want to be alone," (this sentence adds up to Aries). However, what she really said was "I want to be left alone," (this sentence adds up to Pisces). A Pisces vibration can make a person want to hibernate and live in the world of their imagination. It brings mystery to the individual. When you hear the name "Garbo" (Venus) by itself one immediately thinks of Garbo's beauty. (Venus rules beauty).

Joseph Stalin (Taurus) ruled Russia with an iron fist (a Taurus trait). He was stubborn (Taurus) and changed his name from Joseph Vissarionovich (a Neptune-idealistic-name) to Stalin, which means "Made of Steel."

CREATING A NAME

If you are entering into show business as an actor, actress, singer, dancer, or are already in the theatrical profession, you may want to alter your own name, or select a new one. It's important to have a good stage name--it's your trademark, your bread and butter. Your new name should be easy to remember and not too long for a marque. It should suit your personality and vibrate to a harmonious sign/planet in your horoscope.

You may want a name that is a variant or dimitive of a name, such as Laurua--var. And dim., Laurne, Laureen, Laurel, Lora, Lorelie, Loralie, Loretta, Lorette, Lorinda, Lorine, Lorna, Lorne, Lari, Loree, Lori, Lorie, Lorrie. Or you may want to create a different name from one of these names, i.e., Lorni.

You may invent a name that comes from a certain section of the city or country. For instance, if you like driving along Laurel Canyon in the hills of Hollywood, how about using the name Lauri Canyon?

If you have a popular celebrity that you want to name your child after, perhaps you can change the lettering in the star's name around and come up with a name that is unique and interesting. If you have a hero or heroine from a book or real life that you'd like to take for your own, or name your baby after, maybe you can combine part of that person's name with another name, thus making up a name. Or use the Christian or Surname of the person you worship and combine it with one of your names.

When creating a name listen to the sound of the name. Make sure it sounds attractive. Avoid mixing the names of one foreign country with a name of another foreign country such as Alessandro Schwartz or Roberto Krauss.

If a surname (last) is short (one syllable), it usually combines best with a Christian (first) name of two or more syllables. Doesn't the surname of Jones (one syllable) sound good with the Christian name of Melanie (three syllables) Melanie Jones?

If a surname is long (two or three syllables) like Wallenstein, how about adding a Christian name that's one syllable, such as Joyce?--Joyce Wallenstein. If you have a two-syllable surname, try a Christian name of one or three syllables, i.e., Marylou Decker, or with a three syllable surname, a Christian name of one or two syllables, i.e. Dee Landers or Penny Gordon. Most Christian and surnames combined sound best when the syllables of both names are unequal in number. However, this doesn't always hold true as in the case of Jane Doe, Ruth Blair, Beth Jones.

If your name is hard to remember and difficult to pronounce, you'll have problems such as embarrassment or mistakes will be made in the spelling of your name--thus changing its vibration. If you choose an unusual spelling, which people are doing today, make sure it's easy to pronounce. Also, the sound should be pleasant. Usually a Christian name and surname that begin with the same letter don't sound good together. The combination may be awkward or sound phony, i.e., Rose Roberts. Also, you want a name that looks like you; if you're pretty and choose a name that sounds ugly to most people--like the name Chloe is ugly to me, others may be turned off by this new name. However, if you are unattractive and have this name, it will suit you well, that is if it vibrates to a harmonious sign/planet in your horoscope.

Create a name that's easy to remember and spell as well as pronounce; also one that sounds good and is lucky for you according to your horoscope. Keep the Christian name simple if the surname is undistinguished, i.e., Henrietta Butt. Avoid over-weighing a name (combining a Christian long name with a surname that's long) i.e., Raymond Channing--Ray Channing is better.

YOUR ABOUT-TO-BE-BORN BABY'S NAME

In the Jewish tradition it's normal for the parents to name a child after a beloved member of the family who is deceased. In the catholic faith, children are given the name of a saint--either their Christian (first) or middle name. If you want to name your baby after a favorite aunt, or other relative, perhaps you would consider an offshoot from that name i.e., your aunt's name is Anabelle, thus you name your baby either Belle, or Ana.

If the baby is to born at an odd time of the year, on the holiday, you might consider a name commerative of that event. Or you could take the month she's to be born and switch the letters around i.e., September could be either Ember or Sepa.

Read the sign and planet traits in Chapter Five and if there is a planet or sign that has characteristics you'd like your child to have, make sure that his/her name vibrates to that sign/planet. Or if you don't like the traits of a particular sign i.e., Pisces is lazy, may lie or procrastinate--however if your baby is to born under this sign, choose a Sagittarius (honesty) or Aries (energetic) name vibration. This will counteract some the discord associated with his future Sun sign Pisces.

Diminutive names (characterized by small, little, tiny, petite--it comes from certain affixed or words formed by their addition that signify smallness, familiarity, endearment) should be voided especially if it denotes petiteness. The baby may grow up to be tall and statuesque and be ridiculed with a name that denotes smallness. However the first chance she gets, you can expect a name change if she outgrew her diminutive name i.e., from Georgette to Georgia. When giving a baby a name take into consideration that he/she may grow up to be famous, respected, honored, in a high position or prestigious; therefore give him/her a name that will cover these possibilities.

Often parents want their child to have a name that means something; therefore the original meaning of the name may be your method of choosing a name for your baby. There are many dictionaries that contain the origin of names as well as books out on the market. But remember, for your child to be lucky with that name, it has to vibrate harmoniously either with his horoscope (which you don't know because he hasn't been born yet) or choose a sign/planet in Chapter Five that has great characteristics i.e., Sagittarius, Jupiter (the luckiest sign and planet in astrology).

Keep in mind that the name you choose for your baby is to be a part of her/his identify for life. This name can affect her/his personality, popularity (especially at school-she/he may, or may not, be invited to parties because of her/his name) or the name may give her/his certain feelings about herself/himself and can affect how successful or unsuccessful she'll/he'll be when she/he grows up and gets a job; it may even give her/him difficulty in attracting a mate if the name is ugly and unlucky for her/him.

Don't pick a name for a girl that is too masculine because others may laugh at her, especially in school; the other children may call her a boy and make idiotic remarks such as kids in their innocence are known to do. There are many boy's names that are perfectly acceptable for girls. The women's lib has popularized this trend of using boy's names for girls; often boys are given names that are associated with a girl's name. However, nowadays there is less importance attached to the masculine and feminine names especially since short hair cuts for women have been in style and long hair for men been the vogue since the 60's.

If possible try to avoid naming a baby "junior" --it's just an ego trip for the father to have his son named after him. Through the years there have been movies, television shows, books, and magazines articles that have expressed the pitfalls that are attached when a child is named "junior." This is bad psychologically for a child to have to live up to the image of his dad, especially if the father has been successful. It may also prove embarrassing to the father when he's in the middle years of his life and he's called "old Robert" and his son is referred to as "young Robert." People today are searching for their own identity and want to be unique, therefore avoid adding "junior" to his name. If his dad wants his son to be named after him, use a different spelling of the name. If the boy's father is named Robert, call your baby boy Robin, Robi, or Bert. Also you may want to add in a middle name to make it even more distinct from the father's name.

If you are choosing your favorite name of your about-to-be-born baby, make sure it's harmonious astrologically. If she grows up disliking the name, she may use a derivative of the original name; therefore make sure the derivate's of the name are also harmonious astrologically.

CHAPTER THREE

HOW TO USE THIS BOOK...CALCULATING YOUR NAME

Follow the methods outlined in this chapter regardless of whether you are looking for a lucky name for your baby, corporation (business, restaurant, sole propriorship, etc.), title (story, book, song, play, movie), a name for yourself or merely adding up an existing name.

An Existing Name

1. Add the name according to instructions in this chapter under the heading Calculating Your Name.

2. After you've added the name, turn to the sign/planet that it vibrates to in Chapter Five.

3. Read the positive and negative side of sign/planet.

All areas of life are different. You don't attract bad luck with everything, although occasionally it may appear that way. Usually there is something lucky somewhere for everyone. It's up to you to search for good fortune, if you don't have it, and do everything in your power to grasp it. Thus, by having your name vibrate to something harmonious within you, your character and your life can improve. The type of events attracted to you will depend upon the thoughts within yourself that have the same vibratory rate as these events. The events and thoughts are ruled by sign or planetary and their expression depends completely upon you.

4. If you are expressing a sign/planet on its negative side, this implies that you need a name change, especially if difficulties were caused as a result of your expressing these negative traits.

Whenever you realize that you are expressing the negative side of a planet or sign, immediately displace those traits with positive ones. Feel proud of yourself as you do this. However, it is better to have a definite type of thinking planned in advance just in case you goof. Thus, you'll be ready to replace the negative thoughts with positive ones (or positive action); gradually it will become easier and, before you know it, you will have formed a new good habit!

Note: When you start to change your thoughts to harmonious ones, put an enormous amount of *emotional energy* into the new way of thinking. This can be done by tuning in to past memorable occasions when you were extremely happy; thus, this new *joyful emotional* energy will be channeled into harmonious areas.

5. If you are expressing both the positive and negative side, you will experience both good fortune and misfortune with the name. It would be in your best interest to change the vibration and, thus, attract mostly harmony in your life. But there are people who crave excitement and thrive under discord; so, if you are one of these people, keep the name that brings difficulty, but try to follow some of the suggestions for your name vibration (sign and/or planet that your name vibrates to) under "How To Make The Most Of Your Name" at the end of the sign/planet section (Chapter Five) and try to tune into the negative traits and tune in to the positive ones.

6. If you are expressing the sign/planet on its positive side, read the end of the sign/planet section titled How To Make The Most Of Your Name.

7. If you want to be 100% accurate that this name is lucky for you, send for your Astrodynes (See Chapter Four).

8. Read Chapters Twelve and Fourteen to see how famous personalities used the same name vibration (sign/planet your name also corresponds to).

A New Name

1. For 100% accuracy that a name is lucky for you, send for your Astrodynes (see Chapter Four).

2. If you do not send for your Astrodynes and/or you do not know your birth time to do so, then read Chapter Five (Planets and Zodiac Signs). Determine which sign/planet you like best. Perhaps there are several that you like and want as a name vibration.

      a.   Analyze yourself truthfully.

      b.   Did those things happen to you?

      c.   Would you like those things to happen to you?

      d.   If you read all of the planets and/or signs traits, which one describes the actions you most desire? The one you choose, perhaps, should be what your should vibrate to. For example: to be no if you've wanted to be independent, but have been afraid pick a name that will vibrate to Aquarius or Uranus.

3. Once you've decided on the planet/sign that you wish to express (you want your name to vibrate to), you must have your Christian (first) and Surname (last) vibrate to that sign/or planet's corresponding number. The number is given at the beginning of each sign/planet section.

4. Follow the instructions under the heading Calculating Your Name (page 30).

5. If you have difficulty getting the name to come out to the sign/planet desired, perhaps you need to add or delete a letter. To facilitate a name change, read Chapter Six (Changing Parts of Your Real Name), Chapter Seven (Names, Names, Names) and Chapter Nine (Using One Name).

6. Once you have a name that corresponds to the sign/planet vibration that you have chosen, follow the suggestions in that sign/planet section under the heading How To Make The Most Of Your Name (Chapter Five).

With your new name you will attract those things that are representative of the name by planet or sign vibration. Whatever your desires, hopes, or wishes, your new name will be a positive force to help in their realization.

With your new name, you will discover that you have changed. Your personality will take on the traits of the planet or sign that your name vibrates to. Luck will be attracted and your life will be better than it had been previously.

7. Once you decide to use this new name, don't allow anyone to call you by the old one.

Insist that people call you by it, and you will discover that you're nicer to everyone and more at peace with yourself. These are very subtle influences, but they are definitely present and can help to determine what is attracted into your life. Therefore, don't allow pressures from your spouse or family to stop you from using your new name. Don't be passive and give in to their demands; it's your happiness that comes first--that's at stake NOT what THEY want for you, it's what YOU WANT FOR SELF THAT COMES FIRST. It takes time to change your bank account, charge accounts, and establish credit in the new name--but it's easy to do; it can be done with a postage stamp and copy of the court order showing your change of name.

Remember to correct people! Be firm! Don't allow anyone to say your old name without reminding them of the new one. Continue with this procedure until they adapt to the new you. Make others understand how important it is to your well-being and happiness to be called by the new name. If they can't comprehend this, or remain stubborn, then explain that you will not talk to them until they respect your desires. If they really care about you, they will abide by your wishes; otherwise, they don't want you to be happy or lucky--they are being selfish.

Relatives are the most difficult to deal with, or people with planets in fixed, (stubborn) signs (Taurus, Leo, Scorpio, Aquarius), because they resist change. With them, you will have to stand by your rights and demand relentlessly, that they call you by your new name.

Your life will improve simply by having a name that vibrates harmoniously to you. However, depending upon how energetic you are, you can take positive action and reinforce additional harmonious energy to your name; thus even more favorable events will take place. How does one do this? Read on--

If your name is lucky for you probably, without having to think about it, you will express the positive side of the sign or planet most of the time.

8. Read Chapter Twelve to see how celebrities used the same name vibration as your new name.

9. If you decide to change your name, it's best that you do it legally. The only way that a name change will be accepted by authorities on official documents is through a court action. That is if you aren't trying to evade a debt, responsibility, take advantage of someone else's reputation, and if the courts find your reasons proper and understandable. The price to make the change will vary from $50 to $350, depending upon your lawyer's fee.

All legal papers, accounts, social security, stocks, mortgages or loans should be changed to your name. Notify the institutions involved by sending them a copy of the court order of the name change. This should be done even if it's only a letter or initial that is added or deleted from the original name. If you don't follow this procedure, your name will not vibrate entirely to the planet or sign that rules the name. However, if your new name vibrates to a #6 and your given name also vibrates to a #6, there is no need to legally change your name unless you want to for business or other purposes; you will, one way or the other, still vibrate to #6--A Venus vibration. If you use your new name on some things and your old name or other things, you will vibrate to mixed vibrations.

CALCULATING YOUR NAME

RULES: ADDING YOUR NAME

Use the following to find your name vibratory number for your Christian name (first name), surname (last name), middle name, birth name, nickname, pen-name, stage name, or the name you are using or wish to use:

A.   Add all of the letters of your name (for numbers and letter correspondences, refer to table: Alphabet and Astrological Correspondences to Numbers or to Table: Alphabet Combination and Astrological Correspondences to Numbers, both on page 5

Note: For each name or initial every letter should be added as a single entity, unless there is a double letter that vibrates to a particular number (example: 'th' is a double letter that vibrates to number 9. Do not take either the 't' which vibrates to number 22, or the 'h' which vibrates to number 8 separately).

Example: Audrey Smith

A=1   u=6   d=4   r=20   e=5   y=10
Total=46

S=21   m=13   i=10   th=9   (the 'th' a double letter.)
Total=53

After adding each letter in your Christian, Surname and/or middle name or initial, you should have a separate total for each name; however, it's perfectly all right to have one total result of adding both numbers together. But by adding and totaling the names separately, you can continue adding one name and making different totals for many new combinations.

For example: You like the name Audrey, which totals 46; but when you added Smith (in Rule B) you found (in Rules C and D) that the total name of Audrey Smith is unlucky for you; thus, you want to change your Surname to a luckier vibration. Once you have the total of Audrey, you don't have to repeat adding it; just add it's total (46) to any Surname you have chosen.

B.   Add the total figures of each name together, including the middle name or initial (if these are included as your complete name). The result is your new total number. This new total number is broken down to a final vibratory number (The final vibratory number from #1 to #22, cannot go over #22, if it does you have made an error--the table only goes as high as #22.

The Vibratory Number

Example 1:   Audrey totals 46 and added to 53 (total for Smith) your new total is 99. Break the new total number of 99 down to a final vibratory number by adding the 9+9 to each other and the result is your vibratory number of 18.

Example 2:   If your total number, after adding the Christian and Surname to each other, is 320. Break that total down to a final vibratory number of 5 (3+2=5; the 0 is not added).

Example 3:   If your total number, after adding the Christian and Surname to each other, is 566. Break that total down to a final vibratory number of 17 (5+6+6=17).

Example 4:   If you are using a single name (like some famous people—Liberace, Hildegarde, Colette) the total of that single name is broken down to a final vibratory number. For example: Audrey totals to 46; broken down to a final vibratory number it totals to #10.

C.   Turn to page 5 and locate your vibratory number on the Table: "Numbers and Astrological Correspondences to Alphabet." That vibratory number equals a sign or a planet which is listed for the number's correspondence. For example: vibratory number 18 (Audrey Smith's name) corresponds to the sign Cancer; thus, the name Audrey Smith vibrates to the sign Cancer.

Difficult Vibratory Numbers To Obtain

The numbers that are the most difficult to obtain are #1 and from #17 to #22.

Example #1

Liv Ullmann vibrates to Vibratory Number 1., which corresponds to the planet Mercury.

L = 12		U = 6		28 Total
		l = 12		+
i = 10		l = 12		72 Total
+		m = 13		
y = 6		a = 1		100 Total
28		n = 14		
Total		+		100 breaks down to
		n = 14		vibratory number 1
		72 Total		

Example: #2

A vibratory number of 20, which corresponds to the Moon, is difficult to obtain because there are no numbers above 21 that add up to 20 until you reach number 299. This number 299 breaks down to a vibratory number of 20. Since this is so difficult to obtain, and if you wish a Moon vibration, try for vibratory number 18, which corresponds to the sign Cancer. The moon is the ruler of Aries; thus, the characteristics are similar.

Example: #3

A single name that vibrates to vibratory number 21, which corresponds to the Sun is difficult to obtain.

$$L = 12$$

$$a = 1$$

$$.d = 4$$

$$+$$

$$\underline{d = 4}$$

21 Total

Example: #4

To obtain a complete name (Christian and Surname) that vibrates to the sign Leo or the Sun is difficult. Carroll O'Conner has a name that vibrates to Leo, vibratory number 19.

C= 11	O = 16	92 Total
		+
a = 1		107 Total
	C = 11	
r = 20		199 Total
	o = 16	
r = 20		199 Total which
	n = 14	becomes vibratory
o = 16		number 19.
	n = 14	
l = 12		
+	o = 16	
l = 12	+	
92 Total	r = 20	
	107 Total	

Note: Not only does the name Carroll O'Conner vibrate to the sign Leo, but his Sun sign also is Leo; so this reinforces the Leo energy and makes him more of a Leo than he would be if this was only his Sun or name sign vibration. Every time I see a re-run of "All In The Family" television show, which he starred in for so many years, I always identify him with a Leo type of character. The role of Archie Bunker has the traits of being a chauvinist, the head of the family image, and some bigotry--this is the discordant side of Leo.

Doctor, Junior, Senior

If you are a doctor and you sign your name as such, add it in as part of your name. If everyone calls you doctor, you will constantly vibrate to it. However, if you only use the "doctor" in business with clients, you will not vibrate to it all of the time. By using the "doctor" as part of your name on occasions, you will eventually become accustomed to its vibration and adapt to it.

If the name has a Junior or Senior and you sign everything as such, then add in the Jr., or Sr., as part of your complete name. If it isn't used very often, then you will not be stimulating that part of your personality to which it vibrates (sign or planet traits). If you use it all of the time, and people call you by it, you will constantly vibrate to the Jr. or Sr.

Note: When Dr., Jr., or Sr., is part of the name Add these abbreviations. Don't add the letters of the word as it would appear spelled out, such as: Doctor, Junior, or Senior. It's the abbreviation that is signed, not the written form; thus, the abbreviation is the vibration involved. Also see the rules for adding your name.

Titles and the second and the third, etc.

Titles are added to names if you sign the title as part of your name, or are constantly identified with the title. If you sign the title as part of your name, the complete set of words would be the main vibration. If you are identified with the title, but only sign it occasionally, you will only vibrate occasionally to the title.

If Queen Elizabeth II signs documents as Elizabeth II, Queen of England, then she must add her complete title to obtain the correct name vibration. If you have a title, add the II as 1 + 1 = 2. Also see the rules for adding your name.

If you sign as Robert White, III (the third), add Robert White, III by the same method in preceding paragraph (1 + 1 + 1 = 3). Also see the rules for adding your name. Also, see Chapter Eight, Royal Titles.

Business Names

A name of a business may be chosen in the same manner as an individual name. When adding a business name, include the words, the, of, Co., Ltd., Inc., if applicable.

Even though the individual who signs the company checks may have a different vibratory quality than the business name, it will not interfere with the name chosen for the company. The business name will operate independently of other influences--it is the name of the company that people know, not the person in charge of signing the checks. See Chapter 7.

Partnerships

The following applies to married couples and business partners: the "and" is added in when adding the Christian and Surname of each person. When checks are signed the "and" is not included, but the check is made payable to both parties and the "and" is used.

Note: the public will respond to partnership names in exactly the same way as they respond to an individual name. See Chapter 10.

Foreign Names

If you have a difficult name to pronounce and it's always being mispronounced, don't worry about having the wrong vibration sent in your direction. A name vibrates to thought (characteristics ruled by the signs and/or planets), not vocal action. When you see a name written it registers in your conscious and unconscious mind more quickly than if you had heard the name spoken.

The spelling of a name may differ from country to country; but if the English letters are used in the transliteration according to the way they are presented on page 5, the name will vibrate to the same planet or sign as listed on page 5.

The English spelling, therefore, only indicates the vibratory significance of the name to those who use the English spelling. If you write in Spanish, French, German, or other languages, you are still using the English alphabet; although, with the German you may have a few added changes. When this occurs with the language, always use the English transliteration as given in most dictionaries or encyclopedias and use that transliteration with the alphabet printed on page 5. It is the alteration of the spelling of a name, even though the phonetic value is unchanged, that changes the vibratory rate and the inner meaning of the name. Also see Chapter Eight, Transliterations.

CHAPTER FOUR

ASTRODYNES

What are Astrodynes? Astrodynes are a mathematical method of measuring the power, harmony and discord of every sign, planet and house in a horoscope. They have been used for years by many astrologers, especially those who use the Hermetic system of astrology as originated with The Church of Light. The only EXACT ACCURATE METHOD of knowing your harmonious signs and planets is determined by Asttrodynes.

The Church of Light
2119 Gold Avenue S.E.
Albuquerque, NM 87106

They charge a fee for a copy of your birth certificate and you must request, but they may not give or know, your time of birth. Without the time of birth, you cannot have the Astrodynes computed. If this be your case, read Chapter Five and analyze the signs and planets to determine which one you use the most on the positive side. Use that sign or planets number as the final number you need in order to calculate your name. See Chapter Three, Calculating Your Name. Often a person has more than one harmonious sign and planet in their horoscope. If this occurs, an individual has a better chance of selecting a name that will be lucky. However, if none of the planets or sign are harmonious (through Astrodynes) then take the weakest of the bad and use that sign or planet as your best.

This chapter explains how to read the Astrodynes page as computed by Astro Numeric Service. As an example, I will use Fergie which added vibrates to Venus which, you will see, is a lucky name (it's a nickname) for her. Her name Sarah Ferguson vibrates to Aquarius and brings out unconventional behavior and independence. However, this is not a lucky name for her. And she did receive a lot of bad press along these lines—and still does. The Duchess of York vibrates to Mars, the planet of anger, sex, aggressiveness, and impatience, it is not lucky for her. When she uses Sarah Ferguson, The Duchess of York she vibrates to Sagittarius—that is lucky for her. It keeps her optimistic, full of fun, outgoing and happy-go-luck. However, with all of these anmes called by friends, the media and relatives—she is vibrating to mixed vibrations.

Fergie's Astrodynes are on page 6. Therefore, the following is based on her Astrodynes.

How To Read The Computer-Print Out
Astrodynes Page

THE DOMINANT PLANET: The column to the left has PLANETS at the top. Underneath is MC, Venus, Pluto, Moon, Jupiter, Sun, Mercury, Neptune, Saturn, ASC, Mars. (The MC is the 10th house cusp in a chart and does not concern us for choosing a harmonious name. The ASC is the Ascendant, Rising Sign, 1st house cusp) in a horoscope and does not concern us for choosing a lucky name.)

Since Venus is listed below the MC (it is in second place) and Pluto is in third place, this implies that Venus is her dominant planet and Pluto her second dominant planet. The Moon is her third dominant planet and so on down the list. To select a lucky name, we do not need to pay attention to dominant planet.

THE BEST PLANET: Look at the top where the Dominant Planet was found. To the right of the word PLANETS is the word POWER and to the right of it (still under the TOTALS section) is the word HARMONY. Under the HARMONY column, you will notice some numbers with a - minus symbol and other numbers without a symbol in front of them.

Those numbers with a Minus symbol are discordant planets. Those numbers without a symbol in front of them are harmonious planets. To determine the PLANET that is Fergie's First BEST, take the highest figure without the minus symbol which is 20.52; from that number, go to the left (under Planets column) and you will see Mercury. Therefore, Mercury is her first BEST planet. The next highest figure is 17.21, to the left (under Planets) is Neptune---Neptune is her second BEST planet. The third highest figure (number without a minus symbol is 13.16; to the left under Planets is Venus, her third BEST planet. Her fourth BEST planet is Jupiter. Her Fifth BEST planet is Pluto, and in last BEST place is Saturn. Therefore, a lucky name for her could vibrate to any of these planets. If your name comes out to a planet that vibrates to a planet with a minus symbol, you should change your name. A name vibrating to them could cause misfortune or problems.

THE DOMINANT SIGN: In the middle of Fergie's computer print-out page (page 6) is a column on the right that reads SIGNS. Underneath it are Virgo, Scorpio, Libra, Sagittarius, Aries, Taurus, Capricorn, Leo, Cancer, Pisces, Gemini, Aquarius. The sign at the top of the column (Virgo) is her Dominant sign and the sign at the bottom of the column (Aquarius) is the least Dominant Sign. To select a lucky name, we do not need to pay attention to Dominant Sign.

THE BEST SIGN: In the middle of Fergie's computer print-out page (page 6) is a column on the right that reads SIGNS. To the right of it is a column that reads Power and the last column to the right reads HARMONY. Under the HARMONY column, you will notice some numbers with a - minus symbol and other numbers without a symbol in front of them.

Those numbers with a Minus symbol are discordant signs. Those numbers without a symbol in front of them are harmonious signs. To determine the sign that is Fergie's First BEST, take the highest figure without the minus

Those numbers with a Minus symbol are discordant signs. Those numbers without a symbol in front of them are harmonious signs. To determine the sign that is Fergie's First BEST, take the highest figure without the minus symbol which is 41.13; from that number go to the left (under SIGNS column) and you will see Virgo. Therefore, Virgo is her First BEST sign. The next highest figure, under the Harmony column, without a minus number is 25.53; to the left under the SIGNS column is Scorpio, her Second BEST Sign. The third highest figure, under the Harmony column, without the minus number is 16.62; to the left under the SIGNS column is Sagittarius, her Third BEST Sign. The fourth highest figure, under the harmony column, without a minus number is 13.16; to the left under the SIGNS column is Taurus, her Fourth BEST Sign. Her Fifth Best Sign is Gemini, followed by Pisces and Capricorn. Therefore, a lucky name for Fergie could vibrate to any of these signs.

Note: Those numbers with a minus symbol, and the Signs to the left, are discordant signs and are her worst signs; these sign vibrations are her worst; therefore, a name vibrating to them could cause misfortune or problems.

As I mentioned previously, if there isn't any harmonious signs and/or planets, take the weakest one with a minus symbol in front of it under the Harmony column for Planets and/or Signs.

SELECTING A NUMBER THAT YOUR BEST
SIGN AND/OR PLANET VIBRATES TO:

Refer to tables on page 5: Alphabet & Numbers and Alphabet Combinations & Astrological Correspondences To Alphabet. For Example as mentioned previously, her name Fergie vibrates to Venus. On the table (page 6) Venus has a #6 vibratory number; therefore, the letters of her name should be added and the total number should equal 6. See Chapter Three, Calculating A Name. But to give you an example of Fergie:

F = 17   Note: Once the numbers of a name are added, the final

E = 5   number is broken down if it exceeds 22; drop

R = 20   the zero in 60, and the result is 6. The Table on

G = 3   (page 6) indicates that #6 equals Venus.

I = 10

E = 5

+   60 = 6 = Venus

Read Chapter Five, Venus on the Positive side and you will see what Fergie responds to. For her other names, look in Chapter Five also under those planets her other names vibrate to.

You should choose a name that is going to be lucky for you. Make sure it's attractive and will bring you the things you want (see the sign/planet it vibrates to).

CHAPTER FIVE

PLANETS AND ZODIAC SIGNS

There are two sides to a coin and likewise there are two sides to all twelve signs of the zodiac and the ten planets. Because they radiate energy of a specific type they can affect you to the point of expressing their energy on the positive or negative side. Good fortune or misfortune is experienced as a result. By changing your name to vibrate to sign or planet, these qualities will be enhanced. Read the traits and ask yourself, "Do I wish to add these characteristic to my personality?" Read the traits of all the signs in this chapter and see what qualities you admire, want to take on as part of your personality, then choose Your Lucky Name.

ARIES AND MARS

Aries vibrates to #13   Mars vibrates to #16

Mars is the planetary ruler of the sign Aries. They have similar traits, thus they are combined.

POSITIVE EXPRESSIONS

If you've experienced luck as a result of using these positive traits, this indicates that an Aries/Mars vibration would be good for you. Or if you need more of the Aries/Mars characteristics in your make-up, because you feel they are lacking, it then may be advisable to change your name to this vibration.

You are fearless, competitive, and are always in a hurry to accomplish a task or goal. You have tireless energy and an enterprising nature. You are a go-getter and act fast in an emergency. You're full of zest and enthusiasm.

You are moved with inspiration as you impulsively and enthusiastically jump into deals; they usually are concluded to your satisfaction. Your gambling spirit leads you into taking chances that wind up in your favor. You are aweless and go where angles fear to tread. It's necessary for you to compete and win-- usually you do. You strive to be the best in all undertakings. Others have difficulty keeping up with your fast pace.

You've got lots of guts and will do just about anything on a dare. You are a person of action and can create, develop and produce anything you decide to tackle. Your aggressiveness gives you the results desired. You like to keep busy constantly, thus you're always initiating new projects--the bigger, and more challenging they are, the better.

Jobs are quickly done; as soon as one is finished, you are ready to start the next. You are self-assertive and audacious. Your ability to withstand hardship and discouragements is amazing to others. You can work at a job that takes courage, stamina and is venturesome. You thrive with spice and adventure in your life.

You're attracted to someone who is difficult to win. You enjoy conquering the person you're interested in. Excitement is needed in everything, including a relationship. And when it comes to lovemaking, you are ardent, passionate and extremely sexy.

NEGATIVE EXPRESSIONS

If you've experienced conflict, arguments, adversity, problems and misfortune as a result of these negative traits, this indicates that an Aries/Mars vibration would be bad for you. Therefore, avoid obtaining a name that vibrates to Aries or Mars.

When you take chances involving risks or uncertain gain, you usually wind up behind the eight ball. Most of the time when upset, you react with violent rages, especially if you're intoxicated. It seems that you're constantly being involved in feuds, brawls, and fights. Insults are hurled at others without thinking of the consequences. You cuss, rant and rave most of the time especially when things aren't going your way. It doesn't bother you if others think you are rude, coarse, or unmannerly.

You are brazen, bossy, demanding, easily aroused to anger, hasty and reckless in matters of the heart. It is difficult for you to sit still. Slow-moving people drive you up the wall. You can make wrong decisions because you are too hurried and leap impulsively into situations. You may have too many irons in the fire. Risky ventures could result in disaster. You may undertake enormous tasks that are too big for you to handle. Your aggressiveness could cause difficulties with others.

Your main thoughts are on self--it's a "me first" attitude that others see. You couldn't care less what others think of you or your actions. The air around you is tense and you are ready to explode at the least sign of provocation form a loved one, friend, co-worker, boss or employee. You interrupt others so they can barely finish a sentence. Because you blurt things out, you're constantly in hot water. You are energetic, peppery, heedless, noisy, overly-aggressive and quite lustful.

Your rushing about keeps you on a tightrope existence. Deadlines must be finished right now! You take on so many projects that you get all keyed up in trying to complete them; often they are abandoned or given to others. You are impatient and can't stand to wait in line; you push to get ahead. Accidents, fires, fevers, operations and cuts are almost a daily occurrence. You are the horn-honker in a traffic jam. Delays bring your temper out so does just about everything else.

HOW TO MAKE THE MOST OF YOUR ARIES OR MARS NAME

If you have discovered that your old name is beneficial, try to follow these suggestions, thus you will enhance your name vibration and attract even better luck. Also follow these suggestions if this is your NEW NAME VIBRATION.

If you wish to add further harmony into your life, wear the colors or gems for the sign/planet your name vibrates to.

<u>Note</u>: Most people have more than one sign/planet that is lucky for them --I hope you fall into this category.) If you are limited in the colors you wear, use these lucky colors for accessories.

Perk up your energy by wearing all shades of light or bright red--such as fire-engine red! Choose an amethyst to wear as jewelry. Be creative. Build something, perhaps an empire. Get involved in something daring and challenging.

Take an active part in athletics, sports, exercises, Karate, or go to a roller derby, ice skating rink, circus, tennis or bowling tournament. Watch others perform dangerous feats. Do something that has a touch of adventure. Explore new areas and go on a hike in the mountains. Camp out, or go fishing.

You will be inclined to be a daredevil or want to construct something magnificent. Your sex drive will be increased. Excitement in all areas of your life will be craved and can be satisfied by leaping right in and conquering any obstacles put in your path.

Use common sense and moderation in all actions; otherwise danger, accidents or strife can be attracted. Rather than argue, have sex or do something physical like cleaning the house. Enter into competition if you feel quarrelsome or initiate a new project by being nervy and courageous. If someone irritates you, do something protective for a helpless animal or handicapped person. Afterwards, glow.

Give others a chance to finish a sentence. Be courteous instead of ill-mannered. To avoid being late, leave more time than you need so you don't have to rush and become high-strung, tempermental or bump into or drop things or hurt yourself. Get up earlier instead of sleeping late. Stop fidgeting when you have to wait in a line; you'll get there just as fast without tying yourself up in knots. Be creative and make mental plans whenever you're in a traffic jam. Keep in mind that positive action leads to success.

TAURUS
Taurus vibrates to #14
POSITIVE EXPRESSIONS

If you've experienced luck as a result of using these positive traits, this indicates that a Taurus vibration would be good for you. Or if you need more of the Taurus characteristics in your make-up, because you feel they are lacking, it then may be advisable to change your name to this vibration.

Your actions are slow, but steady. You have a methodical mind. You are neat and orderly. Efficiency is a must. You're practical, conservative, reliable and industrious. You dislike taking risks but believe that one has to spend money to make money. You go out of your way to obtain material possessions. You plod along patiently waiting for your plans to materialize. It's easy for you to save for a rainy day. You dislike being rushed. You are charming.

You view everything in a nonchalant manner. You don't get excited about anything until it has been proven to be of value. However, even then, you aren't exuberant but you become more interested in the project because you know it's going to pay off. You're the calm, cool, and collected type; it seems that nothing much fazes you. Your even-temperedness makes you a delight to be around.

The social scene is a highlight in your life, especially if you are mingling with the elite, or those who are on their way to the top. Your friends are usually successful. You entertain elegantly, are courteous and expect good manners from others. Your home must have all the comforts; luxury items are displayed--they are status symbols. You are conscious of what you own and enjoy showing your treasures to others. The price you paid for expensive objects is mentioned when there's a guest you want to impress; you're proud that you could afford them. You won't buy anything that is beyond your means. You are a true collector, not only for investment purposes but, for their anesthetic value. You are attracted to the fine arts, antiques, beauty or fashion.

You bide your time before getting involved in a romantic situation. Yo are quiet and thoughtful with loved ones. And when it comes to lovemaking, you are sensuous and may be overly indulgent. You are possessive but not in a way that attracts problems from others.

NEGATIVE EXPRESSIONS

If you've experienced conflict, arguments, adversity, problems and misfortune as a result of these negative traits, this indicates that a Taurus vibration would be bad for you. Therefore, avoid obtaining a name that vibrates to Taurus.

Your household is run smoothly and orderly, but with an iron fist. You want to own and rule the people you care about. You're a person who asserts your opinions with an overbearing and arrogant manner. Your stubbornness is unbelievable; you won't give an inch. If anyone tires to oppose you, a stalemate is likely to occur.

You think and move at a slow pace. You refuse to budge if someone tries to rush you. Your decisions take a long time and result in losses because you weren't quick enough. You dislike making changes and, thus, get caught in a rut which leads to stagnation.

Your desire for perfection could cause losses or problems with others. You are possessive of property, wealth or people. You get upset if objects are moved without your knowledge. You get disturbed when someone makes a mess in your home or office.

You are materialistic. When it comes to spending money, you're known as a tightwad. Everyone probably says that you've got every penny you've ever earned. You have a horror of debt but can carry it to such an extreme that others are left with making sacrifices, because you are too cheap to buy something that is termed "frivolous" in your estimation.

You are unyielding when it comes to taking a risk. Your obstinacy on a job, or with a loved one, will cause all sorts of problems--but you quietly shut everyone out as you go about living or doing your duties. You could lose the object of your affections because you take too long to make an advance. You are so possessive with your mate that difficulties are attracted. You have strong physical and sexual appetites; however, you tend to do too much eating and drinking. As a result, you could have a weight problem.

HOW TO MAKE THE MOST OF YOUR TAURUS NAME

If you have discovered that your old name is beneficial, try to follow these suggestions, thus you will enhance your name vibration and attract even better luck. Also follow these suggestions if this is your NEW NAME VIBRATION.

If you wish to add further harmony into your life, wear the colors or gems for the sign your name vibrates to.
(Note: most people have more than one sign or planet that is lucky for them--I hope you fall into this category.) If you are limited in the colors you wear, use these lucky colors for accessories.

Wear all the dark shades of yellow and it'll brighten your day. Don copper jewelry or a ring, bracelet, necklace, etc., that has an agate or opal encrusted into its design. Deal with art, fashion, music, dolls, gardening, real estate or finances.

Go to museums, art galleries, jewelry exhibits, fashion shows, concerts, or the ballet, opera or theater. Take lessons in dancing , decorating, designing or something which involves cosmetics or the hair. Make ceramics, pottery, or jewelry. Be creative and add a new dimension to your life.

Entertain, socialize, mix and mingle at gatherings. Make friends by being gregarious, kind and charming. Smile and others will be attracted to you. You will be inclined to go to parties and be companionable and interested in love. All the aesthetic beauties of life will please you. When you listen to beautiful music, you'll feel enraptured and stirred, or perhaps you'll want to dance to it. If you complete a work of art, become elated and show it to others.

Get involved in romantic adventures. Do not think of past bad experiences. Be loving, giving and enjoy the present. But use caution and discretion with all involvements. Watch your emotions and sensitivity.

Get involved with a project that will make you feel important. You'll delight in the recognition you receive from others. Keep in mind that positive action leads to success.

GEMINI AND MERCURY

Gemini vibrates to #17   **Mercury vibrates to #1**

Mercury is the planetary ruler of Gemini. They have similar traits, thus they are combined.

POSITIVE EXPRESSIONS

If you've experienced luck as a result of using these positive traits, this indicates that a Gemini/Mercury vibration would be good for you. Or if you need more of the Gemini/Mercury characteristics in your make-up, because you feel they are lacking, it then may be advisable to change your name to this vibration.

You are popular at parties and gatherings; you've got a bubbly personality that draws others to you. Also, your wit is a great attraction. You can discuss any subject that may pop up. You're an intellectual and enjoy conversing with those who, will not only listen to you but who, will teach you a few interesting things in the process. Seldom is a book read from beginning to end, instead you skip about glancing at a page and getting an instant understanding of what's written there.

You are able to read several books, or watch two television shows simultaneously. Your eternal quest for information leads you down many paths. Every topic interests you. You're known for "knowing a little bit about a lot of things."

You are adaptable able to adjust easily to change. You liven dull and quiet atmospheres to a swinging tempo. You're open-minded and thrive only when you are continually active. It's easy for you to mix with all types of people and make everyone feel at ease. You are good at telling stories or jokes. You like to talk in front of a crowd or to anyone who will listen to you.

Your mind seems to work like a carousal--it just goes round-and-round while you're actively engaged in thinking, talking, writing, reading, learning or teaching. You are aspirant and get mentally carried away with topics you find intriguing. Your memory is excellent. You can unscramble codes, puzzles or solve problems. You are a quizzical conversationalist who ask questions to increase your knowledge. It's important for you to know the "why" and "how" of things. You can make excellent decisions, judgments, or verdicts.

You enjoy traveling to new places--a change of scenery is a must. It would be easy for you to live out of a suitcase. Curiosity about life and people draws to all cultures and all types of acquaintances. You can sing, lecture, teach, write, type, work with figures (accounting, etc.), or as an agent. You are attracted to the communication field. Your awareness of time makes you punctual on the job and in your personal life also.

You constantly seek new and lively companions, excitement and novelty. Communication is a necessity in a romantic relationship. You use reason in matters of the heart rather that physical feelings. You like to be kept guessing in a romantic situation. Love-making is fascinating if you've found the right person who can stimulate your mind. Experimentation with sex is a diversity you enjoy.

NEGATIVE EXPRESSIONS

If you've experienced conflict, arguments, adversity, problems and misfortune as a result of these negative traits, this indicates that a Gemini/Mercury vibration would be bad for you. Therefore, avoid obtaining a name that vibrates to Gemini or Mercury.

You build castles in the air and get high thinking about all the things you want to do. If you attempt them, you get so bored that they are rapidly abandoned. It's difficult for you to stick with things because of your changeable nature. Thus, just as success is around the corner, it slips from your fingers. Most of the time you are tardy and this gets you in hot water with your friends, loved ones and those you deal with in business.

You tend to be a jack-of-all-trades and master-of-none. You job hop. Your home or working environment can be disorganized. Others may see you as a Dr. Jekyll and Mr. Hyde. You are constantly changing your residence, decor, furniture, clothes, mind or thoughts. You're easily confused, distracted and can become jumpy, restless or fidgety, especially if you're not constantly moving. Your energies get scattered.

You love to gossip. And may have difficulties with others because of something you said or wrote. You're a chatterbox. You yak too much. The blabbing you do lacks continuity. When you jump from subject-to-subject others get lost trying to keep up with you. You are a tattle-tale that causes upheavals, especially when you're caught gossiping. It's easy for you to make mistakes because your mind is cluttered with a million things racing through simultaneously. You are easily flustered and words come popping out the wrong way, thus, you're misinterpreted. Your mind is clogged down to the point of getting mental fatigue.

You are indecisive about most things--a job, travel, moving, with love and family. You can't stand this mental mind-pulling, thus you stop it by leaping impulsively into action that is inevitably in the wrong direction. When it comes to romance you get bored with someone who says, "I love you." Usually that's when you dump the person. You lean more toward one night stands than a stable, lasting relationship. Love affairs are taken casuallx. Many romances can occur simultaneously. You run when anyone tries to get close to the real you.

HOW TO MAKE THE MOST OF YOUR GEMINI OR MERCURY NAME

If you have discovered that your old name is beneficial, try to follow these suggestions, thus, you will enhance your name vibration and attract even better luck. Also, follow these suggestions if this is your NEW NAME VIBRATION.

If you wish to add further harmony into your life, wear the colors or gems for the sign/planet your names vibrates to. Note: Most people have more than one sign or planet that is lucky for them--I hope you fall into this category.) If you are limited in the colors you wear, use these lucky colors for accessories.

Perk yourself up by wearing light shades of violet. Don jewelry made of beryl or striped stones. Deal with communications, transportation, education or travel. Become absorbed in something that will keep your mind constructively occupied so you don't have the time to spread tales or talk about others. Go to school, learn a language or something that will aid your career; perhaps starting a hobby will be beneficial and, who knows, it may pay off in the end and wind up as a vocation?

Don't monopolize a conversation. Take an interest in others and learn what makes them tick, Thus, not only will you understand them better, but you'll find your relationships have improved. Try to concentrate your energies on one project rather than scattering in many different directions.

You'll be quite a gad-about, thus make interesting travel plans to places that are nearby or far-away. Go to a different locale on each journey and you'll find your horizons widening--and to your liking.

You will be inclined to increase your cerebral activity and could become involved in writing, studying or teaching. Your memory and perception will improve. You'll be able to judge the size and weight of objects better. It will be easier for you to recognize and develop your talents.

When a problem arises, avoid concentrating on it; instead dismiss it and realize that the answer will come when it's time. Have faith and reliance on some high power (God, a Supreme Being, etc.) that your difficulties will vanish. Just say, "Everything is in divine order." And it is, and will be! Remember that positive action leads to success.

Cancer And The Moon

Cancer vibrates to #18   **The Moon vibrates to #20**

The Moon is the planetary ruler of the sign Cancer. They have similar traits thus they are combined.

POSITIVE EXPRESSIONS

If you've experienced luck as a result of using these positive traits, this indicates that a Cancer/Moon vibration would be good for you. Or if you need more of the Cancer/Moon characteristics in your make-up, because you feel they are lacking, it then may be advisable to change your name to this vibration.

The domestic urges are strong. You enjoy cooking, sewing and doing needlepoint or knitting. The home and its environment is important to you; it's nice and cozy with a welcome mat outside the door greeting your guests. You prefer to entertain from the home; others may have difficulty dragging you out for a night on the town. You enjoy 'mothering' an animal, child or adult. The desire to be needed is overwhelming, thus, you'll cater to the whims of others. You'll even care for the weak, ill, unfortunate or handicapped. You are sympathetic when someone is suffering.

The normal, everyday routine of life bores you, thus constant change is a necessity; however, it doesn't detract from success. You are curious. Your mind is open and receptive to suggestions. You need a job that has variety. When you've found your proper niche in life, you're happy--that's when all of your feelings are put into the performance of a task. You get so emotionally aroused that there's no holding you back from going to the top. You express yourself more through the emotions and feelings than the intellect.

You go by your gut feeling rather than making an intellectual appraisal of a problem. Decisions are based upon hunches that prove to be one hundred percent accurate in the final outcome. In the love-making department, you are sentimental, romantic, and love tenderness in a relationship. You cling to the loved one with your heart and soul.

NEGATIVE EXPRESSIONS

If you've experienced conflict, arguments, adversity problems and misfortune as a result of these negative traits, this indicates that a Cancer/Moon vibration would be bad for you. Therefore, avoid obtaining a name that vibrates to Cancer or the Moon.

You are impressionable, easily bored and swayed and need constant variety. Often you are inconsistent and contradict yourself. Projects are started and often quit in midstream. You tend to be overly sensitive and crave sympathy. Many daily frustrations occur--trivialities. Gossip is enjoyed. You tend to be fickle.

You are capricious and depend upon your whim for the moment. This action gets you into lots of trouble with others, especially if it's merely an innocent flirtation on your part--your mate sees it differently. You are many-sided and thus no one is able to keep up with your moods--not even you! Your emotions can change within seconds--and they range from utter despair to the heights of happiness. You drive those close to you bananas. But you just can't seem to help yourself. When you become emotionally aroused, you goof up a relationship as well as a job.

The determination you lack causes difficulties with those in your intimate circle; also, your career suffers from this same fault of yours. There are times when you shy away from dealing with the public; you just can't cope with everyone. Bad publicity could do you in; you can't take anything that affects your honor and that could possibly mar your family's good name.

Dealing with the female sex in any capacity upsets you easily; it seems that you can't handle yourself when around women. Either they gossip about you or give you a bad time in some way or another depending upon your relationship with them.

You can be a wallflower or play the role of a wanderer with a roving eye. Your reactions are subconscious to just about everything. You can get hurt easily and crawl into a shell when this occurs. Scenes with a loved one are imagined in advance; sometimes they happen, other times they are pure fantasy. You are demonstrative and like attention. However, when you don't get it, you cry until you get the center stage you crave.

HOW TO MAKE THE MOST OF YOUR CANCER OR MOON NAME

If you have discovered that your old name is beneficial, try to follow these suggestions, thus you will enhance your name vibration and attract even better luck. Also, follow these suggestions if this is your NEW NAME VIBRATION.

If you wish to add further harmony into your life, wear the colors or gems for the sign/planet your name vibrates to. (**Note:** Most people have more than one sign or planet that is lucky for them--I hope you fall into this category.) If you are limited in the colors you wear, use these luck colors for accessories.

Wear shades of green--light, dark, chartreuse, forest, olive, emerald, and sea-green. The jewelry you don should be made of silver, or have emeralds encrusted on various pieces. Deal with the public, female sex, retail trade or with food, beverages, vending machines, music, administer to the ill, handicapped or become involved with the sea and its advocations or vocations. Render services to others. Protect the weak and helpless. Take up music professionally or as a hobby; perhaps by performing, writing, or publishing.

Work in an area where you are needed by others; as a result you'll feel a great sense of worth. Provide for the members of your household. Sew, do petitpoint or crochet; try new recipes and cook unusual dishes. Take care of a stray animal. Go on a picnic, to the beach, mountains or nearby scenic places. Be courageous and do something exciting. Keep your house orderly; however, change can be introduced to avoid monotony.

You will be inclined to spark your life with variety. Make a list of all the possible things you could do, in case you got bored; maybe things you've never done--go see the Chinese acrobats or Kabuki dances, if they are in town. Take the initiative and get involved in sports, games (cards, Monopoly) or go the zoo.

Avoid accepting things as they are. Do something about your whims; satisfy them by taking action. Stick with one endeavor; once it's finished be thrilled and pat yourself on the back for having completed it. If you start to get emotional or too sensitive, do something physical--clean the house, paint, play tennis, or ping-pong, have sex. Remember that positive action leads to success.

POSITIVE EXPRESSIONS
Leo And The Sun

Leo vibrates to #19   **The Sun vibrates to #21**

The Sun is the planetary ruler of the sign Leo; they have similar traits, thus they are combined.

If you've experienced luck as a result of using these positive traits, this indicates that a Leo/Sun vibration would be good for you. Or if you need more of the Leo/Sun characteristics in your make-up, because you feel they are lacking, it then may be advisable to change your name to this vibration.

You enjoy power and want to be the boss, leader, supervisor, superintendent, director, producer, star, owner of a business or an entrepreneur.

However, when you are in the top spot, you are kind and never misuse your authority; thus others respect and admire you. When you take command, you manage to hold down your enthusiasm graciously--in fact, quite regally.

Prestige is important to you; a title is preferred over the money. You are always looking and working toward a promotion. You are determined to be successful in spite of any setbacks. Your will power is strong. You stick to your decisions and resolutions: You like a challenge. Personal glory is craved. You are dependable and generous. You're self-assured.

The sun revitalizes you. It's important for you to be elegant and dignified. You feel at home in opulent surroundings. You enjoy the limelight. You are comfortable when in the company of those who are distinguished, successful and influential--you feel equal to them.

You are driven to win votes, honors, prizes or recognition; however, you don't step on anyone's toes to get them. Compliments are bestowed upon you constantly for your many worthy deeds. You are proud of your ability to guide others, however, you're not boastful. Most of the time you have open field to throw your weight around, but you keep a low profile.

You're devoted to your loved ones and want to show them off. Romance is enjoyed and indulged in. Your heart rules your affections rather than your head. Your loved ones are treated as if they were on center stage; photos of them are displayed proudly in your office and home. When it comes to romance you enjoy soft lights and music; wining and dining in plush restaurants are favored also. Words of love are spoken ever so quietly, tenderly. You are passionate, ardent and sensual.

NEGATIVE EXPRESSIONS

If you've experienced conflict, arguments, adversity, problems and misfortune as a result of these negative traits, this indicates that a Leo/Sun vibration would be bad for you. Therefore, avoid obtaining a name that vibrates to Leo or the Sun.

You are power-driven and will do almost anything to get to the top. Once there, you lord it over others trying to play the role of the big-shot. Your orders are given in such a bossy way, others wish they could quit— and often they do! When you try to be the master and exercise control, problems arise in just about every department.

You use your influence so you can have your own way. You're unyielding, domineering, egotistical, vain, bigoted, arrogant, and are a tyrant. You name drop to impress others. You're fond of adulation and flattery. You expect everyone to cater to you. Your desire for approval can make you a big spender. You overwork because you're an overachiever. Your pride could make you lose your job, money, friends or loved ones.

You need a job or position with status. Your pretentiousness is disliked by others. It could hold you back from advancing to the post desired. You are disrespectful of others. People belittle you and put you down, so you feel like nothing. Therefore, you take it out on those beneath you or your coworkers. You are smug, and your high and mighty attitude makes others shun you. When you blow your own horn, you are the only one to hear it. You are a grandstander, wanting all eyes in your direction. You'll go out of your way to get attention; a tactic employed may be to talk loud. If you steal the show from someone else, you'll brag about it. You can't understand why you aren't honored, respected, admired and why the prize always goes to the other person. Often you are qualified to win an award, however, you don't receive the proper credit for your achievements.

You rule the roost and make the lives of your family miserable. A loved one is treated as an inferior. It's difficult for you to ever be pleased with the object of your affections--it's because no one is better than you (that's how you think). You can be too magnanimous with a loved one. You could shine and show off to win the object of your affections. You're ardent and passionate.

HOW TO MAKE THE MOST OF YOUR LEO OR SUN NAME

If you have discovered that your old name is beneficial, try to follow these suggestions, thus you will enhance your name vibration and attract even better luck. Also follow these suggestions if this is your NEW NAME VIBRATION.

If you wish to add further harmony into your life, wear the colors or gems for the sign/planet your name vibrates to. (Note: Most people have more than one sign or planet that is lucky for them--I hope you fall into this category). If you are limited in the colors you wear, use these lucky colors for accessories.

Perk up your vitality by wearing all the shades of the sunset--gold, yellow, orange, tangerine, coral and burnt copper. Your jewelry should be gold or rubies. Deal with bonds, gilt-edge securities, gold, politics, men and influential people who have power, wealth or prestige. Be the boss, a leader, executive or in authority of some kind. Be confident of your talents. Think about positions of importance and work hard to attain them.

Surround yourself with prominent people. Do kind deeds for others, and you will receive the compliments you crave. Get involved in community affairs. Gain the respect and admiration of others through performing a job well; be kind and firm. Avoid all ego trips.

You will be inclined to socialize and entertain people who can help you in business. Your ego will need satisfying and this can be accomplished through worthwhile projects. You will be held in the high regard; your reputation will be impeccable; your power will be felt by others.

Don't exert undue superiority over others. Recognize your own importance and value, but watch being arrogant or condescending. Feel proud of yourself when your income or position has been raised. Take care of your household and give them some attention. When you have fulfilled a desire, feel proud of yourself and start making plans for other achievements. Keep in mind that positive action leads to success.

VIRGO
Virgo Vibrates to #2
POSITIVE EXPRESSIONS

If you've experienced luck as a result of using these positive traits, this indicates that a Virgo vibration would be good for you. Or if you need more of the Virgo characteristics in your make-up, because you feel they are lacking, it then may be advisable to change your name to this vibration.

It's important for you to serve others. You always do more than what is expected of you. You're able to take orders and execute them easily. Imparting knowledge to others is enjoyable. Before making a decision, you discuss a subject with many people, thus getting various views. You are methodical and plan everything in advance. You are good at communicating.

You're busy analyzing everything that is presented to you regardless of whether it's of a personal nature or in connection with business. Your analytical talents also are spent upon yourself; every action and every thought is dissected because you want to know why you said this or did that. You go for facts not dreams of what may be. Your practical nature won't let you waste time or money on impractical schemes or manufacture things that are purely a fragment of your imagination.

All projects are approached diligently and unemotionally. You're a workaholic. You can take the plans of others and tear them apart; flaws are discovered and suggestions are given for improvement. You can solve problems easily by examining and identifying everything. Common sense, logic and reasoning is applied by you daily. You are scholarly, have a good memory and may disseminate knowledge through teaching, writing or conversing. You enjoy explaining to others and do it in a detailed fashion; you don't like to leave anything out.

Your house is neat and everything is in order. In the home you spend a lot of time reading books, magazine and newspaper articles that will increase your knowledge. When it comes to the opposite sex, you are fussy and don't want just anybody; however, you are not that romantically inclined. It will be a long courting before you become intimate with someone—that includes kissing. Lasting relationships are a must. Love is taken seriously; however, you're undemonstrative publicly.

NEGATIVE EXPRESSIONS

If you've experienced conflict, arguments, adversity, problems and misfortune as a result of these negative traits, this indicates that a Virgo vibration would be bad for you. Therefore avoid obtaining a name that vibrates to Virgo.

You waste so much time explaining things that it takes you a long time to accomplish your tasks. Besides you drive others (especially the impatient type of person) bananas when you can't get to the point. You get so wrapped up in details that you overlook the total picture of a project, idea or conversation. When you get bogged down with minute things, business losses are easily attracted. Often your speech is too cutting; your sarcasm causes difficulties with others.

You tend to criticize others constantly. Words are repeated when talking or writing. You are constantly explaining everything. Perfection is demanded in yourself and others. You can talk a blue streak, not letting others get a word in, or you can go to the opposite extreme and appear somber. It's difficult for you to relax, emotionally and physically. You work to the point of fatigue.

Your nit-picking ways are annoying to others. Your desire for neatness and order makes you clean up after everyone the moment an ash tray gets used. This action doesn't put you in the good graces of your guests or loved ones; it makes them feel uncomfortable. People who are around you in your home are afraid to dirty anything or make a mess! No wonder they'll hear about it from you when you start to nag.

You can ruin a relationship because instead of joining in with fun, games, sports, or going outdoors to enjoy nature, you spend most of your time escaping from people by reading books that will expand your mind. You are not the party-goer type, and consider the youthful pleasures as a waste of time, therefore, it's difficult for you to become romantically involved with someone.

Misunderstandings occur when you are cool and cover up your feelings, especially in matters of the heart. Due to shyness, it's difficult for you to express your affections. You are choosy when it comes to a mate. Your chores or business may take precedence over a spouse.

HOW TO MAKE THE MOST OF YOUR NAME

If you have discovered that your old name is beneficial, try to follow these suggestions, thus you will enhance your name vibration and attract even better luck. Also follow these suggestions if this is your NEW NAME VIBRATION.

If you wish to add further harmony into your life, wear the colors or gems for the sign/planet your name vibrates to. (Note: most people have more than one sign or planet that is lucky for them--I hope you fall into this category) If you are limited in the colors you wear, use these lucky colors for accessories.

Feel vibrant by wearing all the darker shades of violet. The earth colors--beige, wheat, flaxen, caramel and light brown--will give you an earthly look that you'll enjoy. Choose a jasper or flintstone as part of your jewelry collection; don these stones and feel the lucky vibes they attract. Deal with books, education, stationary, office supplies, hygiene and health foods. Be creative and write a book.

Increase your knowledge: attend classes, lectures and workshops. Take an assertive training course. Go to seminars dealing with vitamins, juices and health in general. If they are held in another city or state, the trip will be good experience for you. Pep your life up with some physical activity or you'll fritter it away just being a book worm--and that's not the complete answer to happiness.

Guard against being too critical. Try to remember that no one's perfect If you become a nag, you'll chase away those dear to you. Avoid cleaning up so much that others are miserable. Don't overdo orderliness to the point of where the members of your household can't find their belongings--they may make a bigger mess just looking for them!

Your sex life may dwindle down because you are more involved in mental activities. Don't neglect the physical world and those in it--a little indifference or too much moderation may make your spouse look elsewhere for a more satisfying relationship. Keep in mind that positive action, in any endeavor, leads to success.

LIBRA AND VENUS

Libra vibrates to #3   **Venus vibrates to #6**

Venus is the planetary ruler of the sign Libra. They have similar traits thus they are combined.

POSITIVE EXPRESSIONS

If you've experienced luck as a result of using these positive traits, this indicates that a Libra/Venus vibration would be good for you. Or if you need more of the Libra/Venus characteristics in your make-up, because you feel they are lacking, it then may be advisable to change your name to this vibration.

You feel the need to balance colors; the wrong mixtures do you in. Possibly you can paint, draw, sketch, design, decorate, make ceramics or get involved in arts, crafts, beauty, fashion, amusement, entertainment or music--as an avocation or vocation. You lean toward the aesthetic in life and are happy when surrounded by the beautiful.

It's important for you to relax and listen to classical music, at concert halls or on records and tapes. The romantic composers of past centuries and the love songs of the 30's and 40's turn you on. When you have quiet moments alone, you find that the peace and harmony you experience makes it easy for you to bring balance back into your life. Usually you are so busy listening to other people's problems that you temporarily forget about yourself. However, your interest in others make you popular.

You're able to see both sides of every story. You dislike hurting other people's feelings; thus, it's difficult to say "no" to invitations. You're considerate of others, extremely fond of luxuries and enjoy entertaining. You are friendly, gregarious and a good mixer. You are able to turn on charm at the drop of a hat. You love making others happy.

You are a social butterfly. People find you sweet, kind, cordial, pleasing and well-mannered. You are gracious and are the hostess with the mostest. Your friends and acquaintances are as refined as you. Your dinners are works of art; the food is balanced for nutritional purposes, the victuals are all different colors and when combined together resemble a painting. The table setting is elegant--and so are you.

Companionship is a necessity. You're in love with the idea of love. You are affectionate, submissive and extremely sensual. Love-making is like a rhapsody. Your idea of romance is to hold hands, embrace, kiss tenderly, listen to soft music in the background, sip a glass of champagne and nibble on some food every now and then. Often love is your chief interest in life---love of friends, a mate, family, children, and those who befriend you. You're the marrying kind.

NEGATIVE EXPRESSIONS

If you've experienced, conflict, arguments, adversity, problems and misfortune as a result of these negative traits, this indicates that a Libra/Venus vibration would be bad for you. Therefore avoid obtaining a name that vibrates to Libra or Venus.

You're often late because you keep trying to balance your wardrobe with the right colors and accessories. You dislike getting your hands dirty. You tend to take the "easy way out." You must watch laziness. You're easy-going and your chief interest in life is fun rather than a career. You could tell a lie just so you'd avoid an argument. Often your pals and associates are chosen because they cater to you. You expect others to spoil you. You could be ungrateful.

You have difficulty making decisions, thus there's a continual changing of your mind while you weigh the pros and cons of everything. This process may attract losses in business because your competitor may jump into the deal first. You get so mentally carried away with a project that your head stays in the clouds instead of on the ground; thus you wind up not gaining your desires.

It's difficult for you to say no, therefore you attract large expenses, lend others money, sign papers when you shouldn't and wear yourself out going to parties. You may feel slighted at a gathering, bored or just have difficulties when socializing. Attracted is intemperance in fun, pleasure and sex. You lean toward debauchery, dissipation, depravity, promiscuity or immoral practices. You could be jaded depraved, too permissive and pliable.

A craving to be loved could be so strongly imbedded that you might gravitate toward the wrong person. You might be so generous with your mate that you are not appreciated. Difficulties occur withy those you care about. You may think that you are unlucky in love. You are readily influenced and take the direction of the lowest amount of opposition. This is a weakness that can make you suffer.

You tend to live too much in the emotions. Your desire for companionship may make you overly indulge by eating sweets--it compensates for those lonely nights. You're flirtatious because you thrive on attention. Someone can win you through using flattery. You''ll go to any extreme to win the object of your affections. However, you can be inconstant with romance due to indecisiveness toward the person with whom you're involved. You could stay with a mate that you're not compatible with because you dread being alone. Often you're a doormat when with the person you care for. You can easily overindulge in love, pleasure and ease.

HOW TO MAKE THE MOST OF YOUR NAME

If you have discovered that your old name is beneficial, try to follow these suggestions, thus you will enhance your name vibration and attract even better luck. Also follow these suggestions if this is your NEW NAME VIBRATION.

If you wish to add further harmony into your life, wear the colors or gems for the sign/planet your name vibrates to. (**Note:** Most people have more than one sign or planet that is lucky for them--I hope you fall into this category.) If you are limited in the colors you wear, use these lucky colors for accessories.

Perk up your energy by wearing the light shades of yellow-canary, pale, lemon. Don some pink--shocking pink if you're in the mood to trip the light fantastic and make it an evening out on the town. Choose diamonds to wear as jewelry, or the donning of copper bracelets and other pieces might give you the affect you wish to achieve. Deal with art, beauty, fashion, decorating, perfume, flowers, hobbies, confectionary shops, and resort areas. Let your creative talents out--draw or paint something pretty. If it's a hit with your friends, exhibit in a gallery or sell your pictures to a pal. Maybe you've found a new vocation.

Take an active part in athletics that are not too taxing on your nature. Perhaps a game of golf, tennis, ping-pong, or a dip in the pool will suffice. Watch others perform on stage, in a sports arena or ski-jump tournament. Go to parties and social gatherings, however learn to say no to some of the invitations; otherwise, you won't have time for anything else.

You will be inclined to relax and take it easy; therefore avoid goofing off too much. Discipline is need as well as practicality. Avoid going on big spending sprees for those luxury items you adore. Guard against a lazy streak and giving in to the line of least resistance.

Use moderation in all actions and employ common sense in affairs of the heart. If you don't you may have to watch overindulgence in the emotions, ease, pleasure and sex which could lead to an inactive and slothful period. Love and companionship will be craved and can bring you the happiness you've always dreamed was possible to attain. You will be extremely romantic. Tender caresses, warm kisses and a fireside glowing with embers will be the scene desired. Keep in mind that in all endeavors positive action leads to success.

SCORPIO AND PLUTO

Scorpio vibrates to # 4   **Pluto vibrates to # 22**

Pluto is the planetary ruler associated with the sign Scorpio. They have similar traits, thus are combined in this section. Mars also is a planetary ruler of Scorpio but its traits are more similar to Aries, thus it is found in the Aries section.

SCORPIO POSITIVE EXPRESSIONS

If you've experienced luck as a result of using these positive traits, this indicates that a Scorpio vibration would be good for you. Or if you need more of the Scorpio characteristics in your make-up, because you feel they are lacking, it then may be advisable to change your name to this vibration.'

You possess, great determination to succeed in spite of all obstacles. You'll go all the way out to accomplish a set goal. You're resourceful, good at research and will work to the point of exhaustion. Indirect or subtle methods are used to gain your objectives. You have high standards and keep them. You know exactly what you want in life. Everything is done with all your might. You're courageous, mysterious, secretive and have a one-track mind with intense and neverending desires. You dislike others probing into your affairs. It's difficult for anyone to get to know you. You enjoy investigating a person, situation or problem thoroughly. When you follow your instincts, they almost always turn out to be right.

Your never-ending desires are pursued persistently. Once you've won a point, issue, project, deal or person you will turn it into a winning proposition. It's easy for you to follow through on any plans that are made. You stick to your goals relentlessly--success is written all over you, regardless of the position you find yourself in--you exert a certain power that others feel. Your strong emotions are poured into all of your endeavors--everything is done with great intensity.

You are dauntless and don't let anyone stand in your way to get to the top. You've got lots of nerve, guts, and aren't afraid to compete with anyone. You are aggressive and a dynamic go-getter. Others find that you are unpliable and probing. You know how to ask questions to get people to divulge the information you seek. Your steadiness and ability to pay close attention to detail earns you a good reputation. You tend to be creative and productive, disliking wasted effort.

In matters of the heart, you'll capture whomever you've got your eyes on. You emanate animal magnetism that makes you irresistible. A person would have to be very cold to turn away from you. Passion runs deep within you and it is also expressed outwardly. You're sensuous and devoted to your mate.

NEGATIVE EXPRESSIONS

If you've experienced conflict, arguments, adversity, problems and misfortune as a result of these negative traits, this indicates that a Scorpio vibration would be bad for you. Therefore avoid obtaining a name that vibrates to Scorpio.

SCORPIO

You are bitchy, sarcastic, spiteful, malicious and /or jealous. Your mind is preoccupied with one obsessive thought. You spend compulsively and must have what, or whom, you want, regardless of anyone or anything. Often you lack sympathy for the weaknesses of others. You can be forceful, demanding, dictative, revengeful, suspicious, testy. You could carry a grudge forever. Cutting remarks are made which can be hurting to others. You dislike crowds and seek privacy, sometimes to the point of alienating most people. You may be a collector of treasures and keep them hidden because they were bought only for your eyes--this could be an object d' art or a person.

Often you are downright nasty one moment and sugary sweet the next. You can easily become obsessed with a loved one and be a stalker. A loved one's every move and thought can be treated as an interrogation. You're a controller. You smother your mate with possessiveness, and chain the person to you through sex. You force others to do your bidding and they resent it. People are used for your own selfish desires. It is difficult for you to let go of a loved one. You could threaten that person if that individual expresses a desire to leave you.

PLUTO POSITIVE EXPRESSIONS

If you've experienced luck as a result of using these positive traits, this indicates that a Pluto vibration would be good for you. Or if you need more of Pluto's characteristics in your makeup, because you feel they are lacking, it then may be advisable to change your name to this vibration.

You feel drawn toward doing something good for the universe. You could be active in the United Nations, Peace Corps, Civil Rights or some crusade or cause that is for the betterment of the human race. You enjoy being a member of a club, fraternity, cult, society, group or band.

You are a specialist in your chosen field. Astrology, Parapsychology, spiritualism or metaphysics interest you. You are agreeable and extremely cooperative. Crowds make you feel comfortable; the more people around you, the better you feel. You can be forceful, energetic, and persistent. No one is going to stop you from achieving your goals.

You thrive under deadlines and pressure. You're aggressive and persuasive in a nice way. You are a good mediator and usually are right when you follow your first impression. You may devote a lot of time to doing good for mankind. Perhaps, you're very spiritual. You are able to concentrate so thoroughly that you can shut out all talk and noise. When you make changes, it is because you feel compelled to do so.

Once a rapport has been established with a person, you take compulsive action to win that individual's love. It's easy for you to become obsessed with the object of your affections. You'll chase your loved one until you're the victor. Your love feelings are intense. When in the presence of your mate, you feel as if the two of you are one.

NEGATIVE EXPRESSIONS

If you've experienced conflict, arguments, adversity, problems and misfortune as a result of these negative traits, this indicates that a Pluto vibration would be bad for you. Therefore avoid obtaining a name that vibrates to Pluto.

PLUTO

You attract pressure from others or apply it to them. Often it's important for others to do your bidding. You tend to be resentful, ruthless, sadistic, vicious and nasty. You are not afraid of anyone or anything. When you want to be evil, you can't be topped. Regardless of what someone may think, you follow your compulsions. If someone tries to stop you, they'll regret it. You will destroy anyone who tries to oppose you. Various means are used to get your way such as resorting to blackmail, black magic, voodoo or any other forms of witchcraft. You play both ends against the middle and turn one side against the other. Your instigations cause friction and others consider you to be a troublemaker. Often you attack your opponents with underhanded methods, or others apply those tactics to you.

Often you take drastic measures when someone or something displeases you. Crowds can be shunned like the plague. Or you may get involved in causes or crusades that leads to riots or sit down strikes. Shady, criminal or illegal activities may appeal to you, such as bribery, extortion, a racket or something dishonest. You could be uncooperative with groups, or on a team, committee, board or at most meetings. You could badger others, be a double dealer, two-faced or possessed by evil spirits.

You could try everything to seduce the object of your affections. Obsession, jealousy, possessiveness and a desire to control becomes the dominating factor in a relationship. As a result, problems arise. You are passionate and totally committed and devoted to a mate.

HOW TO MAKE THE MOST OF YOUR SCORPIO OR PLUTO NAME

If you have discovered that your old name is beneficial, try to follow these suggestions, thus you will enhance your name vibration and attract even better luck. Also follow these suggestions if this is your NEW NAME VIBRATION.

If you wish to add further harmony into your life, wear the colors or gems for the sign/planet your name vibrates to. (Note: most people have more than one sign or planet that is lucky for them--I hope you fall into this category.) If you are limited in the colors you wear, use these lucky colors for accessories.

Perk up your energy and wear all shades of dark red--scarlet, blood red, deep wine or combined red and black colors together. Jewelry chosen should contain ancient symbols, such as a scarab, serpent or an antique, and/or be made of clay or don a topaz or bloodstone.

Join a cause, spiritual group or fraternity of some type. Study something uplifting. Become a member of a sports team, or club. Get involved in projects that involve peace for mankind. Work with others for the common good of a group. Social or charity work might interest you.

You will be inclined to mingle with the masses rather than with one or two pals. Corporations, companies, mergers and branches of a business may interest you. Psychic healing will fascinate you. A spirit of brotherhood will emanate from you.

Don't be forceful, but persist in a kindly manner with others. Be cooperative at meetings, but be courageous, gutsy and aggressive in accomplishing your goals.

Avoid being bitchy even though you may feel inclined to behave in this fashion. Also stay away from jealous scenes pulled with a loved one. Guard against getting even if someone angers you. Realize that whatever you put out is going to come back double to you.

Your sex life will be increased. An intensity may be felt with a loved one. A strong rapport may be attracted that may seem impossible to break. Watch becoming too obsessed. A one-track mind concentrated on a lover may interfere with business; therefore try to live in both worlds--and you'll have the best of everything. Keep in mind that positive action leads to success.

SAGITTARIUS AND JUPITER
Sagittarius vibrates to # 7   **Jupiter vibrates to # 5**

Jupiter is the planetary ruler of the sign Sagittarius. They have similar traits; thus, they are combined.

POSITIVE EXPRESSIONS
If you've experienced luck as a result of using these positive traits, this indicates that a Sagittarius/Jupiter vibration would be good for you. Or if you need more of the Sagittarius/Jupiter characteristics in your make-up, because you feel they are lacking, it then may be advisable to change your name to this vibration.

You seem to have divine protection, always being saved at the last minute. Your attitude is that everything will turn out all right and it does. You tend to laugh and smile your way through life as if it's one big ball. You are cheerful and lively and thus attract friends easily. You are fun-loving and usually the life of the party. When involved romantically, you radiate happiness.

Your undertakings are performed on a large scale. Money always seems to be on the increase. You have high aspirations. You are attracted to wealthy people. You're optimistic and happy-go-lucky. Travel to foreign or exotic locals intrigue you. Wanderlust is in your makeup. You're restless and like to be on the go. You like to live it up and have a ball. You're an extrovert. It's easy for you to adapt to changes. You're loyal and wish the best for everyone, even your enemies.

You invariably try to encourage those who feel downtrodden. You're a giver, broad minded and perfectly capable of taking care of yourself. Display and pageantry appeals to you. You're always looking for something exciting to do. Sports or the outdoors (could just be scenery) consumes a good portion of your life. If you lose, you're a good sport. You're an ardent and fiery lover and bring great happiness into your life and your mate's. You may run from marriage, but once caught, you go out of your way to make it work.

You are good-natured about everything and don't let anything get you down. Your tolerance for the shortcomings of others is appreciated by one and all. You have a heart of gold and are always doing favors for everyone. Your favorite role to play is Santa Claus---giving to others.

You are impartial and free of prejudice; your belief is that everyone is equal and should be given the same chances. Religious, philosophical and metaphysical areas attract you. You can be quite pious. You have a share-the-wealth attitude. You are a humorist and ever-ready to lift someone's spirits. Your ability to encourage others is amazing. You are sure of yourself and so inspired by projects that you enthusiastically leap right in. When you are kept busy constantly, you're contented.

NEGATIVE EXPRESSIONS

If you've experienced conflict, arguments, adversity, problems and misfortune as a result of these negative traits, this indicates that a Sagittarius/Jupiter vibration would be bad for you. Therefore avoid obtaining a name that vibrates to Sagittarius or Jupiter.

Frolics cost you plenty, but it doesn't bother you. The price you pay healthwise or financially doesn't seem to faze you in the least. Your insane enterprises (and they are just that,) as well as your sprees and escapades cost you a fortune but you couldn't care less. It seems like you enjoy parting with your dough. Unneeded outlays of money and paying more for things than they are worth doesn't disturb you in the least. You rely upon being saved at the last moment just as you are going down under--and usually you are.

You are headstrong, wasteful, impulsive, frank and outspoken even if it means hurting someone's feelings. You take an "I don't care" attitude toward most things and people. You tend to jump to conclusions and look to the future rather than enjoying the present. You're a spoiler of others. You tend to have exhibitionist traits. It's difficult for you to keep a secret.

You may play the field when dating. You can take a loved one for granted. Past intimate relationships are divulged to your present mate/lover. Often, you lose interest when someone gets serious. You like someone difficult to get. If someone bores you, it's possible you'll dump that individual immediately, without a second thought. Sex is like a game--you enjoy it.

In business or personal ventures, your expectations many times are not realized. But you forget about one disappointment and try again in another direction. Everything you do is done in a big way--you overestimate, overspend, overeat, over drink and do things to excess. You gain weight easily from eating rich and fattening foods.

You tend to be unmindful or thoughtless of others. To play a prank and damage someone else's property doesn't bother your conscience--usually because you'll gladly pay for the damages. Your carefree ways could get you into trouble with the law. You trust others implicitly and that could cost you a pretty penny. You can brag and appear quite conceited; however, it's not done because of an ego trip. You toot your own horn because you are sure of yourself. Your loudness comes because you tend to exaggerate everything and do things on a large scale.

HOW TO MAKE THE MOST OF YOUR NAME

If you have discovered that your old name is beneficial, try to follow these suggestions, thus you will enhance your name vibration and attract even better luck. Also follow these suggestions if this is your NEW NAME VIBRATION.

If you wish to add further harmony into your life, wear the colors or gems for the sign/planet your name vibrates to. (**Note**: most people have more than one sign or planet that is lucky for them--I hope you fall into this category.) If you are limited in the colors you wear, use these lucky colors for accessories.

Wear light or dark shades of purple — indigo, plum, orchid, mauve, magenta. Don jade, turquoise, a red garnet or green and red mixed stones for jewelry. Be optimistic and radiate warmth to one and all. Treat everyone as a friend. Encourage others and sell them your wares or beliefs.

Take up an esoteric subject; thus, the wisdom of the ages can be yours and imparted to others in your daily contracts. Travel to far-away lands, and become involved with the customs, traditions and folks you meet. Do favors for others and ask for them in return.

You will be inclined to be philanthropic and may want to donate to worthy causes. You'll feel like being a real do-gooder. You will be extremely confident and outgoing. Your ability to counsel others will be improved; good advice will be given. You can attract an abundance of money--in fact, you can be rich if you go after wealth--you'll certainly attract it.

You will need to think before you leap. Weigh the pros and cons; use logic, then make a decision. Avoid making snap judgments. Be careful of placing too much reliance on faith and good luck. You will have that _and_ divine protection, however don't get too carried away with it.

Avoid overdoing everything. Use moderation with foods, alcohol, finances, pleasure and sex. You will be inclined to be fun-loving and have to watch goofing up. Parties, sports and the outdoors may attract you. You'll enjoy walking through the woods or riding on horseback through a meadow. The smell of fresh cut grass will entice you to stay out longer than you should. Therefore try to mix good times with business--don't go to extremes in either direction although you may have a tendency to do so. Keep in mind that positive action leads to success.

CAPRICORN AND SATURN

Capricorn vibrates to #8   **Saturn vibrates to # 15**

Saturn is the planetary ruler of the Sign Capricorn. They have similar traits thus they are combined.

POSITIVE EXPRESSIONS

If you've experienced luck as a result of using these positive traits, this indicates that a Capricorn/Saturn vibration would be good for you. Or if you need more of the Capricorn/Saturn characteristics in your make-up, because you feel they are lacking, it then may be advisable to change your name to this vibration.

You're ambitious, conventional, conservative, diplomatic, dependable and are good at economizing and saving money. You plan business and personal activities with strategy similar to military tactics. It's easy for you to endure long hours of labor, pressure and painstaking routine. You excel when negotiations are involved in business deals. You're a bargain hunter and enjoy collecting old things; a rat-packer that hangs on to possessions. Regardless of the obstacles encountered, you continue to pursue set goals. You'll forego frivolous or social activities if there isn't any financial or prestigious gain. Organizing and reorganizing is your skill. You obey rules and expect others to do the same. You tend to be an introvert.

Security is a must; it's the feeling of being safe and secure that makes it important for you to have money stashed away in case there's a rainy day. Not only do you have a nest egg, sizable bank account, or money invested in tangibles such as real estate, but you also save your possessions and at later dates manage to find some use for them. You can't stand waste therefore you don't throw out scraps of cloth, food or any other material or product.

Practicality is a strong trait you display daily. You look before you leap; plans are made and stuck with until time to bring them to fruition. Moderation is used in everything. You are self-disciplined, unwavering, responsible and bear your burdens and responsibilities well. You are in control of yourself and are able to meet your obligations. Your strong endurance, foresight, efficiency and rational ideas always seem to pay off.

You are materialistic and don't fritter time away with nonsensical things. People find you down-to-earth even though you display a reserved nature. When you meet others for the first time you are discerning and observe their every action.

You pay attention to every word someone says; your retentiveness comes in handy at some future date. You are calm, cool and collected in all circumstances. Your patience is admirable, so is your diplomacy.

You take love seriously and detest game-playing. In matters of the heart, you are particular with whom you become involved. You desire a lasting relationship. You can be unromantic because business comes before love, though often you'll warm up when your mind is free of problems. It's difficult for you to express your feelings to the object of your affections.

NEGATIVE EXPRESSIONS

If you've experienced, conflict, arguments, adversity, problems and misfortune as a result of these negative traits, this indicates that a Capricorn/Saturn vibration would be bad for you. Therefore avoid obtaining a name that vibrates to Capricorn or Saturn.

You're extremely ambitious and desire security, often, at the sacrifice of fun, loved ones, relatives, family and friends. You have a horror of wasting your time. Others are distrusted. You can be narrowminded, a constant worrier, pessimistic, and a miser. You take rather than give. You tend to scheme and try to out smart those you deal with. Often losses are attracted with negotiations or in your attempt to get a bargain. You are easily depressed or discouraged. You're a workaholic and aim for the top spot; your patient effort can be rewarded but always at the sacrifice of something in your personal life.

You're insecure and lack confidence in your abilities, thus its difficult for you to be successful. Losses are attracted because of negative thinking. Your self-pitying thoughts make others shun your company. You are unsocial, however when you do socialize, it's to meet people so you can use them to gain your own advantage at some later date. You suspect that everyone is out to use you, thus you beat them to the game and use them first.

Others find you cagey as if you've got something to hide (and you probably do). Your answers are evasive because you don't want anyone to get close or discover your plans. You live in fear--fear of failure, fear of being discovered for being deceitful or a user, fear you'll lose money and a deal--- and on and on it goes with your fears.

You are too serious, sullen and as a result, others shun your company. The worst side of everything is seen constantly. You gripe about the sacrifices you made and the losses that have occurred. Your sorrows have dispirited you and made you into a person who is envious of other people's achievements. You are contrite but cover up your sense of guilt by escaping to a solitary world where you can be alone and cry the blues.

You are frigid; your innermost thoughts are suppressed for fear of getting hurt. Thus you put your emotions on ice and don't give to the person you really care about. In romantic situations you are selfish and only think about how everything affects you. Rejection frightens you; thus, often, you'll appear cold, detached and indifferent in matters of the heart--it's a defensive tactic.

HOW TO MAKE THE MOST OF YOUR NAME

If you have discovered that your old name is beneficial, try to follow these suggestions, thus you will enhance your name vibration and attract even better luck. Also follow these suggestions if this is your NEW NAME VIBRATION.

If you wish to add further harmony into your life, wear the colors or gems for the sign/planet your name vibrates to. (**Note:** most people have more than one sign or planet that is lucky for them--I hope you fall into this category.) If you are limited in colors you wear, use these lucky colors for accessories.

Wear navy, steel, sapphire, Dresden, royal and dark blue colors and earth tones--caramel, beige, dark and chocolate brown. Also don black. Put on stones of onyx or sardonyx as jewelry. Be patient and diligent. Take on added work and responsibility. Know your value and worth and use it to your advantage.

Save your money and invest it wisely on something that will take a long time to mature, or a safe investment. Help others get organized. Persist with set goals; always look ahead, never back. Get out and socialize or go to amusing places. Take an interest in the theater, the arts, or people in general. Attend inexpensive or free exhibits, concerts, museums, shows, fairs, or festivals. Go to the flea market and look for bargains.

You will be inclined to be cautious and security conscious. Thus you will be dependable, realistic and practical. You may want to put your house, office and life in order through reorganization. Renovation may be uppermost on your mind.

Avoid thoughts of fear, greed, suspicion, envy, worry, grief, or feelings that you are limited and/or restricted and thus can't take action. Give, rather than take. Keep so busy you don't have time to gripe, complain or think negatively. Be thrilled when you've accomplished a task or reached your goal. Be constructive and take time out to play, be merry and make love. Learn to live life to the fullest. Keep in mind that positive action leads to success.

AQUARIUS AND URANUS

Aquarius vibrates to # 9   **Uranus vibrates to a# 10**

Uranus is the planetary ruler associated with the sign Aquarius; they have similar traits, thus, they are combined. Saturn also is a planetary ruler of Uranus but its traits are more similar to Capricorn, thus it is found in the Capricorn section.

POSITIVE EXPRESSIONS

If you've experienced luck as a result of using these positive traits, this indicates that an Aquarius/Uranus vibration would be good for you. Or if you need more of the Aquarius/Uranus characteristics in your make-up, because you feel they are lacking, it then may be advisable to change your name to this vibration.

You are an individualist and must be yourself at all times. Your associates consider you to be very exceptional and may even say that you're a genius. You tend to be inventive and original. Because you are aroused with inspiration, projects are tackled immediately and finished just as quickly. You are able to communicate your new ideas to others. You make discoveries that leave others in awe. Usually you are the first at something new in your field. You are known to be a real innovator. Anything revolutionary interests you.

You're always searching for a quicker and better way of performing a job. Your business activities are conducted in an unusual way. Most of your actions are spur-of-the moment. 'You enjoy dashing off to new places when you want and where you want. You're perceptive, wide-awake for the new and different and are self-reliant. An interest in the occult, psychology and parapsychology makes you appear as a person who marches to the beat of a different drummer--- and you do. You have an innate understanding of human nature. It is easy for you to handle others, though you don't like to be bossy. Your unpredictable behavior is free of mishap and you can get involved in unconventional things without attracting problems. You thrive on surprises, and even shocking others; however, you are harmless when you shake up others.

Your "I know it all" attitude is displayed because you are intuitively tuned in to a person, event, or product. You are way ahead of the times--sometimes a decade or even a century.

It's important that you are "in" with the latest fashion, gadgets, machinery, equipment, cosmetics, hair-do and frequent the "in" restaurants and disco establishments. You are a free-thinker and dislike joining the mass wave-length way of dressing, thinking or behaving. However you could easily become involved in reform, women lib, strikes, or humanitarian endeavors that will benefit mankind.

Your magnetism attracts the opposite sex. The other person is so mesmerized by you that it appears that you've cast a hypnotic spell on the individual. Communication, freedom and independence is needed in a relationship--you must be unchained.

NEGATIVE EXPRESSIONS

If you've experienced conflict, arguments, adversity, problems and misfortune as a result of these negative traits, this indicates that an Aquarius/Uranus vibration would be bad for you. Therefore avoid obtaining a name that vibrates to Aquarius or Uranus.

Your ideas are so far out, or ahead of the times, that they are discarded and thrown out as useless--even laughed about. The thoughts and opinions of others disinterest you--you make your own rules. Authority is looked down on by you; you'll revolt against anyone in a high position. The establishment or orthodoxy makes you want to overthrow or rebel against it. You tend to drop out of normal conventional affairs in order to do your own thing.

Your interest in reform (for an individual or the world) is so way-out that it's causes difficulties with others. Your views are contrary to most people's.

When you are opinionated and express an "I know it all" attitude, others are turned off. Your independence, unconventional behavior, individualistic ways and unpredictable actions creates problems with others. You tend to be abrupt and erratic. You dislike making or hearing explanations. If possible, you'll choose working for yourself rather than others.

Your goals are turned upside-down constantly. In employment, you could walk off the job, get laid off or fired. Your life is one shock after another. You could get evicted, stranded, abandoned or just disappear. Machinery goes haywire when you touch it; electronic equipment breaks down and electrical equipment, appliances and light bulbs go on the blink continually--it just seems to happen in your presence.

You are undependable, uncoordinated, curt, irresponsible, late, nervous, on edge, controversial and undergo out-of-the ordinary experiences. Plans can't be made because you live your life by doing things on the spur-of-the-moment.

People pop in and out of your life just as quickly as you do theirs. One-night stands may be the order of the day. Yo dislike chains that bind--you'll break them. Lasting relationships are frowned upon unless the person gives you complete freedom and doesn't question you if you don't come home for days, or if you decide to go away for a month or two. Relationships tend to be started suddenly and ended just as quickly. You'll break with a jealous or possessive person. The moment someone becomes serious or tries to get too close to you, you'll be distant and undemonstrative.

HOW TO MAKE THE MOST OF YOUR NAME

If you have discovered that your old name is beneficial, try to follow these suggestions, thus you will enhance your name vibration and attract even better luck. Also follow these suggestions if this is your NEW NAME VIBRATION.

If you wish to add further harmony into your life, wear the colors or gems for the sign/planet your name vibrates to. (Note: most people have more than one sign or planet that is lucky for them---I hope you fall into this category.) If you are limited in the colors you wear, use these lucky colors for accessories.

Perk yourself up by wearing dazzling white, or blue--light, powder, sapphire, sky, electric, baby, royal or sea-blue, Don jewelry, blue sapphires, black pearls or obsidian stones. Deal with new products, devices, methods, electrical objects, electronics, computers, inventions, research, psychology, humanitarian endeavors or the esoteric. Use originality with some creative project such as writing, painting, building.

Make a startling discovery. Invent something useful. Be innovative. Dare to do the novel or untried. Take up astrology or scientology, numerology, palmistry or graphology. Learn to understand your fellowman better. Use your intuition when making decisions.

You will be inclined to be yourself and let your hair down. The latest craze, fad or 'in' thing will mesmerize you, momentarily. You'll be fascinated by unusual subjects, object or people. New friends will enter your life. You'll be magnetic and find yourself drawn into interesting conversations.

Avoid rebelling against those in authority. Take one step at a time in reform projects. Make sure that the crazy stunts you pull are harmless to yourself and others. View things with a greater spirit of give and take. Show, and have, tolerance for the views and shortcomings of others. Be careful of hurting others with your new-found freedom, especially if it consists of one-night stands. If that is what you want, be honest and let the other person know beforehand; thus, suffering and misunderstandings are avoided. Keep in mind that positive action leads to success.

PISCES AND NEPTUNE
Pisces vibrates to #12   **Neptune vibrates to #11**

Neptune is the planetary ruler associated with the sign Pisces. They have similar traits thus they are combined. Jupiter also is a planetary ruler of Pisces but its traits are more similar to Sagittarius, thus it is found in the Sagittarius section.

POSITIVE EXPRESSIONS
If you've experienced luck as a result of using these positive traits, this indicates that a Pisces/Neptune vibration would be good for you. Or if you need more of the Pisces/Neptune characteristics in your make-up, because you feel they are lacking, it then may be advisable to change your name to this vibration.

You have a fabulous creative imagination and can utilize it when you dramatize your emotions through acting, writing plays, movies, novels, poetry or as an artist painting or sculpting. You are interested in the aesthetic world and delve into it as an avocation or vocation. You are starry-eyed and long for your desires to be satisfied. You are idealistic, mysterious, extremely sensitive and easily adapt to your environment. Private play-acting with friends or loved ones is enjoyed. You're fascinated by the bright lights, glamour, entertainment or the exotic. Mysticism intrigues you. A peaceful atmosphere is a necessity. Promises are kept. Successful get-rich-quick schemes are attracted.

You are a wheeler-dealer who makes fantastic things come true for yourself and others. Ballyhoo is the name of the game when you start pushing a product, person or go after a contract with a huge corporation. Large-scale operations and enormous projects are the only type of venture for you. You get emotionally carried away with your feelings, desires and beliefs.

You search for Utopia here on earth. When you think you've found it you may become a recluse. You have psychic visions, prophetic dreams and soul-stirring revelations. Illuminations are flashes that come and go quite often. When you follow your ESP, you're right on target. You are sympathetic, compassionate and have empathy for your fellowman. Often you're attracted to social work so you can help those who are in need. You are selfless and sacrifice for others.

You are romantic and love poetry, soft dreamy music, a glass of wine with your sweetheart, holding hands, warm kisses, tender embraces, words of affection exchanged and to cling to the one you care about. You are enticing, seductive, warm and sensuous. A loved one is idolized. You tend to be subservient to the object of your affections.

NEGATIVE EXPRESSIONS

If you've experienced conflict, arguments, adversity, problems and misfortune as a result of these negative traits, this indicates that a Pisces/Neptune vibration would be bad for you. Therefore avoid obtaining a name that vibrates to Pisces or Neptune.

Your life is filled with disappointments; everything seems to fall through at the last moment or it's not as represented or turns out to be a phony scheme. Fraud occurs. Often, you're easily influenced--the con artists always manage to find you. You are too easily affected by the words of others. Most of the time you believe too much in the wrong people and your hopes are unrealized and shattered.

You tend to be deceived by others because you're gullible. Often your grandiose ideas fail to materialize. It's easy for you to daydream, build castles in the air and withdraw from mundane affairs. You're fascinated when you escape into fantasy and spiritual realms. You've got an overly active imagination, supersensitive system and can worry too much about little things. You tend to be overly emotional, dramatic and can cry easily. Care has to be taken that you don't take drugs or drink to excess. Discipline and 9-to-5 hours are disliked. You can be too idealistic, impractical and wishy-washy.

You tend to deceive yourself and others. Your aims are falsified and you bamboozle people into schemes to get rich overnight. You deviate from the truth and tell lies or exaggerate so much that it seems preposterous that something you promised could possibly come true. There is a tendency to talk without taking action or seeing results--you're lazy and procrastinate. You can be corrupt or become involved in undertakings that later prove useless, futile or unproductive.

You can be shiftless and unrealistic. The world of the unreal is where you find great delight--it's your escape, and you must escape from people and yourself. Everything in your world is magnified and blown out of it's true proportion. Nightmares, delusions, amnesia, blackouts, psychosis or paranoia could surface easily.

You're subservient to a loved one, thus, can be taken advantage of. Romance can be a disappointment when your sweetheart falls off the pedestal you've created. The waking up period can be devastating.

HOW TO MAKE THE MOST OF YOUR NAME

If you have discovered that your old name is beneficial, try to follow these suggestions, thus you will enhance your name vibration and attract even better luck. Also follow these suggestions if this is your NEW NAME VIBRATION.

If you wish to add further harmony into your life, wear the colors or gems for the sign/planet your name vibrates to. (**Note:** most people have more than one sign or planet that is lucky for them--I hope you fall into this category.) If you are limited in the colors you wear, use these lucky colors for accessories.

You'll feel so great when you wear all shades of purple--light, dark, lilac, lavender, mauve, orchid, pinkish-purple, or iridescent, aquamarine or sea-green or mother-of-pearl colors or jewelry. Also wear gems such as the peridot, pearl or coral jewelry.

Deal with the theater, movies, photography, makeup, fantasy, promoting, publicity, aviation, gas, oil, plastics, patent medicines, mediums, psychics or anything that requires a large amount of creative imagination. Use system and practicality, plot and work hard to accomplish the goals you dream about.

Awaken your idealistic longings and share them with others; it will be a great high. Put your visions into action. Paint, write a novel, play, movie or poetry, or utilize your fantasies through a hobby, creative idea or wheeling and dealing in a business; otherwise, they will be just unfulfilled longings. Let your psychic talents out.

You will be inclined to soar mentally into the world of the unreal where everything will appear real. This energy can be channeled into constructive and productive outlets that will bring you many rewarding moments when you reap the profits, aesthetically as well as financially.

Try to be realistic, regardless of the area pursued--work, creative, hobby, or love relationship. Watch exaggerations and viewing things through rose-colored glasses. Weigh all fantastic propositions carefully. Pay attention to details. Make concrete decisions and stick by them. Try to avoid giving imaginary attributes to a loved one. Be romantic, and hold hands. Embrace, kiss, show affection and enraptured states of heavenly bliss will be felt. Just remember to wake up and come back to reality! Keep in mind that positive action leads to success

CHAPTER SIX

CHANGING PARTS OF YOUR REAL NAME

Dropping One Letter

By changing---adding or dropping, one letter, you can change your name vibration which, often, can make a big difference. Many movie stars, before they became famous, dropped a single letter or added one more letter to their name. Dionn Warwick (Venus; artistic, lazy, and love of ease) became more successful when she added an "e" and became Dionne Warwick (Neptune). According to her astrodynes, Venus is afflicted (discordant in her horoscope) and Neptune is her second Best planet; therefore, the Neptune name vibration has brought her good fortune. Neptune represents dramatizing one's emotions which she certainly does excel in, especially when she sings.

Dorothy Malone (Uranus; Uranus represents the unexpected, overnight success, unpredictable events and a magnetic personality) was born Dorothy Maloney; she dropped the "y" and changed from a Neptune (planet of acting and disappointments, things falling through) name vibration to the Uranus name vibration. Her career didn't go anywhere until she made this change.

Diane L. Sawyer (Scorpio; persistence, determination and, often, caustic behavior) dropped her middle initial "L" and uses Diane Sawyer, (Uranus, can bring her many sudden events, make her controversial or deal with controversy which she has done on her many news shows.

Dropping a First Name

The sign/planet in parenthesis after a name represents the sign/planet their name vibrates to. Success and fame came to these celebrities when they dropped their first name: Penny Marshall (Aquarius, independence, daring to be different and original) dropped her first name Carole (Scorpio) was born Carole Penny Marshall) and Bebe Daniels (Aquarius) was born Phyllis Daniels (Neptune). Jane Pauley was born Margaret Jane Pauley (Aries; sign of impatience and temper).. Zsa Zsa Gabor (Mercury; communication, talking) was born Sari Zsa Zsa Gabor (Capricorn; ambition, seriousness). She wrote (Mercury) a tell-all (Mercury) book which revealed everything about her life and loves with friends and relationships. She is known for being quite a talker (Mercury). Anna Eleanor Roosevelt (Uranus) was her birth name; she became famous as Eleanor Roosevelt (Mars, planet of being an activist, aggressive and a go-getter; she was an advocate of human rights).

Clark Gable (Saturn; ambition) was born William Clark Gable (Sagittarius; carefree). Montgomery Clift (Venus) was born Terence Montgomery Clift (Aquarius; unique, different --he certainly was!) Steve Mc Quinn became a Gemini name vibration when he dropped his first name Patrick which gave his birth name a Uranus vibration. You know him as Ryan O'Neal (Pisces; acting) but he was born with a Taurus name, Patrick Ryan O'Neal, Taurus is, also, his Sun sign.

Bob Hope (Pisces); born Leslie Bob Hope, (Jupiter). David Niven (Neptune; born James David Niven, Sagittarius). Gene Autry (Taurus name; born Orvone Gene Autry, Aries). Bruce Willis, a happy-go-lucky Sagittarian name, dropped his first name Walter (total name was Uranus which can make one quite wild). Garth Brooks (Neptune, born Troyal Garth Brooks, Virgo). Neil Simon, Sagittarius; born Marvin Neil Simon (Gemini, sign of writing). Barry Sullivan (Aquarius; born Patrick Barry Sullivan, Neptune).

Robert Redford (Aquarius; born Charles Robert Redford, Jr., Aries). He has odd quirks (Aquarius) when a few years ago he stated that he doesn't like movies and yet he is a top box office draw and founded a movie festival in Utah. Early in his life. He rebelled (Aquarius) at his urbanized upbringing. He believes his children should move independently (Aquarius) through life.

Edith Norma Shearer, (Capricorn birth name) became famous as Norma Shearer, a lucky Sagittarian name. When Gregory Peck (Scorpio) dropped his first name, Eldred (Aquarius) he became successful. She was born Katherine Dawn Lang (Aquarius) and uses her initials K. D. Lang and couldn't escape the Aquarian vibration---Aquarius is original and is the sign of being unconventional such as "gay."

Dropping And Changing a First Name

These celebrities won fame and fortune when they dropped, and changed, their first name. Suzanne Mahoney (Aquarius) became Suzanne Somers (Neptune). Laura Gaynor (Jupiter) became Janet Gaynor (Capricorn). Rosebud Blondell (Sagittarian) became Joan Blondell (Uranus). Gretchen Young (Aquarius) became Loretta Young (Pisces). Virginia Davis (Aquarius) became Genna Davis (Sagittarius). Marilyn Novak (Neptune) became Kim Novak (Pisces).

Richard Klein became Calvin Klein; both vibrate to Sagittarius, thus, he did not change his vibration. William Basie (Scorpio) became Count Basie (Aquarius). Gwyllin Ford (Venus) became Glenn Ford (Venus; thus, his vibration remained the same--Venus rules good looks and he was born handsome). Another person who did not change her name vibration was Meryl Streep who was born Mary Louise Streep---both vibrate to Venus. Or Spike Lee who was born Shelton Lee; both names vibrate to Taurus.

Richard Skelton (Neptune) became Red Skelton (Virgo). Aristotle Savalas (Pisces) became Telly Savalas (Sagittarius). Cornelius Chase (Venus) became Chevy Chase (Uranus). Hubert Vallee (Jupiter) became Rudy Vallee (Aquarius). Susan Ker Weld (Aquarius) became Tuesday Weld (Saturn). Alicia Christian Foster (Aquarius) became Jodi Foster (Venus). Edna Mae Durbin (Cancer) became Deanna Durbin (Taurus; Taurus rules throat, vocal chords; she was a great singer). Joseph Rudyard Kipling (Scorpio) became Rudyard Kipling

(Sagittarius). William Somerset Maugham (Venus) became known as Somerset Maugham (Uranus).

And then there are those personalities that dropped their first and middle name and gave themselves new first names: Eric Hilliard Nelson (Sagittarius) became Rick Nelson (Capricorn). Robert Edward Turner (Jupiter) became Ted Turner (Venus). Edward Bridge Danson, III (Aries) became Ted Danson (a Virgo name.) John Donald Imus, Jr. (Gemini) became Don Imus (Pisces).

Middle Names

Many woman keep their middle name once they marry. Middle names have been increasing in popularity. Possibly because there are so many Christian (first) names and surnames (last) that are similar. With the population expanding, middle names help distinguish one person form another, especially if you have a common surname, such as Smith and a common Christian name such as John; therefore, a middle name may be helpful at the bank and in other similar circumstances--like the telephone directory. Choose an unusual middle name, if John Smith is your first or last name.

However, there are numerous people who dropped their middle name. Tanya Denise Tucker (Neptune) became Tanya Tucker (Venus; love; Tanya Tucker is known for her love affairs as well as artistic talents shown when she sings). Natalie Maria Cole and Natalie Cole both vibrate to Uranus, the planet of originality which she expressed when doing a duet with her father Nat King Cole--- it was dubbed with his voice from his recording of _Unforgettable_. Ella Wallace Rains and Ella Raines vibrate to Aquarius. Julia Fiona Robers (Jupiter) became Julia Roberts (Uranus; =sudden surprises, elopement). Ashley Tyler Judd (Aries) became Ashley Judd (Sagittarius). Bonnie Lynn Raitt (Saturn) became Bonnie Raitt (Uranus). Carrie Frances Fisher (Uranus) became Carrie Fisher (Neptune--- Neptune rules acting, movies). Angela Brigid Lansbury (Aquarius) became Angela Lansbury (Jupiter; the planet of wealth). Danielle Schulein Steel and Danielle Steel both vibrate to Neptune, the planet that rules dramatization.

Thorton Niven Wilder (Jupiter) became Thorton Wilder (Capricorn; --sign of ambition and discipline. He was famous for the play and movie _Our Town_ (Mercury). Jerome David Kern (Aquarius) became Jerome Kern (Neptune). Quincy Delight Jones (Virgo) became Quincy Jones (Uranus). Stephen Joshua Sondheim (Uranus) became Stephen Sondheim (Aries). Guy Albert Lombardo (Neptune) became Guy Lombardo (Scorpio). He has always been associated with New Years Eve (Gemini when added, the sign of change which occurs when a New Year begins. Oscar Emmanuel Peterson (Saturn) became Oscar Peterson (Cancer). Dylan Marlais Thomas (Gemini) became Dylan Thomas (Virgo).

Micheal Jeffery Jordan (Cancer) became Micheal Jordan (Venus). Dennis Keith Rodman (Uranus;--wild, controversial and outrageous behavior) became Dennis Rodman (Neptune; fantastic ability to promote oneself). Andre Kirk Agassi

(Saturn; disciplined) became Andre Agassi (Capricorn; ambitious and disciplined). Colin Luther Powell (Pisces) became Colin Powell (Jupiter). David Mc Clure Brinkley (Mars) became David Brinkley (Uranus). Merv Edward Griffin (Aries) became Merv Griffin (Aquarius).

Steven Allan Spielberg (Neptune; Movies) became Steven Spielberg (Sagittarius, his Sun sign also is Sagittarius, thus, enhancing the Sagittarian traits). David Lloyd Wolper (Neptune) became David Wolper (Virgo). Mel Colunbcille Gibson (Capricorn) became Mel Gibson (Saturn; Saturn rules Capricorn, thus, same traits. His Sun sign also is Capricorn; sign of ambition). Leonardo Wilhelm Di Caprio (Aquarius) became Leonardo Di Caprio (Saturn). Hugh Marston Hefner (Libra) became Hugh Hefner (Aries; his Sun sign also is Aries, thus, enhancing the pioneering traits of Aries). Jack O' Cassidy (Uranus) dropped the O and became Jack Cassidy (Libra).

James Albert Michener (Mars) became James Michener (Capricorn; Capricorn rules historical novels). Famous for his book and movie _Hawaii_, (an Aquarian title). Eugene Gladstone O'Neill (Sagittarius) became Eugene O'Neill (Capricorn). He combined tragedy (Capricorn) and pessimism (Capricorn in his plays. He took his vocation seriously (Capricorn). His plays deal with selfish (Capricorn) people; _Mourning Becomes Electra_ (Neptune title plays and drama. This play is a good example of the Capricorn characters in his plays.

Aldous Leonard Huxley (Uranus) became Aldous Huxley (Capricorn). In his _Brave New World_ he painted a grim (Capricorn) picture of a future Utopia, a scientifically organized (Capricorn) society in which conventional (Capricorn) suffering (Capricorn) has been eliminated.

Arnold Alois Schwarzenegger (Neptune) became Arnold Schwarzenegger (Taurus). His wife, Maria Shriver (Sagittarius) was born Maria Owings Striver (Taurus). Kurt Von Vogel Russell (Aquarius) became Kurt Russell (Pisces; the sign of acting). Brooke Shields (Jupiter) was born Brooke Christa Camille Shields (Mars). Dudley Stuart Moore (Jupiter) became Dudley Moore (Libra; he earned a reputation as a lady-chaser, a Libra trait. He was known as a charming, tender, sweet, romantic and generous person---all Libra traits).

Emily Elizabeth Dickinson (Uranus) became Emily Dickinson (Capricorn). She spent most of her life in seclusion (Capricorn) seeing only a limited (Capricorn) number of people. Had she used her Uranus birth name vibration, her life might have been different. Uranus is the rebel and dares to march to the beat of a different drummer, Uranus is unconventional whereas Capricorn is conventional.

Victor Marie Hugo (Taurus) became Victor Hugo (Uranus). He was a poet, dramatist and novelist who was in exile (Uranus) for awhile; he became a seagirt refugee (Uranus). His sensuality was demanding and led him into many adventures (Uranus), even as an old man. Victor Hugo wrote about the establishment of freedom (Uranus) and love. He advocated political reform

(Uranus).

Sylvester Enzio Stallone (Mars) became Sylvester Stallone (Aquarius). Jesse Woodson James (Sagittarius) became infamous as Jesse James (Scorpio). He was infamous as a leader of a gang that robbed (Scorpio) and murdered (Scorpio) through most of the central states of the USA. (Note: Scorpio when afflicted can be involved in these negative actions.)

Ayatollah Ruhollah Khomeini (Uranus) was known as Ayatollah Khomeini (Capricorn). He used the Capricorn negative side by being stubborn, selfish, ambitious, held a grudge and lived in poverty-like conditions. His birth name vibrates to Uranus, the planet that rules revolution, rebellion, reform and erratic behavior. Joan Henrietta Collins (Uranus) became Joan Collins (Neptune). Her role as Alexis (Uranus) and TV's _Dynasty_ (a Uranus title) was a career boost.

Dropping Your Middle Name And Replacing
It With an Initial

Robert Francis Kennedy (Capricorn) became Robert F. Kennedy (Pisces). Hubert Horatio Humphrey (Uranus) became Hubert H. Humphrey (Aquarius; Aquarius is ruled by Uranus, thus, his name vibration took on the same traits regardless of the spelling of his name). Lyndon Baines Johnson (Venus) became Lyndon B. Johnson (Aquarius).

He was born Huey Pierce Long (Sagittarius). He was known as a demagogue politician. When he was called Huey Long (Neptune) he enhanced the Neptune traits on the negative side---lies, deception, promoting and exaggerations. However, when he used Huey P. Long (Uranus) his vibration changed making him somewhat unconventional and radical in the tactics he used---traits ruled by Uranus. His campaign slogan, "Every Man A King," vibrates to Jupiter, the luckiest planet in astrology = represents wealth, confidence, optimism and is " bigger than life."

Franklin Delano Roosevelt (Aries) was known for his leadership (Aries) ability, especially during World War II---Aries is the sign that rules war. He was admired for his courage (Aries) to continue in spite of polio (ruled by Uranus). Franklin D. Roosevelt (a Uranus name and planet ruling Polio, paralysis). When he used this name he was unconventional, non-conforming and involved with new (Uranus) deals, reform (Uranus) and humanitarianism (Uranus). He furthered a good neighbor (Uranus) policy in foreign (Uranus) affairs.

George Michael Cohan and George M. Cohan vibrate to Sagittarius, thus, he continued to attract the Sagittarius traits regardless of how he spelled his name. He is best remembered for his patriot song _Over There_ (an Aries Title) written during the War (Aries).

Pearl Sydenstricker Buck (Uranus) was known as Pearl S. Buck (Sagittarius). She was a missionary (Sagittarius) who devoted her greatest talents to promoting understanding (Sagittarius and Uranus) between the East and the

West. Her book *The Good Earth* (a Mars title) became a movie.

Dropping Your Last Name And Changing
It to a New Name

Raquel Welch (Aries) was born Raquel Tejada (Sagittarius). Anthony Franciosa (Aries) was born Anthony Papalco (Sagittarius). Christian Slater (Mars) was born Christian Hawkins (Saturn). Ethel Merman (Mars) was born Ethel Zimmerman (Uranus). Doris Day (Taurus) was born Doris Kappelhoff (Pisces). Elke Sommer (Libra) was born Elke Schletz (Saturn). David Janssen (Libra) was born David Meyer (Saturn). Virginia Mayo (Venus) was born Virginia Jones (Jupiter). Pamela Mason (Venus) was born Pamela Kanino (Sagittarius). Howard Cosell (Venus) was born Howard Cohen (Uranus).

Maureen O'Hara(Virgo) was born Maureen Fitzsimmons (Uranus). Emma Samms (Virgo) was born Emma Samuelson (Venus). Lili Palmer (Scorpio) was born Lilli Peiser (Capricorn). Louis Jordan (Scorpio) was born Louis Gendre (Capricorn). Jayne Meadows (Sagittarius) was born Jayne Cotter (Uranus). Fanny Brice (Jupiter) was born Fanny Borach (Scorpio). Milton Berle (Jupiter) was born Milton Berlinger (Saturn). Michael Bolton (Jupiter) was born Michael Bolotin (Venus). Richard Burton (Capricorn) was born Richard Jenkins (Aries). Myrna Loy (Saturn) was born Myrna Williams (Capricorn). Leon Ames (Saturn) was born Leon Wyckoff (Aquarius).

Harry Morgan (Aquarius) was born Harry Bratsburg (Jupiter). Fred Astaire (Aquarius) was born Fred Austerlitz (Capricorn). Bernadette Peters (Uranus) was born Bernadette Lazzaro (Neptune). Walter Matthau (Uranus) was born Walter Matuschanskavsky (Neptune). Diana Dors (Uranus) was born Diana Fluck (Saturn). Vivian Blaine (Uranus) was born Vivian Stapleton (Saturn). Carmen Miranda (Uranus) still remained Uranus, (born , Carmen Miranda Da Cunha).

June Haver (Pisces) was born Jane Stovenour (Capricorn). Frances Nuyen (Pisces) was born Frances Vannga (Neptune). Vera Miles (Pisces continued to vibrate to Pisces as Vera Ralston, Pisces). John Forsythe (Neptune) was born John Freund (Venus). Don Adams (Neptune) was born Don Yarmy (Uranus). Hugh O'Brien (Neptune) was born Hugh Krampke (Scorpio). Elsa Lancaster (Neptune) was born Elsa Sullivan (Scorpio).

Loretta Lynn (Aries) was born Loretta Webb (Jupiter). She is known for singing country music. Typical of her Aries name vibration she endured hardships and withstood discouragement in the early years of her career. She's a woman with guts and drive---Aries traits.

Dropping Your Last Name; Keeping Your
First And Middle Name

Eddie Murphy (Aries; also he's an Aries Sun sign which adds additional

Aries energy to his nature), was born Eddie Murphy Lynch, Pisces. Ray Charles (Gemini) was born Ray Charles Robinson (Scorpio). Tim Allen (Gemini) was born Tim Allen Dick (Capricorn). Robert Preston (Virgo) was born Robert Preston Meservey (Saturn). Leslie Howard (Libra) was born Leslie Howard Steiner (Uranus). Tom Cruise (Sagittarius) retained the Sagittarian vibration because his birth name Tom Cruise Mapother also vibrated to Sagittarius.

Ann-Margaret (Jupiter) was born Ann Margaret Olson (Pisces). Eddie Albert (Aquarius) was born Eddie Albert Heinberjér (Neptune). Audrey Hepburn (Neptune) was born Audrey Hepburn Ruston (Aquarius). Shirley Mac Laine (Sagittarius) was born Shirley Mac Laine Beaty (Neptune). She traveled (Sagittarius) all over the globe and wrote books about her psychic experiences and philosophy (Sagittarius). Her optimistic (Sagittarius), outgoing nature (Sagittarius) and friendly smile (Sagittarius) has endeared her to many fans.

Fidel Castro (an Aries name) was born Fidel Castro Ruz (Uranus). He always carries a knife (Aries), was involved in guerilla warfare (Aries) and battles (Aries). When he is called Castro he vibrates to Uranus (revolution, reforms, modernization, new ideas, government changes, rebellion, erratic behavior). He is known to love gadgets (Uranus).

Dropping Your Last Name; Keeping Your
First And Middle Name

Winona Ryder (Libra) was born Winona Laura Horowitz (Saturn). Jean Gabin (Venus) was born Jean Alexis Moncourage (Leo). Betty Hutton (Taurus) was born Betty Jane Thornburg (Uranus). Carol Lawrence (Capricorn) was born Carol Maria Laraia (Venus). Charles Bronson (Capricorn) was born Charles Dennis Buchinsky (Uranus). Douglas Fairbanks, Jr. (Uranus) was born Douglas Elton Ulman (Mars). Melvyn Douglas (Venus) was born Melvyn C. Hesselberg (Neptune). Joan Leslie (Sagittarius) was born Joan Agnes Theresa Sadie Brodell (Saturn). Maria Montez (Jupiter) was born Maria Africa Fidal de Santos Silas (Pisces). River Phoenix (Pisces) was born River Jude Bottom (Saturn). He died of an overdose of drugs (Pisces when afflicted in a horoscope is easily attracted to drugs, escapism.) If he had kept his birth name he would have been disciplined (Saturn) but would he have been famous?

Using Parts of Your Real Name

Claudette Colbert (Taurus) was born Lily Claudette Chaunchoin (Neptune). Yvonne De Carlo (Capricorn) was born Peggy Yvonne Middleton (Jupiter). Kathryn Grayson (Venus) was born Zelma Kathryn Hendrick (Saturn). Marie Windsor (Venus) was born Emily Marie Bertelson (Aquarius). Nanette Fabray (Capricorn) was born Ruby Nanette Fabare (Aries). Jane Wyman (Neptune) was born Sara Jane Fulks (Jupiter). Jack Palance (Aries) was born Walter Jack Palanuik (Aquarius).

Mitzi Gaynor (Aquarius) was born Francesca Mitzi Von Gerber (Neptune). Merle Oberon (Neptune) was born Estell Merle O'Brien Thompson (Scorpio). Madeleine Carroll(Taurus) was born Marie Madeleine Bernadette O'Carroll (Capricorn). Woody Harrelson (Uranus) was born Woodrow Tracey Harrelson (Aries). Jane Russell (Uranus) was born Ernestine Jane Geraldine Russell (Neptune). Bob Guccione (Saturn) was born Robert Charles Joseph Edward Sabatini Guccione (Aries). Jon Hall (Uranus) was born Charles Hall Locher (Capricorn).

Nat King Cole (Neptune) was born Nathaniel Adam Cole (Pisces). Dirk Bogarde (Saturn) was born Dirk Vander Bogaerde (Sagittarius). Dolores Del Rio (Capricorn) was born Lolita Dolores Martinez-Asunsolo Lopez Negrete (Moon). Van Cliburn (Saturn) was born Harvey Lavan Cliborn, Jr. (Cancer). Alec Baldwin (Saturn) was born Alexander Rae Baldwin III (Neptune). Dana Andrews (Uranus) was born Carver Dan Andrews (Aquarius). Paul Muni (Mars) was born Muni Weisenfreund (Capricorn). Walt Whitman (Sagittarius) was born Walter Whitman (Jupiter). Gene Raymond (Venus) was born Raymond Guion (Uranus). Tennessee Willimas (Capricorn) was born Thomas Lanier Williams (Aquarius). Al Pacino (Uranus) was born Alfredo James Pacino (Taurus).

Ben Affleck (Taurus) was born Benjamin Geza Affleck-Boldt (Capricorn). Lita Grey Chaplin (Uranus) was born Lillita Louise Mc Murray (Aquarius). Katy Jurado (Virgo) was born Maria Christina Jurado Garcia (Neptune). Chita Rivera (Scropio) was born Conchita Del Rivero (Aquarius). Gene Barry (Capricorn) was born Eugene Klass (Jupiter). Faye Dunaway (Pisces) was born Dorothy Faye (Aquarius). Mona Freeman (Neptune) was born Monica Elizabeth Freman (Virgo) . Karl Malden (Pisces) was born Malden Sekalovich (Aries). Mel Brooks (Capricorn) was born Melvin Kaminsky (Sagittarius). Newt Gingrich (Sagittarius) was born Newton Leroy Gingrich (Uranus).

Rod Stewart (Neptune) was born Roderick David Stewart (Pisces). Jon Stewart (Neptune) was born Jon Stuart Liebowitz (Scorpio). Warren Beatty (Neptune) was born Henry Warren Beaty (Uranus). W. C. Fields (Taurus) was born William Claude Dunkenfield (Sagittarius); he merely used the initials of his first and middle name and took the Field part of his last name and made it Fields.

CHAPTER SEVEN

NAMES, NAMES, NAMES
(Pseudonyms, Corporations, Titles, Nicknames, Business)

Pseudonym Names

Pen Names and Pseudonym Names (one and the same) have been used by many celebrities who did not want people to know their real names. The same holds true for the person in a non-celebrity status. Many famous people used these stage names when they first started in show business.

David Copperfield (Saturn) was born David Kotkin (Uranus). By age twelve, he performed under the name, "Davino, The Boy Magician." (Pisces). Kim Basinger (Virgo), before acting, pursued a singing career under the nom-de-chant "Chelsea." (Sagittarius which vibrates to her Sun Sign Sagittarius). Sonny Bono (Venus) was born Salvatore Philip Bono (Neptune). He cut records under the names Prince Carter (Pisces), Ronny Sommers (Pisces) and Sonny Christie (Aquarius---his Sun sign was Aquarius).

Julie Andrews (Venus) was born Julia Welles (Mercury---rules writing and singing). Under her married name Julie Edwards (Jupiter) she wrote two children's books. She is best known for her role in *Sound Of Music* (a Neptune title; rules movies). Stephen King (Jupiter) used the pseudonym Richard Bachman (Libra) for five novels. Did anyone ever hear of him then? Or was it when he used Stephen King that he became popular?

Anne Rice (Capricorn) was born Howard Allen O'Brien (Aries). She was the author of a series of pornographic novels under the name A. N. Roquelaure (also Capricorn) which means "cloak." She is supposedly afraid of the dark. She was originally named after her father and mother's maiden name; she changed her name to Anne by the time she was in the first grade. Rice is her married name.

Joe Pesci (Taurus). He appears in some of his films under the pseudonym Joe Ritchie (Sagittarius). Mark Wahlberg (Libra), actor, model, rap artist. His debut album under nom de rays "Marky Mark" (Venus). It was produced by his brother with his brother's money. Usually people with Libra and/or Venus vibrations to their names, have it easy when it comes to money.

Manolete (Mars) was born Manuel Laureano Rodriguez Y Sanchez (Aries). He was courageous, Aries and Mars). Manolete was known as the most famous bullfighter in history. He was gored (Mars) to death in the ring.

Lola Montez (Uranus) was born Marie Dolores Eliza Rosanna Gilbert (Saturn). She was an Irish dancer who adopted the name Lola Montez when she began to dance, claiming Spanish descent. Her wild and abandoned (Uranus) love affairs were scandalous (Uranus). She had romantic liaisons with Liszt (Aquarius), Alexandre Dumas (Jupiter) and with Ludwig I, King of Bavaria (Uranus). Did the Aquarius (ruled by Uranus) vibration of Liszt and the Uranus vibration of the King, draw Lola to them?

Samuel Langhorne Clemens (Sagittarius; his Sun sign also was Sagittarius) used the pen name Mark Twain (Gemini, sign of writing). He was famous for characters in his books, especially _Tom Sawyer_ (Venus) and _Huckleberry Finn_ (Pisces).

He's known as Charles Dickens (Capricorn); he signed his name as Charles Huffam Dickens (Sagittarius) and was born John Huffam (Virgo). Because he signed his name Charles Huffman Dickens, this is the way he would have thought of himself. But with all of these names he had mixed vibrations. After a sickly, poverty-stricken (Virgo) and bookish (Virgo) childhood he worked briefly in a blacking factory. When he earned money from his writing (Virgo) Charles spent it generously (Sagittarius). He led a life of a dandy (Sagittarius) and was quite flamboyant; however, he worked hard (Capricorn) and burnt the candle at both ends. This was due to the mixed name vibrations--the Sagittarius part would want to live it up and entertain others, which he did; the Capricorn part would labor long hours, which he did; the Capricorn part would labor long hours, which he also did. Dickens wanted to raise (a Sagittarius trait) the poorest (Capricorn) denominator of society.

As a journalist, early in his career, he wrote under the pen name "Boz" (Sagittarius) for the monthly magazine _The Pickwick Papers_ (a Neptune title); this is when he established his popularity. Sagittarius is the luckiest sign in astrology and through this name vibration "Boz," he was able to promote (Neptune) his career. Dickens had humility (Capricorn) and overworked (Capricorn) which hastened his death.

His pen name was Lewis Carrol (Neptune). He was born Charles Lutwidge Dodgson (Venus). He was known as a leading mathematician, ordained as a deacon and was a pioneering photographer (Neptune). He mingled fantasy (Neptune) with satirical observations. The "Alice" (Pisces name) stories (the most famous was _Alice In Wonderland_--an Aquarius title) were written to amuse Alice Liddel (Taurus), the daughter of the dean of Christ Church.

He was born Walter Sydney Porter (Jupiter) and used the pen name O. Henry (Uranus). He was a short-story (Uranus) writer. O. Henry (Uranus) was an author who had ingenious (Uranus) ways of plotting coincidence (Uranus). Above all, his surprise twist (Uranus) endings were much imitated. His life was typical of Uranus traits; he drank plenty of booze, eloped with a girl of 19, and held several different jobs. When he was a bank teller, he was careless with $5500 of the bank's money; to avoid indictment he ran away to Honduras, but returned when he heard his wife was dying. He was apprehended by the authorities and spent three years in jail, where he wrote his unusual (Uranus) stories that later made him famous.

His pen name was Moliere (Aquarius) but he was born with a Leo name (Jean Baptiste Poquelin). Moliere was a 17th century French playwright who broke

(Aquarius) with his classical education and adopted a profession then deplored by all sound citizens and condemned by the Church--all typical of Aquarius doing the reverse of what is considered proper to do. He founded (Aquarius) a theatre which ended in bankruptcy (Aquarius). His plays were distorted (Aquarius) by avarice and showed radical (Aquarius) quirks. His plots displayed these deformities (Aquarius) in all their laughable aspects and showed how an unbalanced (Aquarius) person may unbalance (typical Aquarius action) the lives of others and threaten the social fabric (again typical of Aquarius action).

He was born Lev Davidovitch Bronstein (Aquarius); however, he was known as Leon Trotsky (Mars). He was a Russian revolutionary (Aquarius) who spent years abroad agitating (Mars) others. He organized the victorious Red Army (Mars). Ironically, he was killed by an ax (Mars)!

His pen name was Voltaire (Neptune) and he was born Francois-Marie-Arouet (Aries). He was a writer who lived in constant conflict with authority. He often displayed a great humanity (Neptune) and generosity (Aries), particularly in rehabilitating the victims of unjust oppression (Aries). His career gave literature a new prestige (Aries, Neptune). He was also a playwright (Neptune).

Edna St. Vincent Millay (Aquarius) wrote unusual (Aquarius) poetry about a woman who did the leaving (Aquarius) in a relationship. She would stop (Aquarius) her romances before they led to marriage. Once she married, her husband did the housework (a typical Aquarian trait). She wrote her serious work under the name Edna St. Vincent Millay, but her satire was written under a pseudonym — Nancy Boyd (a Uranus name). She loved being called Vincent when she was young and no wonder, it also vibrated to Uranus. She was a woman's libber (Uranus) long before it became popular.

George Eliot (Aquarius) was a woman who used a man's name (an Aquarian action) to conceal her identity. She made the daring decision (in the 1800's) to live with her mentor as his common-law wife (he was married and couldn't obtain a divorce). Therefore, she defied (Aquarius) convention and it caused a cut off (Aquarius trait) of all communications with her brother. She rebelled (Aquarius) from her family as a child at an early age. Her greatest distinction as a novelist is her insight into human psychology (Aquarius).

She used the name George Eliot as a pseudonym; her maiden name was Mary Ann Evans (Libra) or, some sources give Marian Evans (Sagittarius). Regardless of whether she used the Libra, Sagittarius or Aquarius name vibration, all of these signs are somewhat similar in that a person having them would do and live as desired. However, when she married her name became Marian Evans Cross (Saturn) and with this new vibration, she settled down (Saturn) --Saturn is the planet of conventional behavior and the establishment.

She was born Amandine Aurore Lucie Dupin (Aquarius). She married Casmir Dudevant (Aries) and became Baroness Dudevant (Aquarius). She left him for another man. She wrote many successful novels under her pen name George

Sand (Neptune) and dressed in men's clothes. Her famous lovers were Frederic Chopin (Aries) and Alfred de Musset (Pisces; born Louis Charles Musset, Aquarius). To this day Chopin (Neptune) and George Sand (Neptune) are a famous couple whose names when joined become a Taurus, love and artistic vibration; a deep friendship existed. She was known also for her infidelity (Neptune) as well as her writing.

Agatha Christie (Libra) wrote detective stories. Her real name was Mary Clarissa (Venus); Venus rules Libra --- her pen-name). She was a recluse during the latter part of her life--the Sun sign Virgo tends to make one withdraw and work hard; however, with her Libra and Venus name vibration, she lived in luxury and refrained from using the same vibration for entertaining and love. Her play *Mousetrap* (a Libra title) set the record for the longest continuous run in a theatre. Isn't it ironic that the title of her play and her pen name are both a Libra vibration? She became Dame Agatha Clarissa (Taurus; Taurus is ruled by Venus, Venus also rules her real name).

BUSINESS, TITLES AND CORPORATION NAMES

CORPORATION NAMES

Even the Hollywood producers have gotten into the act because the August 30, 1980 issue of *TV Guide* contained an article about names--that of naming your production company. They suggested using your own name. However, if you don't want your family name, be creative and try the initials of all your partners. They advised, "...be careful if your partner is your wife. While both marriages and production companies are born in bliss, they don't always endure. So you might be on firmer ground to name your production company after your child."

You may want to name your company after your pet as Marione Dione Hensley of Maggie Vanda Enterprises did, when she named her corporation after her cat, Maggie Vanda. There's an endless variety of names that you may select for your company. The corporation may be named after your given name, stage name, nickname, a dog, cat, favorite city, place, state, street, river, lake, mountain, apartment building, hotel--such as the Andover Apartments, could be changed to your company name --Andover Productions. You may want an arcane or esoteric name, perhaps a name after a famous ruin such as Parthenon Productions. Or how about a name from one of the Greek God or Goddesses right out of mythology -- Venus Corporation, Apollo Productions, or Zeus Manufacturing Company?

Historical names are popular and are used more with a corporation that an individual name; however, certain historical names may be good for a Christian or surname. Bonaparte (Napoleon) may be a good surname for someone or Bonaparte Productions could be auspicious for a company. However, stay away from historical names connected with loss such as *Waterloo* Productions.

You may want to change a name to a favorite expression of yours, or to a feeling you once enjoyed, i.e., Fiddle Faddle Manufacturing Corporation or Happiness, Inc. Maybe you want to give the name of the business you'll be operating--i.e., a solar production company may be called, "Sunshine Unlimited." Or perhaps you want to take the initials of a foreign language expression, i.e., " Mon Cherie Productions."

Invent a name from a title of a song, story, poem. Perhaps you are searching for a name for the new corporations you want to form. If you like the song, *"The Object Of My Affection,"* take the first letter of each word and name your company "Tooma"--or switch the letters around and call it "Oomat" Corporation or "Matoo" Corporation.

Samuel Goldwyn (Venus) was born Samuel Goldfish (Pisces, sign of film, promoting, glamor). He was a film producer and established his own Goldwyn Pictures Corporation (Taurus, ruled by Venus). He later merged with Louis B. Mayer (Capricorn; he was strict with old-fashioned rules, disciplinarian to the stars). With the merger Metro-Goldwyn-Mayer (Uranus) became known as MGM (Neptune, planet ruling movies).

Jack Warner (Cancer), producer and founder of warner Brothers Pictures (Uranus)---they were four brothers who owned it. Their company produced the first "talkie" (Sagittarius word when the letters are added), classical films and were the first Hollywood studio to produce TV programs. Uranus, is the planet of being "First,"---original. *The Jazz Singer* (Scorpio title) was the first talkie film.

Mary Tyler Moore (Pisces) and her husband at that time, owned MTM Productions (Pisces title) and her TV show was named after her.

Barry Gordy, Jr. (Uranus) is the founder (Uranus) of Motown Record Corporation (Uranus title---the planet of daring to be original and different). New (Uranus) sounds came out of Motown (Saturn when spelled by itself; planet of ambition and perseverance and training---the performers were trained). Motown Record Corp. vibrates to Neptune, the planet of being visionary and promoting.

Paul Newman (Gemini) is a philanthropist (Sagittarius trait) and humanitarian (Aquarian trait; his Sun sign is Aquarius). As of 1999, his food company "The Newman's Own" (Sagittarius name) has donated more than ninety million dollars to charity.

The names "Barnum and Bailey" combined vibrate to Sagittarius (large-scale operations). When P. T. Barnum (Taurus) and J. A. Bailey (Venus; Venus rules Taurus -- thus, sharing similar traits) joined forces and combined with "Ringling Bros." (Taurus) the total name became "Ringling Bros. and Bailey" which vibrates to Libra (Venus) rules Libra and represents fun, frolics, merriment, beauty, costumes, make-up, the expression of artistic abilities and ready cash — which they made plenty of). With such a combination, is it any wonder that this has been called "The Greatest Show on Earth?"

TITLES

Are you aware that you can add up the title of a movie, book, story, poem, television show or song so it will come out harmoniously for you? It's done in the same fashion as adding a name.

You may ask, "How important are titles?" In the July 25, 1981, *TV Guide*, an article appeared, "Have we sold you dear viewer?" This article was about names. If you have a show and want a good Nielsen rating, the television movie or show should have a good name. It seems like words involving love combined with words of action in the same title, almost guarantee success.

The networks use a computer service, ASI Market Research, Inc., in Hollywood , that can tell whether a title is marketable (has high rating possibilities). This article in *TV Guide* states that, "The best titles come from intuitive people." It seems that producers like titles that "...express jeopardy, conflict, passion, thrills and chills...looking for certain buzz-words that will get an audience's blood pumping ...combine sex with violence ...or a title must have sex, love, but especially human abuse...words that evoke a feeling of mystery--words like 'stranger' or 'happen' or 'mystery' itself...titles that contain one word and one syllable are fantastic."

However, you can go one step beyond this and add the title's name to see if it has the type of vibration that you want--or that is lucky for you according to your horoscope. Perhaps you like the title, *"Death Kisses"* for a sex-murder play you are writing for the television screen; if Venus is in Scorpio in your horoscope and it's harmonious, this would be a lucky title for you, especially if it involves your house of fame and money. The preceding may be too technical for the average layman. However, if you don't want to get this technical, you can still come up with an interesting name vibration.

"Death Kisses" vibrates to Aquarius, the sign ruling the sudden and unexpected. But let's say it vibrated to Scorpio, the sign of sex, murder and intrigue--then this tittle would take on this additional Scorpio energy (traits) and make the public more interested in turning into the channel it's appearing on. And, furthermore, if this sign Scorpio is harmonious in your horoscope, this could be a lucky break for you.

George (Sagittarian) is the name of a political magazine published by John F. Kennedy, Jr. (Taurus; Sun sign is Sagittarius, the same name vibration as his magazine's name). Sagittarius is the luckiest sign in astrology. Taurus is a sign that perseveres; thus, hopefully his magazine will be a success. When the name *Titanic* is used the movie, book and ship all vibrate to Aquarius. Aquarius on the negative side can be sudden events; the unexpected which occurred when the ship sunk. When the movie became an overnight success (perhaps, for the producers and people involved Aquarius is harmonious), that was an overwhelming (Aquarius action) surprise (Aquarius the sign of surprise).

The television shows *Kojak* and *Columbo* vibrate to Aries (sign of adventure, violence, accidents and often involved in murder).

Margaret Mitchell (Taurus) labored with great perseverance (Taurus trait) to write her only novel *Gone With The Wind* (Libra title; romance vibration). Vivien Leigh, (Aries; a spitfire and builder) played the heroine. Her real name was Vivien Mary Hartley (Neptune; movies, acting).

Gabrielle Chanel (Libra) was famous as Coco Chanel (Aries). Coco by itself, as many called her, vibrates to Aquarius. Aquarius is original, Aries indicates an enterprising nature and Libra is the sign ruling fashion and perfume. Chanel, as her designer clothes are called, vibrates to Scorpio, an energetic and resourceful sign. Her most famous perfume *Chanel No. 5* vibrates to Aries (the same vibration as her name Coco Chanel. Another perfume under her banner is *Chanel No. 19*, which adds up to Aquarius, the same vibration as her name "Coco." She was also known for her love (Libra) affairs, daring and adventuresome (Aries) in her personal life. She was fearless (Aries) in her conquests (Aries) and would take chances--real risks--(Aries) in business. She had the courage (Aries) of her convictions.

NICKNAMES

Avoid derogatory nicknames. Take into consideration all abbreviations of a nickname because maybe your about-to-be born baby will change her name later to one of these abbreviations. Often nicknames can be embarrassing and interfere with one's popularity and cut down on one's chances to have a happier life.

Don't use a nickname unless it's lucky for you. The following is a hypothetical situation which will give you some idea of how important this can be. For example, if your name is Catherine it will vibrate to the sign Pisces. When people call you Catherine, or when you use the name by itself, you are subconsciously and inadvertly expressing the characteristics associated with the sign Pisces, which would make you sweet, kind, timid, romantic, mysterious, indolent, self-sacrificing and easy to live with because you desire harmony for self and the world and will do almost anything to maintain it.

However, if people call you Cathy, which is a nickname for Catherine, you are now vibrating to the planet Pluto. This will bring out Pluto's traits in your personality, which mean you could alternate between being cooperative or uncooperative, or on the negative side you might become dictative, sarcastic, forceful, underhanded, rebellious, energetic, compulsive and difficult to live with. However, on the positive side, you could have spiritual feelings and become involved in some worthy cause to aid mankind.

Now I'm not saying that the preceding is fated, or that this is the way you will absolutely react, because everybody responds in a different manner. This is dependent upon one's basic traits, planets, condition and environment. (Everyone has all of the twelve signs and ten planets in his or her horoscope; some are harmonious and others are inharmonious.)

In your horoscope if Pisces (Catherine) or Pluto (Cathy) is discordant and you use this name, you'd reinforce the name with additional discord and attract misfortune; however, if Pisces (Catherine) or Pluto (Cathy) is harmonious and you use this name, you'd reinforce the name with additional harmony and attract good fortune. And, it's just as easy to have one that is discordant (unlucky). This will help you utilize the most favorable influences in your horoscope.

One of the most popular nicknames that people use is the common nickname of their first name, such as "Jimmy" for James and "Tommy" for Thomas. He was born James Scott Connors (Neptune) and is called"Jimmy" (Neptune) or uses the name Jimmy Connors which changes his name vibration to Saturn. James Stewart (Pisces) was called Jimmy Stewart (Aquarius). James Howard Doolittle (Capricorn) was called James Doolittle (Mars) by many; however, he's also known as Jimmy Doolittle (Aries). He led (Mars, Aries) the first (Mars, Aries) successful bombing (Mars trait) of Tokyo in world War (Mars) II. He was a courageous (Mars, Aries) aviator and army officer.

He was born James Earl Carter, Jr. (Gemini) and called Jimmy Carter (Aquarius) and when in office it was President Jimmy Carter (Uranus). These Aquarius, Uranus traits he used represent reform, changes, freedom, independence and humanitarianism. His habitat for humanity projects of building homes for the needy is also Uranus/ Aquarius ruled.

Thomas Jones Woodward (Leo) is known as the singer Tom Jones (Aquarius). Thomas Connery (Venus) was as a boy called Tommy (Neptune) but became famous as Sean Connery (Jupiter, the luckiest planet in astrology; is this when success came---using the name Sean Connery?) He was born Joseph Paul DiMaggio (Pisces) but the world knows him as Joe Di Maggio (Uranus). Anthony Charles Lynton Blair (Pisces, an idealistic sign) is Prime Minister of the U.K. but is called Tony Blair (Capricorn; ambitious) by many.

Kathleen Doyle Bates (Pisces) uses Kathy Bates (Uranus) as her professional show business name. Katherine Couric (Taurus) is called Katie Couric (Jupiter). Professional baseball player Samuel Sosa is called Sammy Sosa--both names vibrate to Aquarius. William Penn Adair Rogers (Uranus) became known as Will Rogers (Capricorn). He was an actor and humorist who was killed in a plane accident with aviator Wiley Post (Neptune, planet of aviation) and Will was known for his dry (Capricorn) humor.

Charles Rogers (Capricorn) was often called Buddy Rogers (Libra) or Charles "Buddy" Rogers (Mars). You know him as Al Capone (Taurus); his nicknames were Al (Aries, gutsy sign, fearless) and Scarface (Saturn). His birth name was Alphonse Capone (Aquarius).

Jacqueline Joyner (Saturn) is her birth name. When she married she hyphenated her name; however, she did it with her nickname---Jackie Joyner-Kersee (Uranus, planet of breaking records, which she did as a track and field athlete). Often she is called "Jackie"---Pisces.

You know Lucy Ann Collier (Uranus) by her professional name Ann Miller. She's known for her tap dancing (whose letters adds to a Mars vibration; Mars is ruled by Aries, her Sun sign---Mars is, like Aries, energetic and rhythmic). Ann Miller (Cancer) was very protective (Cancer) of her mother since she was eleven years old and went out and sang to make money for food (Cancer) for herself and her mother (Cancer). Her nickname, Annie (Capricorn) probably is a stabilizing influences which may be needed if she ever expresses the Cancer emotional and changeable traits.

Often, nicknames are given to people by others. Will Smith (Pisces; acting) earned his nickname, "the Prince" (Uranus) from a teacher in Overbrook High School because of his regal attitude and ability to talk his way out of difficult situations.

Marguerite Annie Johnson (Venus) is known as Maya Angelou (Uranus). She was nicknamed "Maya" (Sagittarius) by her brother who called her "My" (Jupiter) or "mine." (Venus). Gwyneth Palthrow (Venus) is called Gwinny (Pisces) by her pals. His real name was Eric Clapp (Jupiter) but he's famous as Eric Clapton (Aries). He earned the nickname "Slowhand" (Uranus)because his powerful playing regularly broke his guitar strings, which he then changed on stage to the accompaniment of a slow handclap from listeners.

Sean "Puffy" Combs (Aquarius) got the nickname "Puffy" (Aries) as a child because he would huff and puff when angry. His clothes label, Sean John (Gemini), is monikered after his first and middle names. His real name is Sean John Combs (Capricorn). Howard Hughes (Sagittarius) was born Howard Robard Hughes, Jr. (Leo, sign of the entrepreneur). When growing up, he was called "Sonny" (Pisces, sign of acting, aviation) or "Little Howard" (Pisces). However, his greatest luck came by using the lucky Sagittarius name "Howard Hughes."

Cameron Diaz (Libra) was nicknamed "Skeletor" (Scorpio) as a child for being so skinny. Her first name, Cameron, means "crooked stream" in Gaelic. She was born Sofia Scicolone (Capricorn, ambitious) beauty (Venus) with her gracefulness (Venus) and feminity (Venus). She donated her art (Venus) collection to the Italian government. When she was a child she was as skinny as a "stick" (Pisces) and was called "Stechetlo" (Libra, ruler of Venus) which means stick in Italian.

John Wayne (Pisces, acting) was born Marion Michael Morrison (Uranus). By the time he was seven years old, kids ridiculed him for having a "sissy" first name and boys loved to beat him up. The kids called him a "little girl" (adds to Neptune) and asked him why he wore pants instead of a skirt.

Katherine Hepburn (Pisces, acting) called herself "Jimmy" (Neptune, acting) when she was eight years old, after brother Tom's friend. She wore boys clothes to school and beat up the biggest bully in the neighborhood. To keep kids from pulling her hair, she cut it so it was only a hair inch long. She was a rebel who wanted to be a boy like Tom.

Jane Fonda (Uranus) is known for her controversial (Uranus) crusades as well as her movie roles and marriage to Ted Turner. She almost arrested for treason. She spoke out against the Vietnam war; she took a trip there which earned her the nickname Hanoi Jane (Mars, planet of war and speaking out, the activist planet).

The statesman who was Britain's Prime Minister, Benjamin Disraeli (Sagittarius) was called "Dizzy" (Neptune, trait of dizziness). Walter Mondale (Jupiter) was born Walter Frederick Mondale (Aquarius) and was known as "Fritz" (Neptune). The revolutionary and Mexican bandit known as Pancho Villa (Neptune, idealistic) was called "Pancho" (Capricorn, ambitious) and often used the name Francisco Villa (Aquarius, revolutionary) but was born Doroteo Aranga (Aries, fighting). As Pancho Villa he used the Neptune traits, i.e., grandiose ideas and wanting better conditions for mankind.

His real name was Charles Augustus Lindberg (Sagittarius, travel) and used Charles A. Lindbergh (Pisces, aviation). But he was known as "Lucky Lindy" (Mercury; travel). He made the first solo nonstop transatlantic flight from New York City to Paris. Did his name vibrations influence him along these lines?

Charles "Lucky" Luciano vibrates to Mars (violence, murder, fights, temper) and Charles Luciano vibrates to Pisces (drugs, corruption, lies, escapism). By using his nickname "Lucky" Luciano (Libra), the known Mafia leader was able to flee from danger (Libra is the second luckiest sign in the zodiac). The name lucky vibrates to Jupiter, the luckiest planet in astrology. Luciano by itself vibrates to Sagittarius, the luckiest sign of the zodiac which is ruled by Jupiter.

Louis (Satchmo) Armstrong (Saturn) never forgot his early poverty (Saturn). Critics said his lips and strong teeth gave him a natural advantage with a trumpet or cornet. That vast mouth led to his having a variety of nicknames. The first nickname was "Dippermouth" (Aquarius) the second was Satchelmouth (Jupiter) and the third and last nickname which stuck was "Satchmo" (Aquarius, the same vibration as his first nickname). With the Aquarius vibration, he became known for being unique (Aquarius) and original (Aquarius) and with the Jupiter vibration his smile (Jupiter) became his trademark.

Edward Kennedy Ellington (Scorpio) was creative (Scorpio) and persistent (Scorpio) but worked harder and became ambitious (Capricorn) when he used his nickname "Duke" Ellington (Capricorn).

Anna Mary Robertson Moses vibrates to Mars (a pioneer, competitive, fast worker) and with this name vibration, she could push (Mars) her career even though she didn't start it until she was in her seventies; her name Grandma Moses vibrates to Venus (symmetry, beautiful shapes and forms). Her art (Venus) work sells at luxury (Venus) prices! She was a self-taught artist.

Elizabeth Bayley Seton (Mars), known as Mother Seton (Venus, love) was called by her nickname Betsey (Neptune). She was known to be fun-loving, man-loving (both typical of Mars, Venus and Neptune mixed vibrations. She turned the sorrows of her life and the strength (Mars) with which she not only met them, but turned them to spiritual advantage (Neptune). She was known to have fits of temper (Mars) and jealousy (Mars)--she is the first (Mars) native American to be declared a saint by the Catholic church. Her courage was typical of Mars on the positive side. She was made a Saint, her name now is Saint Elizabeth Ann Bayley (Scorpio).

You know her as "Mother Teresa" (Neptune, planet of idealism and wanting better conditions for womankind). Her birth name is Agnes Gonxha Bojaxhiu ("Capricorn; hardworking, sacrificing, dedicated, reliable and poverty conscious).

Charles Dillon Stengel (Uranus) is known as "Casey" (Pisces) and "Casey" Stengel (Scorpio), a baseball player and manager. Flo-Jo and Dee-Dee (both Capricorn names; ambitious, persevering) were her two nicknames. The former, when she was famous, and the latter, as a kid. Her name Florence Delorez Griffith Joyner vibrated to Venus and as Florence Griffith Joyner she vibrated to Aquarius. She was a field and track star who broke records (Aquarius).

Ed Byrnes (Aries) appeared in a TV show *"77 Sunset Strip"* and played a character named Gerald Lloyd Kookson, II (Taurus). His nickname in the show was "Kookie" (Saturn). From that time on he was called, in real life, Edd "Kookie" Byrnes (Venus). Louis Burt Mayer (Neptune; movies, promoting) was known as "L. B. (Taurus). He was in charge of MGM (Neptune title movies) a giant movie studio.

William Shakespeare (Saturn; ambitious, hard working) was also called Shakespeare (Jupiter) and also spelled "Shakespere) (Gemini; writing). He was known for his sonnets and as the greatest writer in English literature. He was an actor, playwright and poet. He wrote tragedies (Saturn). Some of his famous plays were *"Hamlet"* (Sagittarius), *"Othello"* (Sagittarius), *"Macbeth"* (Jupiter, *"King Lear"* (Aries). The old English spelling of his name William Shakspere vibrated to Aquarius, sign of originality. He was called "Bard of Avon" (Mars, planet of creativity, energy and guts). In England a bard is an exalted national poet. Shakespeare was born and buried in Stratford-on-Avon, thus called "Bard of Avon."

There are terms of endearment we call our loved ones. These terms also, vibrate to a sign/planet. When you call someone "Sweetie" or honey bee"---these names vibrate to Neptune, the planet of idolization. "Honey bun" is Pisces, romantic sign ruled by Neptune. "Honey" is Capricorn, serious, stable, true blue and loyal sign. "Sweetheart" and "sweetie pie" is Sagittarius, a happy-go-lucky and contented sign.

Jennifer Anniston (Aries) calls Brad Pitt (Gemini) by the pet name of "My Willie," (Uranus), which is based on his birth name William Bradley Pitt (Cancer). Barbara Streisand (Uranus) was born Barbara Joan Streisand (Mars) and was married to Elliot Gould (Uranus; birth name Elliot Goldstein, Aries). Her second husband, James Brolin (Sagittarius) was born James Brunderlin, Aries. Reportedly Barbara Streisand has a pet name her husband calls her, "Beezer," (Capricorn; ambition).

Cher (Venus) uses her nickname "Sheryline" (Aries) with her pals. She dated Robert Camilletti (Jupiter). He uses the name Rob Camilletti (Pisces). The press dubbed him "The Bagel Boy," (Neptune) and Cher called him "Mookie," (Capricorn).

F. Scott Fitzgerald (Leo) became famous (a Leo goal) with his first novel, and he became a legend as a playboy and traveled in the company of the rich, including royalty (Leo); also, he was a chronicler and idol of *The Jazz Age* (a term he coined, Pisces). His socializing and entertaining was done in a grand way (Leo) amidst an opulent (Leo) background. He had a fat ego (Leo) that craved satisfaction constantly.

His birth name was Francis Scott Key Fitzgerald which vibrates to Jupiter, the planet of wealth and opulence. However, he signed his name F. Scott Fitzgerald. Often he was called Scott Fitzgerald (Neptune, dramatization, drinking, movies). He married Zelda Sayre (Taurus) who became Zelda Fitzgerald (Neptune). As Mr. and Mrs. Fitzgerald, they vibrated to Capricorn, sign of stability and ambition. Zelda had many terms of endearment she called him, either in person or when she wrote him notes or letters. "Dear Do-Do" (Sagittarius), "Dear D.O." (Jupiter, planet which rules Sagittarius, thus same traits and same vibration. She called him "Scott"' (Neptune), "Scott King of the Roses" (Saturn), "Scottie" (Capricorn ruler Saturn, thus, same name vibration and traits,)"Monsieur Scottie" (Jupiter). She called the two of them "The Goofus" (Pisces, an endearing sign of the zodiac, romantic).

CHAPTER EIGHT

TRANSLITERATION AND ROYAL TITLES

TRANSLITERATIONS

Also refer to page 27 under the heading "Foreign Names."

Amenohotep (Scorpio) was also called Amenophis (Mars). He was known to have a strong sex drive (Scorpio -- Mars) and many children as a result. He changed his name to Akhenaten (Aquarius) when he undertook a complete reform (Aquarius). His new name is spelled in various way by people of different countries. When it is spelled Akhenaton, it vibrates to Neptune (idealism) and when it is spelled Ikhnaton, it vibrates to Mars (sex).

His wife had many spellings of her name, due to transliterations. When her name was spelled Nofretete or Nephretiti (both Aquarius vibrations) she had the same name vibration as her husband after he changed his name. Thus with both of them having this same name vibration (Aquarius), they were attracted to reform, astrology, the occult, the arts and humanitarian causes. When her name is spelled Nepretiti, she vibrates to Capricorn which is ambition, duty, as well as ruling the bones, and she had high cheek bones that gave her a sculptured look. She was known for her beauty (Venus) and also used the name Nefretete (Venus).

Akhenaton's son-in-law was Tutankhaten (Aquarius) for the first twelve years of his life. When he became King, he revised (Aquarius) Akhenaton's policy and returned to worship the God Amon. Some sources refer to his birth name as Tutankhaton which vibrates to Neptune (dreams of grandeur, idealism). When he changed his name to Tutankhamun, he vibrated to Uranus (reform). Thus, his name sign vibration did not change because his original name vibration is Aquarius which is ruled by Uranus — thus, giving similar traits. And what is most interesting is that before he died, he chose the name he would use in the afterlife -- Nebkeperure --which also vibrates to Uranus. It seems like he couldn't get away from Uranus. However, when he's called King Tut, he takes on a Mars vibration. The boy King was known to go out and hunt (Mars) in his chariot.

His wife was one of the daughters of Akhenaton and her name Ankhesenpaaton vibrated to Venus (love and beauty) which is noticeable on the Egyptian carvings. At the same time, Tutankhamun changed his name, she changed hers to Ankhesenamun (Jupiter) and when this occured her religion (Jupiter) was changed from worship of the Sun-god Aton to the God Amon.

Whomever uses the title "The Shah of Iran" is vibrating to Neptune (grandiose ideas, idealistic, dreams, lies, deception). When the late Shah was in the military (Mars) he was Reza Pahlavi (Mars) and also used the name Muhammed Reza Pahlavi which vibrates to Capricorn (ambition, strategy, planning, campaigning, greed, and seriousness). When he became Shah Mohammed Rexa Pahlavi he vibrated to Gemini (intellectual, good at talking, thinking, making changes, and multiple personalities). In some countries, the spelling is Mohammed and in other places it is Muhammed; either way, the vibration changes with the spelling. Muhammed Riza Pahlavi vibrates to Sagittarius. Shah Muhammed Riza Pahlavi vibrates to Mars, planet of war. Muhammed Riza Pahlavi, Shah of Iran vibrates to Aries, sign ruling wars. Thus, he had mixed vibrations.

His wife, before she became Empress vibrated to Farah Diba (Capricorn, the same name vibration as her husband before he became Shah). As Empress Farah (Pisces) and Empress Farah Diba (Neptune; Neptune rules Pisces) she vibrated to her husband's title "The Shah of Iran." There are different spellings of her name due to transliteration; one variant is Dibba instead of Diba. When she was called Empress Farah Dibba, she vibrated to Aries (war, military, anger, violence, courage), but she is no longer an Empress and if she uses Farah Dibba, she will vibrate to Uranus (uprising, revolution, reform, shocking changes, liberation for women's rights --which she did fight for and was granted in some and unexpected upheavals. If she uses Farah Diba (Capricorn) she would have to guard against living in fear which can be representative of Capricorn.

The name Rembrandt (Virgo) is famous around the world. However, there were many spellings of his name due to transliteration in various countries. Thus, he had mixed vibrations. The different spellings of his name are: Rembrandt van Rijn (Taurus), Harmensz van Rijn (Taurus), Harmenszoon van Rijn (Libra), Rembrandt van Ryn (Aries), Rembrandt Harmenszoon van Rijn, (Neptune).

He was the first (Aries) to establish that the blending of paint (Libra, Taurus), light and color (Libra, Taurus) can equal subject matter in importance. He could portray old age without sentiment (Virgo, Aries) or revulsion. This attitude enabled him to penetrate (Virgo) into the essence of the subject, to lay bare (Virgo) its structure and find the visual complaint. Paint (Libra, Taurus) became a tool with which to express feeling (his Sun Sign was Cancer --the sign of feeling).

Rembrandt (Virgo) was preoccupied with detail (Virgo) so much that it was evident in his paintings that have become masterpieces. He was known to be the greatest etcher in the history of art and sometimes took several years to finish a plate to his satisfaction (a Virgo trait). He was know to be a tireless worker (typical of Virgo).

The famous Renaissance painter whose paintings are priceless and hang in museums all over the world is known to many as Raphael (a Neptune name); however, his name in many countries is spelled Raffaello (a Virgo name). His birth name is spelled two different ways: Raffaello Sanzio (Capricorn) and Raffaello Santi (Mars). Thus, his name vibrates to all these different signs and/or planets, depending upon how you spell it.

The artist known as George Braque (Venus, planet ruling art) is also known as Georges Braque (Aquarius, sign of abstract, originality and doing things one's own way). As "Braque" he vibrates to Capricorn.

The Hungarian spelling of Franz Liszt is Ferencz Liszt. But this does not change his name vibration of Jupiter (broad mindedness, fun-loving, extravagant); however, as Liszt, he vibrated to Aquarius (unconventional, individualistic and original).

He is known as Tchaikovsky (a Capricorn name). His birth name was spelled two different ways due to transliteration. Piotr Ilyich Tchaikovsky (a Sagittarian name) and Peter Ilich Tchaikovsky (an Aquarius name). The composer, married one of his pupils but, unable to overcome his homosexuality (Aquarius) left her after a few weeks.

Arthur Rubinstein (Aries), the pianist, is also spelled Artur Rubinstein (Pisces).

He was born Publius Vergilius Maro (Aries) and gained fame with one name spelled two different ways: Vergil (Taurus) and Virgil (Sagittarius). The dutch philosopher called Spinoza (Taurus) was also called by two different names: Baruch Spinozo (Venus) and Benedict de Spinozo (Saturn) which are two opposite vibrations---Venus is artistic and can be lazy; Venus is love. Saturn is hardworking and serious. Venus is affectionate, Saturn is cool.

He is famous as Tolstoy (Neptune), author and philosopher who wrote *War and Peace* (Aries title) and *Anna Karenina* (also Aries title). He has many spellings of his name: Leo Tolstoy (Capricorn), Leo Nikolayevich Tolstoy (Pisces; also Pisces when spelled Tolstoi), and Count Lev Tolstoi (Jupiter, also Jupiter when spelled Tolstoy).

He was born Mikolaj Kopernik (Mars) and through transliteration there has been many different spellings of his name: Nicolaus Copernicus (Jupiter) and Nicholas Copernicus (Venus). He was an astronomer who calculated planets. He discovered (believed) the Sun was the center of the universe and planets moved around it. His system is known as the "Copernicus System" (Scorpio) and often he is called by one name, Copernicus (Scorpio; the sign involved with fact-finding research).

He is known as Galileo (Taurus), also spelled Galilei (Capricorn). He was an astronomer and mathematician who developed his own telescope. He believed Copernicus was right, and for this he was persecuted by the Inquisition. However, he used the diplomacy of Capricorn (name vibration for Galilei) and recanted under his breath and was let go.

Christopher Columbus (a Uranus name) discovered (Uranus) the Americas. He believed (Pisces trait) the earth was not flat. He was an Italian explorer in the service of Spain. His Italian name was spelled Cristoforo Colombo (Pisces); his Spanish name was spelled Cristobal Colon (Aries).

Nostradamus (Aries) due to transliterations, is Michel de Nostradamus (Mars; Mars is ruler of Aries) and Michel de Nostre-Dame (Mars). He was a French astrologer and physician (Mars) who wrote "Prophecies." However, I, the author, have been in his house in Salon, France and there is nothing in it to indicate he was an Astrologer. In fact--there was mostly things there that indicated he was a PSYCHIC.

Joan of Arc (Sagittarius) is in French Jeanne d'Arc (Aries). Saint Joan of Arc (Pisces) in French is Saint Joan d'Arc (Aquarius). She is known as "The Maid of Orleans," (Neptune, planet of idolization and canonization).

He was known as "Chairman Mao" (Mars). His name is spelled two different ways: Mao Tse-T'ung (Venus) and Mao Ze-dong (Mars, planet of aggression, war). The Chinese general and statesman, Chiang Kaishek (Neptune) is spelled in Chinese as Jiang Jieshi (Uranus, the planet of revolution).

Confucianism (Aquarius) is based on the teachings of Confucius. Confucius vibrates to Scorpio (hidden meanings, subtle action, resourcefulness). The Chinese spelling of his name is K'ung Futse (Venus); Kongzi (Sagittarius) and Kong-Fuzi (Pisces). Thus he vibrated to the Chinese spellings of his name as well as the English one. He was a philosopher (Sagittarius) and an ethical teacher who urged a system of morality (Scorpio) and state to bring about peace (Venus) justice (Venus) and universal order (Scorpio).

ROYAL TITLES
Also refer to page 33 under the heading "Titles."

Anastasia (Neptune) also known as Anastasia, Grand Duchess of Russia (Jupiter, wealth and opulence). She was the youngest daughter of the last Czar of Russia, Nicholas II (Uranus name of entire title). Franz Josef (Neptune), also known as Emperor Franz Josef (Capricorn ambition), Franz Joseph Emperor of Austria (Taurus) and Francis Joseph, Austrian Emperor (Pisces). Maximilian I, King of Bavaria (a Jupiter name and title combined). Ludwig I, King of Bavaria (Uranus; he was the son of Maximilian I) and had the affair with the dancer, Lola Montez, which stimulated his downfall.

Louis XIII, King of France (Saturn) married Anne of Austria (Aries) and started Versailles (Jupiter, name vibration; most opulent palace in the world). Louis XIV, King of France(Mars) married to Marie-Therese of Spain (Libra) was known as the "Sun King" (Mars). He enlarged Versailles. Louis XV, King of France (Pisces) married Maria Leczinska (Neptune)---Note: Pisces ruled by Neptune, can be a wishy-washy sign. He was a weak ruler and influenced by his mistresses (Pisces afflicted can be a philanderer) Madame du Barry (Mercury) and Madame de Pompadour (Pisces).

Louis XVI, King of France (Scorpio) also called Duc de'Berry (Saturn) and Louis XVI, King of France, Duc de'Berry (Uranus; planet of revolution). Marie-Antoinette of Lorraine, Archduchess of Austria (Saturn) was his Queen. When she was called Queen Marie-Antoinette she vibrated to Aries, the sign of courage and the guillotine.

Marie Antoinette (Aquarius) was alleged to have had no warmth or understanding (Aquarius on the negative side). She was independent (Aquarius) and wouldn't listen to anyone (Aquarius). When she faced the guillotine, it was with composure (Aquarius) and firmness (Aquarius).

King Farouk I (Aquarius) was called King Farouk (Uranus). He was known for his strange (Uranus) sexual appetites along unconventional (Uranus) lines. He had an extravagant lifestyle and was the last King of Egypt. He was in exile (Uranus) because a revolution (Uranus) forced him to abdicate (Uranus).

Aga Khan (Pisces) and The Aga Khan (Capricorn) are names of a hereditary title of the religious and spiritual leader of the sect of Ismaili Muslims. Aga Khan III (Venus), the title of Aga Sultan Sir Mahomed'Shah (Pisces), he was a leader. Prince Aly Khan (Capricorn) was married to Rita Hayworth (Venus); he was the son of Aga Khan, III. Aga Khan IV, (Sagittarius) the appointed successor of Aga Khan III was the son of Prince Aly Khan.

Hussein (Aries) was King of Jordan (Uranus); also known as Hussein, King of Jordan (Jupiter, planet of optimism, wealth and sharing). His name was Ibn Talal Hussein (Saturn) and his complete name and title was Ibn Talal Hussein, King of Jordan (Capricorn). His last wife was Queen Noor (Sagittarius).

A Shah is a Monarch. Shah Jahan (Sagittarius) also spelled Shah Jehan (Neptune) was a mogul emperor of India. He brought the moguel empire to its golden age. A patron of the arts, he was a great builder. His Taj Mahal (a Taurus name, beauty) was erected. He had it built (Aries trait), the Indian spelling is Khas Mahal (Aries).

He was known as Hirohito (Virgo) as well as Emperor Hirohito (Capricorn), Emperor of Japan (Neptune) and Hirohito, Emperor of Japan (Pisces). Thus, he had many vibrations.

Mary Stuart (Uranus) was Mary Stuart, Queen of Scots (Pisces). King Edward II (Capricorn) King Edward III (Aquarius); King Edward, IV (Taurus). Queen Victoria (a Uranus name) was known for her humanitarian (Uranus) traits. The Duke of Windsor (Idealistic Neptune name) also known as Edward, The Duke of Windsor (Venus, love, romance name). He abdicated the throne and married Wallis Simpson (Pisces). Her nickname was Wally Simpson (Aquarius). She was known as The Duchess of Windsor (Jupiter, wealth, opulence, happiness, lucky), though, she was called Wallis Simpson, The Duchess of Windsor (Gemini, her Sun sign also was Gemini, thus this enhanced the Gemini traits of communication and duality).

Queen Elizabeth II (Libra). Most people think of her as Queen Elizabeth (without the II), thus she vibrates to Venus which is the ruler of the sign Libra; thus, similar traits. Her husband is thought of by most people as Prince Philip which is a Capricorn vibration; however as Prince Philip, Duke of Edinburgh, or as Philip Mountbatten, The Duke of Edinburgh he vibrates to Saturn, the planet which rules Capricorn---thus similar traits, such as ambition and seriousness. As Philip Mountbatten he vibrates to Jupiter which can make him lighten up and smile. As the Duke of Edinburgh he vibrates to Uranus.

Princess Margaret (vibrates to Venus; thus, her love life receives lots of publicity). Her name, Princess Anne (vibrates to Aquarius---thus indicating, independence and humanitarianism). Prince Charles vibrates to (Aquarius) or as Prince Charles, The Prince of Wales (Sagittarius). His mistress, Camila Parker-Bowles (Mars, planet which represents a fiery, sexy nature, a hunter and adventuresome).

Her title Lady Diana Spencer (vibrates to Venus, love, affection, beauty) and as Princess Diana (Taurus, ruled by Venus, thus similar traits). As Princess Di (Sagittarius, sign of confidence) and as Diana, The Princess of Wales (Sagittarius, the luckiest sign of the zodiac). Her romance with James Hewitt (Venus---romance, love) received enormous publicity. When she was involved with Hasnat Kahn (Virgo), she wanted to marry him; however, his Virgo vibration is not harmonious to her Sagittarian vibration so it was not to be. Dodi by itself is Sagittarius and Dodi Al Fayed is Aries (his Sun sign is Aries) and she was happy with him---(Aries and Sagittarius are harmonious signs together); Aries rules accidents due to its planetary ruler Mars. His father introduced them, Mohamed Al Fayed (Libra, love, romance and the sign that brings people together). He owns Liberty Radio (Venus name) and Harrods (Aquarius name) department store.

Prince William vibrates to Venus so like his mother he will be known for his loving nature and romances. Prince Harry vibrates to Uranus, the planet of rebellion and humanitarism. Prince Edward vibrates to Aquarius, the sign of independence and being unconventional. He likes to be called Eddie Windsor (Neptune, movies---he works in TV as a documentary producer). As of this writing, he's engaged to Sophie Rhys-Jones (Taurus). Prince Andrew (Uranus, an independent sign which dares to be different and gets along great with Sarah Ferguson's name vibration---Aquarius (both have similar traits). As Prince Andrew, The Duke of York he vibrates to lucky and carefree Sagittarius which is the same sign vibration for Sarah Ferguson, The Duchess of York or as The Duchess of York. No wonder they can not seem to end their relationship...it's as if they were meant to be together.

Hereditary title---Prince of Monaco is a Uranus vibration. Prince Ranier III and Prince Rainer are Pisces vibrations. He has 142 titles (Dukes, Marquises and Counts). Grace Kelly (Aquarius) and Princess Grace (Saturn) or as Princess Grace of Monaco (Neptune, the planet of movies, acting, promoting and idealism). If they were called Mr. and Mrs. Grimaldi they would vibrate to Gemini.

She is called by the press, Princess Stephanie, a Sagittarius vibration---carefree, with an "I don't care attitude". As Princess Stephanie Grimaldi of Monaco she vibrates to Aries, a sign that is sexy, takes risks and is adventuresome. When she uses Princess Stephanie Marie Elisabeth Grimaldi she vibrates to emotional, moody, changeable and motherly Cancer. She is more disciplined when she vibrates to Saturn as Princess Stephanie Marie Elisabeth.

Prince Albert is an Aries vibration which according to his Astrodynes, is unlucky; also unlucky is Prince Albert of Monaco (Aquarius, independent, unconventional) and Prince Albert Louis Pierre Grimaldi (Capricorn). His lucky name vibration, according to his Astrodynes, is Prince Albert Louis Pierre, a Neptune name which represents acting, promoting and idealism.

Rumors are that Prince Albert doesn't have the strength of character to be a powerful modern decision-making Prince(his Sun sign is Pisces which can be wishy-washy). It is said that he does not want to marry because he doesn't believe in marriage and is happy as he is ---a playboy (Neptune) and says, "I can live happily without the throne." He is not interested in perpetuating the family line.

As Princess Caroline she vibrates to Uranus, the planet of rebellion. When she uses Princess Caroline of Monaco she vibrates to Venus --- love, socializing, entertaining. As Princess Caroline Louise Marguerite she vibrates to Taurus, ruler of Venus. When she uses Princess Caroline Louise Marguerite Grimaldi she vibrates to serious and disciplined Saturn; also the sign of ambition. She is married to Prince Ernst (a Neptune name). Her son's name Andrea Casiraghi vibrates to Scorpio.

Princess Caroline changed her son's (Andrea, Aquarius by itself) last name from Casiraghi (his late father's name) to Casiraghi-Grimaldi (Taurus), thus Andrea Casiraghi-Grimaldi (Jupiter, planet of wealth and happiness) is his name. Prince Ranier and his seven-member advisory council gave official approval which was needed for the name Grimaldi (by itself, Uranus) --the ruling family's last name; thus, he could be eligible to assume the throne as Prince Andrea Casiraghi-Grimaldi of Monaco (Saturn, discipline). When he uses Prince Andrea Casiraghi-Grimaldi he vibrates to Uranus, planet of rebellion, reform.

CHAPTER NINE

USING ONE NAME

One Name To Fame

Vaslav Nijinsky (Pisces name and Sun sign) was a ballet (Pisces; Pisces rules the feet) dancer. He was famous for his characterizations (Pisces), height of leaps and length of time he stayed in the air. His career was cut short by insanity (Pisces); he suffered a mental breakdown from which he never fully recovered. Note: Nijinsky (Mercury) Mercury rules the mind and is involved in mental problems. He kept a diary (Mercury) which was a strange (Pisces) mixture of spiritual (Pisces) insight and hallucination (Pisces).

These stars have a one-name that vibrates to the sign Aquarius---independence, daring to be different and original: Madonna, Charo, Fabian (born Fabian Forte, Capricorn), Capuchine (born Germanine Lefebre, Sagittarius). The super model, Fabio, vibrates to Uranus, planetary ruler of Aquarius; thus, similar traits.

These celebrities vibrate to Pisces, the sign of dramatizing the emotions, creative imagination, acting, promoting: Shaq, Bono, Seal, Wynonna, Jewel (born Jewel Kilcher, Jupiter) and Liberace (born Wladziu Valentino Liberace, Jupiter).

Cher (Venus, love, romance, artistic expression), Brandy (Venus, born Brandy Norwood, Capricorn), Oprah (Capricorn, hard working, ambitious, serious; born Oprah Winfrey, Aquarius name and Sun sign, independent, magnetic), Sinbad (Sagittarius, born David Adkins, Taurus), Sting (Sagittarius, born Gordon Matthew Sumner, Uranus), Usher (Aries, born Usher Raymond, Jupiter) and Yanni (Aries, born Yanni Chrysomallis, also Aries).

In the world of fashion, many designers are known by one name: Givenchy (Pisces, sign of designing), Valentino (Mercury), Pucci (Uranus---born name Emilio Pucci, Scorpio), Schiaparelli (Aquarius; born Elsa Schiaparelli, Pisces), Halston (Aries; pioneer in fashion), Versace (Saturn; born Gianni Versace vibrates to Scorpio, the sign which represents sex and murder--when afflicted). Supermodels Iman (Neptune) and Vendella (Neptune; dramatic, glamourous and promoting).

The author Colette (Pisces, real name Sidonie Gabrielle Claudine Colette, Aquarius). She was the author of Gigi (Capricorn title). Her works were sensuous and idyllic.

Moses (Aries), the Hebrew prophet and lawgiver who bravely (Aries) led (Aries) the Israelites out of Egypt. He is known for The Ten Commandments (adds to Saturn, the planet which represents rules that are to be obeyed).

Ovid (Aquarius; born Publius Ovidius Naso, Leo) was a poet who went into exile (Aquarius). Cicero (Uranus) had a typical Uranus life---he lost his left arm in battle and was held five years in captivity until his family ransomed him.

Dante (Uranus); born Dante Alighieri (Capricorn, ambitious and serious) is famous for Dante's Inferno (Uranus), La Divina Commedia (Scorpio) and The Divine Comedy (Jupiter). He also went into exile (Uranus).

Socrates (Aquarius) he initiated (Aquarius) question-and-answer methods of teaching as a means of achieving self-knowledge (Aquarius). He said that his wisdom (Aquarius) consisted in knowing (Aquarius) that he knew nothing, finally. He was condemned to die for introducing (Aquarius) strange (Aquarius) divinities and new (Aquarius) ideas to youth. His theories (Aquarius) have survived through the writing of Plato, his most famous pupil.

Plato (Taurus), a philosopher who was a devoted admirer of Socrates. He presented his philosophy in the form of dramatic "Dialogues" in which Socrates conducts the discussions.

Aristotle (Pisces) was a metaphysical and political philosopher who wrote on most branches of learning, including physics and biology, and whose influence extended for more than a thousand years. He saw the world as an ideal (Pisces) universe. He studied under Plato and was tutor to Alexander The Great.

SO FAMOUS THEY ARE CALLED BY ONE NAME

Houdini, (Taurus), was a magician and could make things, including himself, disappear (Uranus). Harry Houdini (Uranus) invented (Uranus) daring escapes which catapulted him into international fame. Upon death of his mother, he became interested in the occult (Uranus) and went to mediums in an effort to reach her. He became the relentless (Taurus) enemy of spiritualism and used all the tricks he could to discredit (Uranus) it.

The name Picasso is known the world over; it vibrates to Mars. Typical of Mars is a physical body that is stocky, virile, firey-eyed, fast-moving and temperamental. He was known to be adventurous (Mars) in his work. He pioneered (Mars) the development of collage. His name Pablo Picasso (Aquarius) was used when he was young--he invented cubism (both cubism and inventions are ruled by Aquarius). He took risks which is typical of Mars. As a young artist, he signed his paintings P. Ruiz (Venus; Art) and occasionally he signed his paintings as P. Ruiz Picasso (Mars) until he was about 11 years old. That's when he settled on the name Picasso. He dropped the Ruiz (his father's name) because their views different on art (his father didn't approve of his son's deviating from the old strait-laced way of painting; therefore, he underscored his differences with his father by using only his mother's name "Picasso" from that time on. Pablo Picasso was known for being unusual (Aquarius) and everything about him is bizarre (Aquarius).

Michelangelo Buonarroti (Uranus) was a genius (Uranus). Michelangelo (Cancer; the name he's identified with more than his birth name) expressed the Cancer traits with his work. He put feeling (Cancer) into everything he did. Michelangelo did not rush, he worked slowly (Cancer) and painstakingly long hours for years on end without much rest or food. Lots of his commissioned work was abandoned when he got bored with it (all typical of Cancer's influence), thus, there are many incomplete tombs, statues, etc. The tomb for Pope Julius II was constantly being interrupted (Uranus) and was uncompleted (Uranus) for years. He couldn't hack it emotionally (Cancer) he admitted--there were too many problems when he had to wait for the decisions of others in connection with certain jobs. By the time they got around to deciding, he lost his enthusiasm (typical of Cancer's influence).

Both Cezanne and Paul Cezanne vibrate to a Pisces name; he was known for his distortion (Pisces) of natural forms in their paintings (Neptune).

Whistler (Jupiter) is a famous artist who spent lots of money foolishly and on a grand scale (typical of the negative side of Jupiter). However, he signed his painting as Whistler, this thought of himself with this Jupiter vibration. However, he always managed to get saved at the last minute Jupiter influence. His birth name, James Mc Neill Whistler vibrates to Venus the planet ruling art.

James Whistler (Uranus) was a painter who was eccentric (Uranus). His uninhibited (Uranus) behavior was a stratagem to get his art noticed--and it worked. He wore jaunty hats, carried a long cane, used a mobile monocle, donned yellow gloves and had dandified dress and mannerisms--he had a lock of white hair that would bounce around with his defiant movements--all typical of Uranus. He was an apostle of artistic freedom (Uranus). He introduced (Uranus) the cult of the Japanese porcelain into art.

Rodin (Uranus) shocked (Uranus) people with his nudes and couples entwined in love embraces (Sun sign Scorpio--the "obsession with sex" sign). Auguste Rodin, vibrates to Neptune and his sculptor and poetic (Neptune) works were unrealistic. His first salon success reflected a rippling life-style vitality and was such a sensational contrast (Uranus) to academic conventions that he was accused of using life-casts. He rebelled (Uranus) and to disprove (Uranus) these accusations, he made "St. John The Baptist" larger than life.

His real name was Francois Auguiste Rene Rodin (Gemini, the sign whose keyword is "I Think"---is it any wonder that he is famous for his sculptor of "The Thinker"? (Neptune). He won an immense reputation for the originality (Uranus) of his compositions. He had controversial (Uranus) public commissions. Some of his sexual orgy sculptures were scandalous (Uranus). His famous sculptor The Kiss vibrates to Taurus, love and kisses.

Other famous artists that are called by one name: Matisse (Pisces, creative imagination), Rubens (Taurus, artistic sign; real name Peter Paul Rubens--Neptune, creative imagination), and Van Gogh (Venus, planet ruling art; real name Vincent Van Gogh--Sagittarius). He was born Henri Marie Raymond de Toulouse Lautrec (Taurus, sign rules art) and also used the name Henri de Toulouse-Lautrec (Aries, creative, pioneering) but was most famous as Toulouse-Lautrec (Uranus). He painted an unconventional (Uranus) side of life among the music halls of

Montmartre in Paris. He was deformed (Uranus) from childhood and led a life of debauchery (Uranus).

Renoir (Aries) and Pierre Auguste Renoir (Uranus) was an impressionist (Uranus) who contributed to this art form the rainbow pallette and broken (Uranus) color. Tp retain the momentariness (Uranus) of nature's changing (Uranus) appearance, he developed (Aries) a technique (Uranus) of broadly painted brush-strokes, which gradually evolved (Aries) with the help of fellow-artist, Monet.

Monet (Sagittarius; born Claude Monet, Uranus), founder (Uranus) of impressionism. It was his painting titled, "Impression: Sunrise" (Uranus title) that gave the Impressionists their name. The word "Impressionists" vibrates to Mars, a Pioneering, creative and enterprising planet that influences a person to be gutsy.

Cervantes (Venus; born Miguel de Cervantes Saavedra, also, Venus). He's famous for his book _Don Quijote_ (Virgo title). Steinbeck (Virgo; born John Ernst Steinbeck (Sagittarius and used John Steinbeck, Taurus). Balzac (Sagittarius) is also known as Honore De Balzac (Jupiter). He was noted French author, was heavy (Sagittarius and Jupiter) and had a weight problem.

He is called Chekhov (Aquarius). Anton Pavlovich Chekhov (Gemini), was an author who was forced to live at resorts. He had tuberculosis (Gemini on the negative side) which killed him. You know him as Spinoza (Taurus). Benedict Spinoza (Saturn) and Benedictus de Spinoza (Saturn) wrote his _Ethica_ which contains a systematized (Saturn) collection of definitions, axions (Saturn) and theorems (Saturn). Both Goethe or Johann Wolfgang van Goeth vibrate to Neptune; he had a philosophy that was mystical — pantheism (Neptune). He was a writer, scientist and major figure in world literature. Poetry, novels, drama (all ruled by Neptune) were his forte. He was famous for his poetic (Neptune) drama _Faust_, (Aries title also called _Faustus_---Aries title).

Famous composers that you know by one name: Puccini (Mars, born Giacomo Puccini, Aries, sign ruled by Mars, thus same type vibration and traits). Brahms (Neptune; born Johannes Brahms, Uranus). Bach (Neptune; born Johann Sebastian Bach, Sagittarius). Schumann (Taurus; born Robert Alexander Schumann, also Taurus). Grieg (Jupiter; also known as Edvarg Greig, Aquarius; born Edvard Hagerup Grieg, Venus--melodious and artistic planet). Schubert (Uranus; also known as Franz Schubert, Capricorn; born Franz Peter Schubert, Jupiter). Chopin (Neptune; Frederic Chopin, Aries and born Frederic Francois Chopin, Pisces--sign ruled by Neptune).

Other famous composers who are called by one name now that they are famous are: Rachmaninov (Scorpio; Sergei Rachmaninov, Taurus; born Sergei Vasilyevich Rachmaninov, Aries). Verdi (Aquarius, born Giuseppe Verdi, Pisces--creative imagination sign; the title _Aida_, Mars, when it is called Verdi's _Aida_ it is Uranus; Verdi's _La Traviata_ is Aquarius).

Bizet (Uranus; Georges Bizet, Neptune; born Alexander Casar Leopold Bizet, Neptune; thus dramatic. His famous opera _Carmen_, Uranus, same planet ruling his <u>one name</u> Bizet). You know him as Rimsky-Korsakov (Mars; born Nikolai Andreyevich Rimsky-Korsakov, Pisces, dramatic; Mars, creative, most famous for Gemini name title *Scheherezade*. Mozart (Mars, Wolfgang Mozart, Sagittarius, Wolfgang Amadeus Mozart, Scorpio), is considered one of the most highly gifted and prolific composers in history. He was a child prodigy; his Scorpio name vibration gave great powers of concentration and persistence. The Mars vibration gave him guts, creativity, and ability to work fast. The Sagittarius vibration gave him luck, though often he was destitute---he was a big spender' which is a Sagittarian trait, as well as Mars and Scorpio traits.

Igor Stravinsky (Taurus; born Igor Feodorovich Stravinsky) and called Stravinsky (Uranus) dared to be different (Uranus), he composed to please himself (Uranus) and his rhythms are often bold (Uranus).

He is called Beethoven (Capricorn, serious, deep and heavy, dedicated to his work, ambitious.) Ludvig van Beethoven (Sagittarius) is regarded as the last of the classicists and the first of the romantic composers. In his personal life he was wild and carefree (Sagittarius on the negative side).

Debussy (Saturn) was born Claude Achille Debussy (Neptune) and as Claude Debussy (Aquarius) started a new (Aquarius) style of music. He had a mistress, then left her to marry someone else, only to abandon (Aquarius on the negative side) her for a rich woman that he finally married. His interests in the arts (Aquarius) made him desirous of bringing music, literature and painting into one single communicative world of art.

Other famous people called by one name are: Caruso (Pisces and his Sun sign also is Pisces; his name Enrico Caruso vibrates to Sagittarius). Dillinger (Aquarius, the erratic and unpredictable sign when afflicted; born John Dillinger--a Pisces name). Edison (Sagittarius; Thomas A. Edison, Jupiter--wealth , luck; born Thomas Alva Edison, Venus).

He was born Grigory Yefimovich Novykh Rasputin (Neptune, idealistic) and often used G. Y. Novykh Rasputin (Cancer). He was a Russian monk and faith healer. People thought of him as a demagogue, Grigori Rasputin (Aries) changed his vibration to the complete opposite when people called him Rasputin (Libra) thus, from violence (Aries) and war (Aries) to peace (Libra). He was murdered because others feared his power at court with the rulers.

He was born Nikita Sergeyevich Khrushchev (Pisces, idealistic) and was often called Nikita Khrushchev (Venus, which might have softened him to being charming by those who called him that name.)

Krushchev (Uranus) and Nikita S. Krushev (Aquarius) spoke out (Uranus, Aquarius), was known to be erratic (Uranus, Aquarius) and given to revolutionary (Aquarius, Uranus) ideas, as well as imbued with a desire for a new (Aquarius, Uranus) order. His career came to a sudden halt (Aquarius, Uranus). He disappeared (Aquarius, Uranus) and was in exile (Aquarius, Uranus) until his death.

CHAPTER TEN

FAMILY NAMES AND RELATIONSHIPS

Family Names

Family tradition may be your strongest deciding factor when selecting a name. The Greeks devised a method of alternating names with every generation, each grandson is named after his grandfather. The Chinese, American Indians and Latins collect many names. Often the Spanish added a roster of names that honored various godparents, relatives and saints. And at the end of a long string of names came two more names--the Christian (first) and surname(last): one in honor of the mother (her maiden name), the other for the father (his surname)--as is Spanish custom. The famous artist, Picasso, was baptized Pablo Diego Jose Francisco de Paula Juan Nepomuceno Maria de los Remedios Cipriano de la Santisima Trinidad--these names honored various godparents, relatives and saints. These long strings of names are becoming passe.

It's best to select a name that you and your spouse both like rather than going by a relative's desire. Create a name that identifies your child, make him unique and don't embarrass him with a name that is too odd or he'll be ridiculed in school. You may want to give a baby a middle name, maybe the mother's maiden name. If you want to change your name for professional reasons, or to attract luck, perhaps your grandmothers's maiden name will be to your liking.

If you want to name a girl after her father, and his name is Dan, call her Danielle. If you want to name a baby after his mother, take her name and switch the letters around or try her middle or maiden name. If the mother's maiden name is Hendrix, call your boy Henry, etc. Perhaps you want to name your baby after both you and your husband. Thus, take part of your name and combine it with part of your mate's name. If your name is Patricia and your hubby's is Stuart, try Stucia or use Tricia S. Endings like "ina" may be added to a name, for instance the name Patricia could be changed to Patina. Often these "ina" endings sound lyrical. Keep in mind the sound of a name is also important when choosing a name-but not as important as the astrological vibration.

William Randolph Hearst (an Aquarius name) was controversial, independent (Aquarius) and did as he pleased (Aquarius). He founded (Aquarius) a news empire. Mr. Hearst didn't care who knew about his relationship with Marion Davis (Scorpio). She was his mistress (Scorpio) and kept plenty of secrets (Scorpio) to herself. Patricia Hearst (a Mars name) attracted violence and was full of anger and hatred (typical Mars traits on the negative side). At the same time she had courage, nerve, and spunk (Mars on the positive side). She will be much happier when using Patty Hearst (Taurus) because with this name she tends to be sweet, kind and loving (Taurus on the positive side); however, she could also be too stubborn (Taurus on the negative side).

Both Donny Osmond and Marie Osmond are Sagittarius name vibrations; ironically they are brother and sister and their religion (ruled by Sagittarius) has helped make them both famous. Donny and Marie Osmond as a team vibrate to Libra, an artistic sign. As Donny and Marie, they vibrate to the independent sign Aquarius.

Billy Carter (Capricorn) is brother of ex-President Jimmy Carter and turned Plains, Georgia into a commercial (Capricorn) investment. He operated a sight-seeing tour and has made a lot of money on lecture tours. He certainly has ambition (Capricorn) and made use (Capricorn) of his brother's name to make his own fortune (a typical Capricorn trait).

Peter Graves (Sagittarius; born Peter Arness, a Capricorn vibration. His brother, also, is an actor---James Arness (Venus). The Marx Brothers (Sagittarius, sign of comedy) are famous. Groucho Marx (Uranus) was born Julius Marx (Venus). Chico Marx (Capricorn) was born Leonard Marx (Scorpio). Harpo Marx (Libra) was born Arthur Marx (Venus; both Libra and Venus are artistic, he could play the harp well). Zeppo Marx (Libra) was born Herbert Marx (Jupiter, planet of comedy).

The Wright Brothers (Taurus) made the first successful flight in a heavier-than-air machine. Wright Brothers vibrates to Aquarius, the sign of doing something different--an Air sign. Wilbur Wright vibrates to Capricorn, perseverance, and hard working. Orville Wright vibrates to Venus.

Joann Strauss, Sr. (Aquarius) created (Aquarius) the waltz. Johann Strauss, Jr. (Sagittarius) was the greatest dance composer in history; he was famous for his waltzes. He was extremely zealous (Sagittarius), flamboyant (Sagittarius) and lived it up (Sagittarius) with his many love affairs.

They are known as *The Barrymores* (Sagittarius) John Barrymore (Neptune, acting, movies), Ethel Barrymore (Pisces, acting, movies), Lionel Barrymore (Taurus, artistic sign, staunch, strong), Diana Barrymore (Neptune, she was heavily into alcohol ruled by Neptune; Sun Pisces, sign of drugs, drinking) and Drew Barrymore (Sagittarius, carefree, willing to live it up and was into drugs and drinking; Sun Pisces, actress).

The Judds (Saturn) is famous in show business. Naomi Judd (Saturn, disciplined, ambitious, Sun Capricorn has same traits), Ashley Judd (Sagittarius) and Wynonna Judd (Cancer, sensitive, emotional and sings with feeling; Cancer keyword is "I Feel."

Lloyd Bridges (Neptune, acting, movies) was born Lloyd Vernet Bridges II (Aries). His son Beau Bridges (Sagittarius name and Sun sign) was born Lloyd Vernet Bridges III. Jeff Bridges, his other son is also a Sun sign Sagittarius and a Venus name vibration.

Martin Sheen (Jupiter); born Ramon Estevez (Aquarius). Charlie Sheen (Gemini, changeable, dual and talkative), born Carlos Irwin Estevez (Jupiter). In 1999 he told the media he wants to be called Charles Sheen (Uranus, planet of being erratic, magnetic and unpredictable).

Aaron Spelling (Neptune, acting, creative imagination, promoting, visionary) is married to Carole Gene Marer (Neptune) and as Carole Spelling she vibrates to Saturn (true blue, loyal, steadfast) and with her nickname Candy Spelling (Capricorn--same traits as Saturn). They have two children who also are into acting: Tori Spelling (Aquarius, unpredictable), also called Victoria Spelling (Uranus, same traits as Aquarius) and Victoria "Tori" Spelling (Saturn, stable). He uses Randy Spelling (Taurus) professionally and was born Randall Gene Spelling (also Taurus).

They are called *The Jacksons* (Neptune, planet of show business) and The Jackson Family (Capricorn, ambitious). Michael Joe Jackson (Neptune) uses Michael Jackson (Sagittarius, lucky sign). His father is Joe Jackson (Sagittarius) and his mother is Katherine Jackson (Saturn). His sister is Janet Jackson (Uranus, magnetic and unpredictable). La Toya Jackson (Neptune) and Jermaine Jackson (Aquarius) are Michael's siblings.

Michael was married to Lisa Marie Presley (Pisces) and as Lisa Marie Jackson she vibrated to satable Saturn; she called herself Lisa Marie Presley-Jackson, also ruled by Saturn which can make her serious and ambitious. Debbie Rowe (Pisces, idealistic and said to worship, a Pisces trait, her husband Michael.) As Debbie Jackson she vibrates to the sexy, possessive and jealous negative side of Scorpio. Their son is named Prince Michael Jackson, Jr. (a Venus, sweet, loving and kind vibration).

His birth certificate had an error; his name was spelled Elvis Aron Presley (a serious, ambitious and stable Saturn vibration). It was corrected to read Elvis Aaron Presley (Mars; planet of temper, aggressiveness, creativity, adventure, guns and excitement). His twin brother died at birth (he was stillborn); he was named Jessie Garon Presley (Capricorn, same as his Sun sign would have been if he had lived). Elvis Presley (Aquarius) did crazy (Aquarius) things. He has always been up to mischief (Aquarius). Elvis was obsessed by cars (Aquarius) and trucks. And, occasionally, he liked to frighten (Aquarius) his visitors.

Priscilla Presley (Venus) is known for her beauty (Venus) and her marriage (Venus) to Elvis Presley. Ironically, her maiden name, Priscilla Beaulieu vibrated to Capricorn---that's the Sun sign Elvis was born under. Her married name is used now and with it she opened a clothing boutique (ruled by Venus) and became a model (Venus) before becoming an actress. As Priscilla Beaulieu she vibrates to Neptune, show business and promoting). When she is called Lisa Marie (Pisces) and Lisa Marie Presley (Pisces) she could take interest in a show business career, if she doesn't get lazy, procrastinate or wishy-washy (all Pisces traits on the negative side).

Frank Sinatra (Capricorn) was married to a Capricorn Sun sign, Ava Gardner. It's interesting but when you mention women and Frank Sinatra, everyone immediately thinks of Ava and Frank. Is it because the combination of the Capricorn name identification (on his part) and her Capricorn Sun sign (on her part) makes people remember them as a couple--even decades later?

Frank Sinatra's first wife's maiden name was Nancy Carol Barbato (Aries name harmonious to his Sagittarian Sun sign) and as Nancy Sinatra she still vibrated to Aries. When Nancy Sinatra, Sr. (Aquarius) gave birth to her daughter, the daughter became Nancy Sinatra, Jr. (Mars, aggressive and enterprising). Tina Sinatra vibrates to Uranus and so does Barbara Sinatra (As Barbara Marx--she was married to Chico Marx---she vibrated to the cool and ambitious sign Capricorn which is the same name vibration as her husband Frank had.) As Barbara Sinatra she vibrates to Uranus, an independent, unpredictable and magnetic sign.

Frank Sinatra, Jr. (Neptune) is called by the nickname of Frankie (Saturn, disciplined and similar traits as his Sun sign Capricorn. His sister Tina, also vibrates to Saturn when she is called Christina Sinatra. Frankie was born Franklin Wayne Sinatra (Capricorn, like his Sun sign); he was named after Franklin D. Roosevelt. When he uses Frank, Jr. he vibrates to Pisces.

The name Jon Benet (Mars, planet of violence and sex when afflicted) has been in the news. Her birth name Jon Benet Ramsey (Taurus, love and beauty) has also received lots of publicity. Her mother, Patsy Ramsey (Venus, beauty) and her brother Burke Ramsey have the same name vibration---Venus. John Ramsey vibrates to Uranus, the sign of being erratic and unpredictable; often, unconventional and weird interests sometimes attract those with a Uranus name vibration.

PARTNERSHIPS

In show business, it's quite common to have a partner. In many partnerships, some last, others make frequent appearances together, and there are those who have split and gone their own ways. Not only the names together but, also their individual name vibrations are significant. Certain names combined (with the 'and' included) are remembered and seem to go well together; others just don't seem to jell.

Lucy and Desi vibrate to Gemini; Lucille Ball and Desi Arnaz, also, vibrates to Gemini (talking, singing, multiple personalities, situations). But the sign Gemini is usually not a lasting combination. However, they lasted for years, which is shown in their individual horoscopes and by her individual name. The name Desi Arnez vibrates to Neptune (show business) which rules Pisces (his Sun sign). The name Lucille Ball vibrates to Taurus and her Sun sign is Leo; both signs fixed, stubborn and resistant to change. Desi, went into semi-retirement (Neptune) while she continued working (Taurus).

When Barbara Walters and Harry Reasoner worked together, their combined names vibrated to Uranus which represents sudden breaks or changes in a format, presentation or with each other. The events, which their combined names attracted, would be quick (Uranus) and unexpected (Uranus)--and that's what happened when they both went separate ways, professionally.

Barbara Walters (Capricorn) had a slow (Capricorn), steady (Capricorn) climb (Capricorn) to success and, on the way, made many sacrifices (Capricorn) both personally and professionally. She is ambitious (Capricorn) and self-disciplined (Capricorn), which has aided her in accomplishing as much as she has. Harry Reasoner (a Capricorn name), shared the spotlight with her. He is known as a serious, staid, respectable and hardworking man (all typical Capricorn traits). Two Capricorn name people working together can be detrimental--both have their eye on the same top sports.

Hugh Downs, a Taurus name, is harmonious to the Capricorn name vibration of Barbara Walters. They have been successful working together on their TV show *20/20*. Also, their Sun signs are compatible, she is a Libran, he's an Aquarian.

Two other Capricorn name-vibrations who worked together, but did not last was Tom Snyder and Rona Barrett when they appeared on the TV show *Tomorrow*.

The famous comedy team of Laurel and Hardy (Uranus): Oliver Hardy (Scorpio; born Norwell Oliver Hardy, Gemini) and Stan Laurel (Venus, easy going; born Arthur Stanley Jefferson, Aries). Another successful comedy team: Bud Abbot and Lou Costello (Sagittarius, sign of comedy). Individually, Bud Abbot (Uranus) and Lou Costello (Taurus, a fixed sign with lasting qualities; which stabilized Bud Abbot's Uranus vibration.

Steve Rossi vibrates to Pisces (impractical) and Marty Allen to Virgo (practical) which are opposite signs; thus, opposite name vibration traits can balance one another. Oddly enough, Steve Rossi and Marty Allen, combined, vibrate to Virgo, which adds stability and hard work to the team. When they are called Rossi and Allen, they vibrate to Sagittarius (comedy).

Dean Martin and Jerry Lewis (Capricorn. Individually, Dean Martin (happy-go-lucky Jupiter; born Dino Crocetti (Capricorn, ambition, same vibration as team name). Jerry Lewis (Neptune; Joseph Levitch, Venus), his Sun sign Pisces is compassionate--his Muscular Dystrophy TV marathon, Neptune title is ruled by Pisces; thus same traits.

Jerry Lewis (Neptune) was addicted (Neptune) to the drug (Neptune) Percodan for thirteen years in order to relieve a pain due to a back injury. To get off of the drug he spent five years sedated (Neptune) into unconsciousness (Neptune).

Sid Caesar (Aries; leader, aggressive, wanting to be "first," and often desirous of being the boss) and Imagine Coco (Libra, easy going, liking fair play but dislikes arguing); thus, she might tend to give in (Libra) whenever he took the initiative or stole the spotlight. As a team, Sid Caesar and Imogene Coco, their combined name vibrates to Capricorn (ambition).

The singers and songwriters, Simon and Garfunkel (Neptune, show business, dramatizing the emotions), have parted on many occasions. Individually, their names signs are incompatible: Paul Simon (Virgo) and Art Gunfunkel (Gemini). A popular comic strip that became a successful TV show, *Blondie and Dagwood* (Venus, love, affection, marriage). Arthur Lake (Aries) played Dagwood (Jupiter) and Penny Singleton (Saturn) played Blondie (Aquarius). All these signs and planets are harmonious together.

The TV show *X-Files* (Aries, action) stars Gillian Anderson (also an Aries vibration) and David Duchovny (Gemini). Their signs are harmonious to one another, despite rumors to the contrary.

RELATIONSHIPS

When it comes to love one thinks of Romeo (an ardent male lover; the name vibrates to the fiery sign Sagittarius) and Juliet (Neptune; romantic, worshipful of a loved one, the ideal). Their names combined as Romeo and Juliet vibrate to Uranus, which can be a magnetic, fascinating, unpredictable and swept off one's feet attraction. However, with Uranus things don't always last. Of course, these characters are from Shakespeare's play of the same name.

The names Antony and Cleopatra vibrate to Libra (love and affection). Is it any wonder they had a love affair that has been remembered through the ages? Cleopatra (Venus, goddess of love); Cleopatra, Queen of Egypt (Uranus, independent). She was noted for her beauty (Venus) and charisma (Uranus). Her lovers included Julius Ceasar (Sagittarius) or as Caesar (Taurus, sign of love). Mark Antony (Venus, love), Marcus Antonius (Taurus, his birth name), Mark Anthony (Uranus and Marc Anthony also Uranus). When the names Caesar and Cleopatra are combined, a Pisces, romantic, poetical vibration occurs. Another spelling: Anthony and Cleopatra, changes the vibration to Gemini, the sign of communication, adaptability and changeableness.

Napoleon Bonaparte vibrates to Aries (war, battles, courage, dynamic energy). By proclaiming himself Emperor Napoleon I (Pisces) he changed his vibration. He had illusions (Pisces) of grandeur (Pisces) which made him desirous of conquering (Aries) new territories.

Napoleon (Taurus), Napoleon I (Saturn, disciplined, good at strategy) was married to Josephine (Gemini) born Josephine Rose Tascher de la Pageric (Saturn, stability). As wife of Napoleon I, Empress of France she vibrated to Saturn and as Josephine, Empress of France she vibrated to Saturn and as Josephine, Empress of France she vibrated to Scorpio. Their names as lovers in history combined, "Josephine and Napoleon," vibrate to Jupiter, the planet of wealth and happiness.

Juan Peron vibrates to Scorpio (dictatorship) and his wife Eva Peron vibrates to Aries (courage, leadership, guts, battles). Thus, his dictatorship combined with her leadership made quite an extraordinary team. He was born Juan Domingo Peron (Gemini). She was known as "Evita," (Capricorn ambitious) but she was born Maria Eva Duarte (lucky, confidant, outgoing Sagittarius). As Maria Eva Duarte de Peron, Mars), she was aggressive, sexy, fearless and could lead and command others---all Mars traits.

The poetry of Robert Browning (Capricorn, serious, true blue and loyal) and Elizabeth Barrett Browning (Pisces, sign of romance, poetry) will live in our hearts forever. Another ideal Pisces name vibration couple, Roy Rogers and Dale Evans will be remembered. Roy Rogers (Jupiter; born Leonard Slye, Libra) and Dale Evans (Saturn; born Francis Smith, Sagittarius). Both were Sun sign Scorpio's. Trigger (Neptune, movies) the horse was famous and everyone knew who Roy Rogers and Dale Evans will be remembered. Roy Rogers (Jupiter; born Leonard Slye, Libra) and Dale Evans (Saturn; born Francis Smith, Sagittarius). Both were Sun sign Scorpio's. Trigger (Neptune, movies) the horse was famous and everyone knew Roy Rogers and Trigger (Capricorn combined names).

A well-known couple who work together or separately is Ruby Dee and Ossie Davis (Saturn combined names, which gives stability). Their individual names vibrate to Sagittarius (optimistic, happy, contented) which is his Sun and her rising sign. When she uses Mrs. Ruby Davis, she vibrates to Capricorn, ruled by Saturn, which is the total of their names together and this reinforces the long-lasting quality evident in their relationship. In fact, their marriage, as of 1999, has lasted fifty years.

The singer and actress Dolly Parton (Aquarius) says that she must be a free-spirit (Aquarius). She can't live life stern. However, her free-spirit belief got her into trouble when she was growing up. She bases her marriage on freedom (Aquarius), she sees her husband now and then, he lets her be herself (typical desire of Aquarius) and she does what she feels (Aquarius). Her husband Carl Dean vibrates to solid and stick-to-it Taurus. His name and her name vibration are not harmonious; however, his Taurus name and her Capricorn Sun sign are compatible. As Dolly Dean she vibrates to Saturn (rules Capricorn, similar traits). Her theme park, *Dollywood* also vibrates to Saturn (stability, ambitious and status conscious.

Maury Povich (Capricorn name and Sun sign) and Connie Chung (Virgo) have name signs that are compatible. Steve Laurence (Sagittarius; born Sidney Leibowitz, Capricorn) and Edye Gorme (Aquarius) are a married couple who work together as a team; their name signs are compatible. John F. Kennedy, Jr. (Taurus, Sun sign Sagittarius) married Carolyn Bessette (Mars, Sun sign Capricorn). Her Sun sign and his name sign are compatible. As Carolyn Bessette Kennedy she vibrates to Sagittarius, her husband's Sun sign which is an aid to the relationship.

Nicole Kidman (Scorpio, sexy) and Tom Cruise (Sagittarius) have name signs that are compatible, so are their Sun sign's---he is a Cancerian and she is a Geminian. Nicole has been on the London and New York City stage performing nude (typical of her Scorpio name). They made a movie together titled *Eyes Wide Shut* which, it's title ironically, vibrates to Scorpio. It is a film in which they do nude sex (Scorpio) love scenes.

Howard Stern (Neptune, promoting, grandiose ideas) and his wife, Alison Berns Stern both vibrate to Neptune. As Alison Berns (her maiden name) she vibrated to Pisces, rules Neptune, similar traits). He was born Howard Allan Stern (Saturn, ruler of his Sun sign, Capricorn; thus, similar traits of ambition and status). He promotes himself as *The King of all Media,* (lucky sign of Sagittarius title). His co-host, Robin Quivers has a name that vibrates to Taurus, which is compatible with Howard's Sun sign.

Stedman Graham is known as the steady boyfriend of Oprah Winfrey. His name sign and her name vibrate to Aquarius; thus, they can give each other independence and still be fascinated with one another. Ex-president James Madison (Neptune) married a wife who was called Dolly Madison (Sagittarius, confident) and as Dolly Payne Todd Madison (Uranus) she was independent. She was a genial (Sagittarius) White House hostess. She heroically carried important government (Uranus) documents and a portrait of George Washington to safety during the British invasion of Washington.

Will Smith (Pisces) and Jada Pinkett (Aquarius) have name signs that are compatible. As Jada Smith and as Jada Pinkett Smith she vibrates to Capricorn.

Christie Brinkley (Aquarius name and Sun sign) was married to Billy Joel (Gemini name compatible with her name; their Sun sign's were not compatible). Her third husband, Peter Cook vibrates to Venus, love, sign of modeling. Richie Sambora (Uranus), dubbed as a "rocker," (Neptune name), is lead guitarist of Bon Jovi (Neptune) band. His wife, Heather Locklear also vibrates to Uranus. She is known for her vixen role in the TV show *Melrose Place,* (a Neptune title).

Madonna (Aquarius) was married to Sean Penn (Uranus, unpredictable) and it was a stormy marriage. A Uranus type of relationship with plenty of shocks (Aquarius is ruled by Uranus; thus similar traits). Carlos Leon (Neptune) is the father of her child, Lourdes Maria Ciccone Leon (also ruled by Neptune); they probably adore (Neptune) each other. Bobby Brown (Aquarius) and Whitney Houston (Mars, anger, fights, sex, fiery) have a tumultuous marriage. His Sun sign is also Aquarius and is opposite hers; thus, they are not all that compatible, though opposites attract. Aquarius is erratic, unpredictable, independent and can mesmerize others.

Gene Simmons (Aquarius) is the bassist for heavy-metal band *Kiss,* (Aquarius title). He's married to Shannon Tweed (Neptune, actress). He had an affair with Diana Ross (Aquarius) and Cher (Venus). Cher's real name was Cherilyn Sarkisian (Gemini, sign of communication, singing, duality, adaptable).

Their combined names, Sonny and Cher, vibrate to Uranus (originality, the unusual), overnight success, electric magnetism, sudden and unforeseen events and separation). The name Cher, by itself, and Sonny Bono, by itself, vibrates to Venus (good looks, clothes, artistic expression, love). Cher Bono (her name when married to Sonny) vibrates to Aquarius, the ruler of Uranus; thus, giving the same type of vibration as their combined names. Their combined name vibration (Uranus), affected them time and again: they suddenly (Uranus) broke up (Uranus), later, surprised (Uranus) their fans when they worked together again, but that didn't last (Uranus). As long as the public continues to think of them as Sonny and Cher, a mass of Uranus energy will be sent in the couple's direction. In the fall of 1981, he appeared on a TV show stating that he thought of himself as Sonny and Cher, and that it was difficult for him to think of himself as Sonny Bono. No wonder! The public's mass energy bombards him in this direction. They will always vibrate to Uranus; thus, their life has been constant ups and downs. Nothing would last (a Uranus negative side trait) with these two. However, their signature song *I Got You Babe,* (Pisces) will always be identified with Sonny and Cher. He was born Salvatore Philip Bono (Neptune, he was born, Salvatore Philip Bono (Neptune, promoting, idealistic). Their daughter, Chastity Bono vibrates to Sagittarius. After the divorce from Cher, he married Mary Whitaker (Uranus) who became Mary Bono (Neptune) and used Mary Whitaker Bono (Aries, activist, aggressive sign). As Sonny he vibrated to Pisces, Chastity's Sun sign.

Cher married Gregg Allman (Pisces, born Gregory Le Noire Allman, Libra) and had a son by him, Elijah Blue Allman (Sagittarius). The son's Sun sign blended with his father's Sagittarian Sun sign. Both of Cher's children had a Sagittarian name vibration.

Bianca Jagger and Mick Jagger, combined, vibrate to Mars (sex, quarrels, impulsiveness). The name Bianca Jagger, by itself, vibrates to Aquarius; Mick Jagger, by itself, vibrates to Saturn. When they were together they attracted strife; however, their individual name vibrations would affect one another: When Bianca is eccentric, wild or unconventional (Aquarius), Mick could stabilize (Saturn) her and bring conventionality (Saturn). However, this individual vibration did not work. If he expressed the selfish side of Saturn and she expressed the freedom loving sign of Aquarius, it would terminate fast on her part. They were divorced. He took up with Jerry Hall (Gemini, adaptable) who bore him many children.

The Beatles, as a group name vibrates to Uranus (sudden rise to fame, termination). They were instrumental in bringing to the world a completely new (Uranus) and different (Uranus) sound. They were individualistic (Uranus) and each went his own way (Uranus) to do his own thing (Uranus). But with Uranus, don't be surprised (Uranus) if they reunite again. However, with John Lennon's death, this is now impossible. If they do, (without John Lennon), it might only be temporary (Uranus). Individually, the Beatles have the following name vibrations: Ringo Starr vibrates to Pisces (acting, dramatizing the emotions, drugs, pills, booze, creative imagination). His real name Richard Starkey vibrates to Aquarius (independent, intuitive, original) and his wife Barbara Bach vibrates to Aries. Their name signs are compatible as well as their Sun sign's--his is Cancer, hers is Virgo.

George Harrison vibrates to Aquarius (independence, originality, unpredictable). The name, John Lennon, vibrates to Venus which rules artistic expression, charm, love, (no wonder there was so much love centered on him when he was killed!) socializing, and taking the easy way out. Yoko Ono (Cancer) has written with feeling (Cancer) numerous songs and poems. She was in touch with the masses (Cancer) through newspaper messages from her to the public concerning her husband, John Lennon's murder. Her name sign (Cancer) makes her maternal and protective; traits expressed toward her husband.

Paul Mc Cartney vibrates to Capricorn (ambition, stability, self-imposed privacy) and he used this Capricorn energy to seek seclusion, live the simple life on a farm, and then to turn around and make a successful comeback on his own. He was born James Paul Mc Cartney (Aries) and married Linda Eastman (Uranus) who became Linda Mc Cartney (Aries).

Her maiden name was Alana Collins (Capricorn). She married George Hamilton (Aries) and she became Alana Hamilton (Capricorn). Thus, she did not escape her name vibration which was not compatible with George, nor was her Sun sign Taurus compatible with his Leo Sun sign. Their son's, (Ashley Hamilton), Sagittarius name vibrates harmoniously to his parents. She married Rod Stewart (Neptune name, Sun Capricorn) and became Alana Stewart (Aquarius). That name was inharmonious to her Taurus Sun sign; they're now divorced.

Stefanie Powers (Aquarius; born Stefanie Federkiewicz, Capricorn) has her own line of perfume *Rare Orchid,* (Jupiter) and is the founder and president of William Holden Wildlife Foundations (Pisces, idealistic, promoting). If it is called "The William Holden Wildlife Foundations," (Gemini). She dated William Holden (Venus) for years. He was born William Franklin Beedle (Mars, alcohol, aggressive; supposedly he was an alcoholic).

He was born Derek Harris (Sagittarius) and used the name John Derek (a Pisces). He starred in movies as an actor (Pisces) and has promoted (Pisces) his wife Bo Derek into fame and made a fortune for her for the movies she's been in. He enjoys doing photography (Pisces) and took nude photos for *Playboy* magazine of three different wives. Bo Derek (Aquarius) is magnetic (Aquarius) and has a unique (Aquarius) look. She was born Kathleen Collins, (Aquarius); thus, she did not escape from her name vibration. Aquarius is ruled by the planet Uranus; she was an overnight (Aquarius) sensation when she played in the movie *10* (a Uranus title).

He was born Donald John Trump (Saturn, lucky planet by his Astrodynes). He's also called Donald Trump (Pisces, lucky sign for him) and Donald J. Trump (Aries, lucky sign for him). He's not lucky when referred to as "The Donald," (Neptune). His birth name vibration, Saturn, is the planet of real estate (He's a real estate developer). He married Ivana Zelnicek (Taurus) who became Ivana Trump (Virgo). Their Sun signs (hers, is Pisces, his is Gemini) are not compatible. His Donald Trump name vibration is not compatible to her when she uses the name Ivana Trump. He married Marla Maples (Capricorn) and she became Marla Maples Trump (Taurus). Both of these name vibrations of hers were compatible with his Donald Trump (Pisces) name. However, her Taurus married name sign was not compatible with her Sun sign, Scorpio. They are divorced.

Burt Reynolds (Capricorn; born Burton Leon Reynolds, Aries) married Loni Anderson (Pisces; born Loni Kaye Anderson, Pisces). He dates Pam Seals (Uranus). Pam Anderson and Pamela Anderson both vibrate to Aquarius. She married Tommy Lee (Saturn) and became Pamela Anderson Lee (Aries) and also used Pamela Lee (Capricorn). He is a drummer with the band *Motley Crue,* (Libra).

Carmen Electra (Lucky Jupiter name vibration was born Tara Patrick, Uranus). She married Dennis Rodman (Uranus, outrageous, unpredictable). Both are Sun sign Taurus, possessive, sensual. Tammy Faye (Neptune, dramatic, glamorous, exaggerations like her false eyelashes) married Jim Baker (Neptune, wheeler dealer). Ike and Tina Turner (Gemini, changeable, communication, singing) were a famous vocal team. However, their private life was a nightmare for her. She was born Anna Mae Bullock (Neptune) and as Tina Turner (Capricorn) she was ambitious. Her Sagittarius Sun sign is the sign that rules "Legs,: which she is famous for. Ike Turner vibrates to Jupiter. Their name as a team was harmonious for him but not for her (it was opposite her Sun sign). They are divorced.

Oscar Wilde (Sagittarius; born Oscar Fingal O'Flahertie Wilde, Venus) was a poet, dramatist and humorist. Renowned as a wit (Sagittarius.) He achieved recognition with the novel *The Picture of Dorian Grey,* (Pisces, imagination) turned into a film. He was imprisoned for a homosexual relationship with Lord Alfred Douglas (Pisces).

Two Capricorn name vibrations, Robert Wagner and Natalie Wood, were married, divorced and remarried. The Capricorn influence seemed to make them hold onto each other. Her birth name was Natasha Gurdin (Venus) He was devastated when she drowned. He dated Jill St. John (Aquarius; same as his Sun sign Aquarius) and then they married. At one time she dated Henry Kissinger (Uranus) and received sudden (Aquarius, Uranus) publicity. Their involvement was of short duration which is typical of the traits ruled by Aquarius and Uranus.

Courtney Love (Capricorn; born Courtney Menely, Uranus) married rocker Kurt Kobain (Virgo). Their name signs were compatible. Phil Hartman (Uranus, shocks, surprises, the unexpected and unpredictable) was shot by his Aries Sun sign wife Brynn Hartman (an Aries name, fiery, temperamental and rash when expressed on the negative side).

As Mrs. Andy Williams (Saturn), she might have felt restricted (Saturn), but as Claudine Longet (Aquarius) she was free to express her individuality (Aquarius) and independence (Aquarius). Under this Aquarian name vibration the unexpected is likely to happen. And it did when she accidently (Aquarius) shut her lover! Her ex-husband, Andy Williams (a Venus name), kindly (Venus) and affectionately (Venus) stood by her side during her trial and imprisonment.

He as born Orenthal James Simpson (Taurus). His nickname is O.J. (Capricorn, ambitious). He uses O.J. Simpson (Pisces) and, if called, Orenthal

James vibrates to Uranus. Nicole Brown (Aquarius) married him and became Nicole Simpson (Aquarius). His birth name and her Sun sign were both Taurus, however, that Taurus vibration was not lucky for them. They divorced and she was murdered. The civil suit jury voted him guilty. His horoscope's astrological evidence indicates that he killed her. Their progressed chart comparison, solar and lunar returns, both his and Nicole's progressed chart, transits to the exact time of the killing as well as their daughter, Sydney's horoscope showed that her father killed her mother!

Adolph Hitler (Uranus) refused to follow the crowd, wanted a new order and was high-strung, crazy and eccentric (all Uranus traits). When he was called Hitler, his vibration changed to Aries (war, hatred, sadism). He disappeared suddenly (Uranus) when the wheel of fortune (Uranus) was suddenly reversed (Uranus) on him.

Eva Braun (Uranus) was Hitler's mistress. On their first (Uranus) meeting, she was suddenly (Uranus) attracted to him. Her unconventional (Uranus) sexual behavior fascinated (Uranus) Hitler and was the gossip of the day. She knew (Uranus) how to handle him. Hitler and Eva were magnetized (Uranus) by each other. No wonder they disappeared (Uranus) together although rumors are that they were married and committed suicide. Others say they were married, shot and their bodies burned together (Aries) at his request. As long as Uranus is involved in their name vibration, it is unpredictable (Uranus) as to what really happened.

Kathie Lee and Regis vibrate to the unpredictable planet Uranus. Her various name vibrations are Kathie Lee (Aries), Kathie Lee Gifford (Uranus), Kathryn Lee Epstein (Uranus) and her nickname Kathy (Scorpio). Regis Philbin vibrates to Sagittarius which is harmonious with Kathie Lee. Frank Gifford (Venus, love; born Frank Newton Gifford, Neptune which on the negative side can be a philanderer) was entrapped in a sex scandal with Suzen Johnson (Pisces, sign of deception, promoting, wheeling dealing when expressed on the negative side) who calls herself Suzy Johnson (Capricorn, sign of ambition). Her husband, Harold Johnson vibrates to Sagittarius, a happy-go-lucky sign.

Lynn Redgrave (Venus; born Lynn Scudemore, Sagittarius married John Clark (Scorpio, sexy). Her sister Vanessa Redgrave (Sagittarius) was born Vanessa Scudemore (Capricorn). Her Sagittarian name vibration could influence her to be the outspoken activist that she has been; however, her birth name would make her diplomatic.

Mia Farrow (Jupiter, confidence, optimism) was married to Frank Sinatra (Capricorn). Their name and Sun signs were harmonious; however, they didn't have a good compatibility in their horoscopes together. Her father was John Villiers Farrow (Capricorn). Her mother Maureen O'Sullivan (Aquarius) blended with Mia's Sun sign, though her mother's Sun sign Taurus did not blend with Mia's Aquarius Sun sign.

Andre Previn (Capricorn) was born Andreas Ludwig Priwin (Aries) but uses Andre George Previn (Saturn). Woody Allen (a Saturn name, ruler of Capricorn, thus has similar traits as Capricorn) was born Allen Stewart Konigsberg and uses as his legal name Heywood Allen (Uranus, the unpredictable planet). He married their adopted daughter, Soon-Yi Previn (Aries) and she became Soon-Yi Allen (Libra, love).

Hillary Rodham (Aquarius, independent) became Hillary Rodham Clinton (Venus, sweet, loving, charming, gracious) when she married Bill Clinton (Aquarius, unpredictable); if she uses Hillary Clinton she also vibrates to Aquarius He was born William Jefferson Blythe Clinton IV (Venus). Their name signs are compatible but their Sun signs are not compatible (she is Scorpio, he is Leo). When he is called ("Bill" he still vibrates to Aquarius. If called Billy, he vibrates to Uranus, the ruler of Aquarius. He still vibrates to Uranus when called William Clinton and President Bill Clinton. Uranus is involved in scandal. As President William Jefferson Blythe IV, he vibrates to Aquarius. Chelsea Clinton vibrates to Sagittarius; her birth name Chelsea Victoria Clinton vibrates to Aries. Her name signs are compatible with her parents' name signs. Note; Aquarius and Uranus rule unconventional behavior.

Monica Lewinsky vibrates to Gemini, the sign of talking---gossip---and she did plenty of that. It's the sign that rules adaptability and changeableness, two personalities or more. According to her Astrodynes, Gemini is a discordant, unlucky, sign for her. Thus, her name is not a lucky name. Will she change it? Possibly she will. However, her Gemini name sign and Clinton's Aquarius name sign, are compatible. They have the same Leo Sun sign and Libra Rising sign and ruler of the house of sex (Uranus Saturn--Uranus is kinky sex and, like Saturn, is not attached; Saturn can be cold, Uranus can be similar to a one night stand---not a lasting relationship.) Uranus is the planet of shocks and oral sex.

The word *Zippergate,* vibrates to Libra, sign of love, and giving in to the line of least resistance. The girls at a beauty parlor, it was reported, called Linda Tripp *The Royal Bitch,* the title vibrates to Sagittarius. Linda Tripp (Uranus) was born Linda Rose Carotenuto (Neptune; deceptive and tell lies when expressed on the negative side. Her Sun sign is Sagittarius, blunt, candid and outspoken). Often she used Linda Carotenuto (Pisces, ruled by Neptune; thus, similar traits). She vibrates to Cancer when she uses Linda Rose Tripp, an emotional and changeable sign.

Ken Starr (Venus) was born Kenneth Winston Starr (Neptune). Vernon Jordan's Pisces name sign is harmonious with Bill Clinton (Aquarius); both are Leo Sun signs. The name Paula Jones is a Jupiter vibration (confidence, optimism and happy-go-lucky and the name Paula Corbin Jones (Taurus) is a materialistic (Taurus) name vibration. Her Sun sign is Virgo which is harmonious with her Taurus name sign. However, her Sun sign and Bill Clinton's name sign are not compatible. Gennifer Flowers (Pisces name) is an Aquarian Sun sign and she is not compatible with Bill Clinton's Sun sign Leo.

WHO IS YOUR NAME COMPATIBLE WITH?

If you're an employer, and want to hire someone who is compatible to your name sign vibration, add the person's name to discover what sign or planet he/she vibrates to. If this individual is not compatible with you, it would be in your best interest not to hire him/her. However, if the two of you are compatible, it would be to your advantage to have this person on your payroll.

The name signs that are compatible with one another are as follows:

Aries does best with another Aries (although you two may be competitive with one another), Gemini, Leo , Sagittarius, and Aquarius. The next most harmonious signs are: Taurus, Virgo, Scorpio and Pisces. The signs that are most difficult in a relationship are: Cancer, Libra, and Capricorn.

Taurus does best with another Taurus (although stubbornness may be a problem), Cancer, Virgo, Scorpio, Capricorn, and Pisces. The next most harmonious signs are: Aries, Gemini, Libra, and Sagittarius. The signs that are the most difficult in a relationship are: Leo and Aquarius.

Gemini does best with another Gemini, Aries, Leo, Libra, Sagittarius, and Aquarius. The next most harmonious signs are; Taurus, Cancer, and Capricorn. The signs that are the most difficult in a relationship are: Virgo and Pisces.

Cancer does best with another Cancer, Taurus, Virgo, Scorpio, Capricorn and Pisces. The next most harmonious signs are: Gemini, Leo, Sagittarius and Aquarius. The signs that are the most difficult in a relationship are: Aries, Libra and Capricorn.

Leo does best with Aries, Gemini, Libra, and Sagittarius. The next harmonious signs are: Cancer, Virgo, Capricorn, and Pisces. The signs that are the most difficult in a relationship are: Taurus, another Leo, Scorpio, and Aquarius.

Virgo does best with Taurus, Cancer, another Virgo, Scorpio, and Capricorn. The next most harmonious signs are: Aries, Leo, Libra, and Aquarius. The signs that are the most difficult in a relationship are: Gemini, Sagittarius and Pisces.

Libra does best with Gemini, Leo, another Libra, Sagittarius and Aquarius. The next most harmonious signs are Taurus, Virgo, Scorpio, and Pisces. The signs that are the most difficult in a relationship are: Aries, Cancer, and Capricorn.

Scorpio does best with Taurus, Cancer, Virgo, Capricorn and Pisces. The next most harmonious signs are: Aries, Gemini, Libra, and Sagittarius. The signs that are the most difficult in a relationship are: Leo, another Scorpio and Aquarius.

Sagittarius does best with Aries, Gemini, Leo, Libra, another Sagittarius and Aquarius. The next most harmonious signs are: Taurus, Cancer, Scorpio, and Capricorn. The signs that are the most difficult in a relationship are: Virgo and Pisces.

Capricorn does best with Taurus, Virgo, Scorpio and Pisces. The next most harmonious signs are: Gemini, Leo, Sagittarius, and Aquarius. The signs that are the most difficult in a relationship are: Aries, Cancer, Libra, and another Capricorn.

Aquarius does best with Aries, Gemini, Libra, Sagittarius and another Aquarius (at times if they don't become too opinionated and erratic.) The next most harmonious signs are: Cancer, Virgo, Capricorn and Pisces. The signs that are the most difficult in a relationship are: Taurus, Leo, and Scorpio.

Pisces does best with Taurus, Cancer, Scorpio, Capricorn, and another Pisces. The next most harmonious signs are: Aries, Leo, Libra and Aquarius. The signs that are the most difficult in a relationship are: Gemini, Virgo and Sagittarius.

CHAPTER ELEVEN

WHERE DID THEIR NAMES COME FROM?

INDIVIDUALS

Edith Piaf (Uranus) and Edith Giovanna Gassion (Mars) was a famous French chanteuse who had a rough life from the time she was born. Her whole life is typical of Uranus and Mars events: she was born on a street; abandoned by her mother several months later; went blind at three years of age; eyesight was restored when she was seven years old; got pregnant and baby died when she was sixteen years old; changed her name to Piaf, which is the Parisian slang for 'sparrow' (she was 4' 10" and sang like a sparrow); the man she loved was killed in a plane crash; she had a broken arm from an auto accident, followed by another car accident, and an ulcer operation; the next month she had intestinal block surgery, six months later a gall bladder operation, three months later she collapsed and was confined to bed; a year and a half later surgery for intestinal constriction; a year and a half after that had arthritis; nine months later had pneumonia and jaundice, and six months later died of an internal hemorrhage resulting from a liver ailment.

Gunther Gebel-Williams (Mars) is one of the most courageous men alive. He is known as the greatest animal trainer in the world and Ringling Bros. & Barnum Bailey Circus is lucky to have him. If you've ever seen him you'd know how he uses his Mars vibration with his name. He took the name Williams when he was in Germany growing up (it was the name of the circus owners who he lived with from an early age). His name without the Williams vibrates to Pisces, the sign ruling the circus; isn't it ironic he was attracted to it (although it was his mother who needed a job and went to work for the circus) and, with his name vibration, he'd be happy in this environment--and he is ! By the way his wife was in the circus also. She uses the name Sigrid Gebel, without the Williams which vibrates to Aquarius and she is magnetic, extremely beautiful and charming.

Many stars changed their names when they began---it was part of the process of being reborn, of bringing a romantic character to life. Often they took a name from a heroine in a book, or a part they played on stage or in a movie.

Michael Caine (Aquarius; born Maurice Mickle White) took his name from the title in _The Caine Mutiny_. Nathan Lane (Capricorn; born Joseph Lane, Virgo) took the name Nathan at age 22 after playing Nathan Detroit in _Guys and Dolls_ (Sagittarius title) in a dinner-theater show. Anouk Aimee (Uranus; born Francoise Sorya, Pisces) took the name of a servant she played in her screen debut in _La Maison la Mer_. Bette Davis (Gemini; born Ruth Elizabeth Davis, Neptune acting planet) dropped the Ruth Elizabeth and took the Bette from a book by; Balzac called _Cousin Bette_.

Hedy Lamarr (Aries; Hedwig Eva Marie Keisler, birth name Uranus) took her last name from a well known screen star, Barbara La Marr. Parker Posey

(Capricorn) was named after the super model Suzy Parker (Uranus). Barbara Stanwyck (Venus; born Ruby Stevens, Venus) was given her name by Willard Mack; it came from a character in a play called Jane Stanwyk. Sigourney Weaver (Aries; born Susan Weaver, Sagittarius) took her name from a character in _The Great Gatsby_. Anne Shirley (Uranus) was a child star using the name Dawn O'Day (Neptune) and changed her name when she played the heroine in _Anne of the Green Gable._

Natasha Richardson (Aquarius) was named after the heroine in Tolstoy's _War and Peace_ (Aries) Note: Title _Tolstoy's War and Peace_ vibrates to Aquarius. Gig Young (Neptune; born Byron Barr, Venus) took the name of the character he played in _The Gay Sisters._ Dustin Hoffman (Uranus: born Dustin Lee Hoffman, Taurus) was given his first name by his mother who named him after an early cowboy star she liked---Dustin Farnun (Sagittarius). Bob Dylan (Sagittarius: born Robert Allen Zimmerman, Saturn ; often used Robert Zimmerman, Uranus) took his stage name from Dylan Thomas (Scorpio). He is called by his nickname Robert (Aries).

Elton John (Aquarius, sign of being original, unconventional; born Reginald Kenneth Dwight, also Aquarius) combined the first name of two friends: John Baldry (Mars) and Elton Dean (Pisces). Most of his performances are typical of Aquarius: Weird and unusual costumes which he utilizes to create a magnetic effect. Judy Holliday (Scorpio,; born Judy Tuvim, Saturn) took the Hebrew word and its meaning "holiday" and added an "l" to get her stage name.

Gilbert Roland (Venus; born Luis Antonio Domaso De Alonso, Jupiter, ruler or Sagittarius, thus similar traits) took parts of the names of his two favorite movie stars: John Gilbert (Jupiter) ruth Roland (Libra). Elle MacPherson (Capricorn; born Eleanor Gow, Gemini) the super model, actress, took her name from the magazine _Elle;_ she appeared in every issue from 1982 to 1988. Nicholas Cage (Venus; born Nicholas Coppola, Uranus) changed his last name to have an identity independent of his famous uncle. He assumed the name "Cage," (Moon) in admiration of the avant-guard composer John Cage (Taurus) and comic book character Luke Cage (Aquarius).

She was born Marguerita Wendy Jenkins (Aquarius) and changed her name to Wendy Barrie (Mars). She was called Wendy (Pisces) after the character in _Peter Pan_ by her playwright god-father who wrote it ---M. Barrie (Capricorn). Bette Midler (Libra) was named after Bette Davis, which her mother mistakenly thought was pronounced "Bet" (Neptune, planet that can be foggy in thought). Loretta Young (Pisces; born Gretchen Young, Aquarius) was named by the star who discovered her when she worked as an extra at 14 years of age.

Tony Bennett (Neptune; born Anthony Dominick Benedetto, Aries) used the name Joe Bari (Uranus) until Bob Hope(Pisces) introduced him as Tony Bennett in 1950. Regis Philbin (Sagittarius) was named after Regis High, a Manhattan Catholic boy's school and his father's alma mater. Bridget

Fonda(Uranus) was named after Bridget Hayward (Capricorn), a woman her father (Peter Fonda, Scorpio) had a love affair with and who had committed suicide.

Kenneth "Baby Face" Edmonds (Aries) was given the name "Baby Face,"(Aries) in the early 1980's by funk guitarist Bootsy Collins (Taurus) because of his youthful looks. Uma Thurman (Neptune, acting) was given her name by her father, a professor of Asian religion; he named her after Uma (Moon) a Hindu Goddess. Hammer (Venus; born Stanley Kirk Burrell, Sagittarius) rapper turned minister was called "hammer" when he worked as a bat boy for a baseball team (Oakland A's) and it stuck as his professional name. The basketball player, Kobe Bryant (Scorpio) was named for the Kobe(Uranus) steak house in suburban Philadelphia. His hip-hop (ruled by Aquarius, Uranus) is Kobe One Kenobe the Eighth," (Aquarius). Magic Johnson (Neptune; born Earvin Johnson, also, Neptune) was given the nickname "Magic" (Neptune) in high school by a local sportswriter after a game which he scored 36 points and had 18 rebounds.

Seal (Pisces; born Sealhenry Samuel, Uranus), singer, songwriter. His name comes from his Brazilian father's custom of having the grandparents select the name (they chose Seal) coupled with his parent's fascination with British Royalty. They wanted Henry (Pisces), thus, his first name Sealhenry.

Prince (Taurus:), "Prince, the Artist Formerly Known As Prince,"(Taurus) and Prince Roger Nelson (Sagittarius---his birth name) was named after the Prince Roger Trio (Neptune)---a jazz group led by his father. Now known as an Egyptian symbol, or referred to as"The Artist Formerly Known As Prince,"sometimes abbreviated to Tafkap (Saturn). Tiger Woods (Venus; born Eldrick Woods Uranus). The Nickname Tiger (Venus) come from father Earl's Green Beret army past; it was the moniker of a South Vietnamese officer who saved Earl's life on several occasions.

Bono (Pisces; born Paul Hewson, Sagittarius), singer, songwriter, got his nickname from a billboard advertising "Bono Vox," (Aries), a hearing aid retailer. Carole Lombard (Sagittarius; born Janice Alice Peters, Aquarius) reportedly came up with the name from a pharmacy in New York City called "Carroll-Lombardi,"(Capricorn). Luther Vandross (Neptune; born Luther Ronzoni Vendross, Aquarius). His middle name came from the Ronzoni food producer; it was the only food his mother could keep down during her difficult pregnancy.

Wynonna Judd (Cancer; born Christina Claire Ciminella, Uranus) adopted her name "Wynonna," (Pisces after the town of Wynona (Sagittarius), Oklahoma. It's mentioned in the song "Route 66," (Aquarius). Jack Oakie (Aries; born Jack Lewis Offield, Saturn) got the "Oakie," (Sagittarius) from his home state's nickname "Oakie" for Oklahoma (Saturn). People were called Oakies if they were from Oklahoma.

Johnny Cash(Libra; born J.R. Cash, Venus) changed his birth name to another name when the military would not accept the initials he was born with; he changed it to John R. Cash, Gemini). He is known as *The Man in Black* (Scorpio);

he adopted this persona while working in a trio that only wore black matching outfits. Scorpio is ruled by the planet Pluto whose color is black; Pluto rules recordings.

She was born Frances Ethel Gumm (Neptune, acting, dramatizing the emotions) and took the name Judy Garland (Aries) from the Hoagy Carmichael song *Judy* (Libra). Her last name came from the theatre pages of a Chicago newspaper whose reviews were written by Robert Garland (Jupiter). Jacqueline Susann (Capricorn, ambition) was born Jacqueline Susan(Pisces); she added an "n" to the Susan. Often she was called Jackie (Pisces), Jackie Susann (Capricorn) or her father and husband called her "Skinny bones" (Pisces). Her husband Irving Mansfield (Capricorn, ambitious, hard-working) publicist made her book *The Valley Of The Dolls* (Uranus, overnight success planet). He was born Irving Mandelbaum (Capricorn).

Erykah Badu (Taurus; born Erica Wright, Capricorn), wanted to change her "slave name"; when her mother objected, as a teen she respelled her first name with the "y" symbolizing "origin" and the "kah", ancient Egyptian for "pure inner light." Later she changed her surname, choosing a riff she favored. She is influenced by mathematics, a type of numerology that equates numbers with personal growth and self-knowledge. She gave birth to a son, Steven Sirius (Saturn) and named him "Seven" because that number cannot be divided by anything but itself.

Rock Hudson (Uranus, unconventional sign) was born Roy Scherer Jr. (Neptune). When his stepfather adopted him, his name became Roy Fitzgerald (Uranus). His agent wanted his name to look good on a marquee and told him he would have to have a name change. He suggested Hudson, then eventually said the name Rock, which he agreed upon with his agent, Henry Wilson. At first, he spelled it Roc, then changed it to Rock (either way it still vibrated to Uranus).

Joe E. Lewis, the comedian vibrates to Aquarius. He was born Joe Klewan (Capricorn, same as his Sun sign). He first changed his last name to Lewis (Joe Lewis, Aries) because a press agent had been unable to spell his birth name. There was confusion when he tried to get publicity as Joe Lewis. A copy desk writer at the newspaper kept changing it to Louis. He was getting it confused with the boxer Joe Louis (Saturn; born Joseph Louis Barrow, Leo and known as *The Brown Bomber,*---Jupiter, the lucky planet). So, he was told he had to do something about his name.

The publicity agent suggested that Joe Lewis should have a middle name or initial. At first, they thought of the letter "K," then tested the other twenty-five letters of the alphabet and came up with Joe. E. Lewis. The press agent told him, "Lots of people call you Joey (Jupiter), so use Joe E. Lewis. His friends called him Joe E. (Aquarius) after his name change. They never called him "Joe," (Scorpio)

At the time of his name change, he was a singer and worked in a nightclub in Chicago. He had an offer to change to another club, but the mob threatened him.

He rebelled (Aquarius name); gangsters cut-his face, just missed the vocal cords, but damaged his voice. It took him a year to speak, his voice was raspy and he became a comedian. His Aquarian name vibration was used constantly, during the remainder of his life. He was original (Aquarius), inventive (Aquarius) great at alibiing (Aquarius) and for decades past his demise, comics are still stealing the lines he made famous.

Joan Fantaine (Jupiter; born Joan de Beauevoir de Haviland, Saturn) assumed the name her mother's second husband. Her sister Olivia de Haviland (Sagittarius) did not change her name. Jean Harlow (Pisces name and Sun sign); she was born Harlean Carpenter (Sagittarius), she took her mother's maiden name. Neve Campbell (Scorpio) took as her first name, her mother's Dutch maiden name which means "snow." Calista Flockhart (Mars) was named after her great grandmother. Calista means "most beautiful" in Greek.

Susan Sarandon (Uranus; born Susan Abigail Tomaling, Aries) took the last name of her ex-husband from her first marriage. Charlton Heston (Gemini; born Charlton Carter, Sagittarius) got his middle name from his mother's maiden last name.

Madonna (Aquarius) used part of her mother's maiden name (Madonna Louise Forten, Neptune). Her mother married Tony Ciccone (Jupiter). Madonna's birth name is Madonna Louise Veronica Ciccone (Saturn). Often she was called Madonna Ciccone (Venus); however, to distinguish her from Madonna senior, as a child, she was called "Little Nonni,"(Sagittarius)

Debbie Reynolds (Capricorn) was born Mary Frances Reynolds (Uranus). Frances was her father's middle name and Mary was the name of her mother's sister. Her mother called her Mary (Capricorn or Mary Frances (Sagittarius); others in the family called her"sis," (Sagittarius). Jack Warner, of Warner Brothers Studio, changed her name to Debbie Morgan (Taurus). She did not want the name Morgan and spoke up (her Aries Sun sign trait) about keeping her family name of Reynolds(Libra).

Marilyn Monroe (Neptune, screen Goddess, worship is ruled by Neptune, so are films). She has become and idol (Neptune) to her followers (fans). She was born Norma Jean Baker (Sagittarius) and was named in honor of the actress Norma Talmadge (Capricorn), who was her mother's favorite silent screen star. Her mother's second husband was Edward Mortensen (Capricorn); thus, she became Norma Jean Mortensen (Aries). It was rumored that her real father was Stanley Gifford (Uranus, a rebel). Often she called herself Norma Jeane (Cancer).

Once she became a starlet in films, the studio decided she needed a name change. It is rumored that "Marilyn" came from her grand mother's side of the family; however, other sources say that she was given the first name of Marilyn by a Fox studio talent scout, Ben Lyon (Uranus); he named her after the famous star of Broadway, Marilyn Miller (Capricorn) It is said that the name "Monroe" came from her maternal grandmother's husband.

Marilyn Monroe was notorious for being addicted (Neptune) to sleeping pills (Neptune). It's alleged that she swallowed an overdose and thus ended her life

However, there's a mystery (Neptune) surrounding her death because an investigator from the coroner's department said she was murdered. Her horoscope, at the time of her death, indicates she was murdered. But because she vibrates to Neptune, will her demise always be a mystery (Neptune)?

WHERE DID THEIR NAMES COME FROM?---GROUPS

Pablo Cruise is the name of a pop rock group which vibrates to Scorpio, a water sign; interestingly enough, they say that their name comes from a friend of theirs who has been cruising (in the water) off Columbia for years. The group consists of Dave Jenkins, Bruce Day, Cory Lerios and Steve Price. Their individual name sign vibration is harmonious to each other: Dave Jenkins (Virgo) and Bruce Day (Taurus) have names that are trine (good luck) to one another. Cory Lerios(Venus) and Steve Price (Jupiter) have name vibrations that belong to the two luckiest planets in astrology. And they in turn, blend with Dave's Virgo and Bruce's Taurus name vibrations; plus they all go well with the group name *Pablo Cruise*.(Scorpio)

The late Jerry Garcia (Libra), leader of the group *The Grateful Dead* (Mercury, rules communication, singing), randomly picked the words from a dictionary. The group was originally called *The Warlocks* (Scorpio) but had to abandon that occult designation because it was already taken.

The Beach Boys (Mars) were originally called *The Pendletones* (Taurus) but their name was changed by the record company to cash in on the surfer music craze. Frankie Valli (Neptune), lead singer of *The Four Seasons* (Uranus), named the band after a bowling alley lounge in New Jersey. *The Go-Go's* (Uranus) thought up the name while having breakfast in a Denny's (Pisces, sign of creativity) restaurant in Los Angeles. Glenn Frey (Mercury), guitarist for the *Eagles* (Sagittarius) and called *Eagles* (Neptune)by many. This rock group borrowed their title from American Indian folklore. The eagle is said to transport spirits from this world to the next.

Lauryn Hill (Venus), singer of the group *The Fugees* (Capricorn), said the name springs from the trio's feeling of being refugees from mainstream culture, and even hip-hop, and from their sense that they find refuge in the music they make. *The Doors* (Uranus) which is a psychedelic band, found their namesake in the title of a book about hallucinogenic drugs----Aldous Huxley's (Capricorn) *The Doors of Perception* (Aquarius, sign of awakenings, ruled by Uranus, which is the name sign of the group; Aquarius and Uranus represent the traits of daring to be different and rebellion against the establishment).

Rick Ocasek (Aquarius, sign that rules automobiles), lead singer of the group *The Cars* (Pisces), gave them their name because it was easy to spell and had a "z" sound on the end. _Grand Funk Railroad_ (Pisces) got their name from a Michigan state landmark the old _Grand Trunk Railroad_ (Leo). _The Who_ (Capricorn) got their name because it was short and, thus, would print up large on posters for the concert. They thought people would be so confused by it that it would not be easy to forget.

Jimmy Page (Uranus), guitarist, unsuccessfully tried to get John Entwistle (Pisces) and Keith Moon (Aries) to join his new group he was starting. John Entwistle of the group _The Who's_ (Neptune, spelled with the apostrophe "s"), remarked, "We'll call it _Led Zeppelin_ (Aquarius), because it'll go down like a lead balloon." _Tranzlator Crew_ (Saturn) was forced to change the name of the group when a long-forgotten 1980's new wave act called Translator objected.

Stewart Copeland (Saturn) of the group The Police(Aries, violence) chose the bands title thinking it would bring police escorts and free publicity. He gained his nickname by wearing a black-and -yellow striped shirt, like a bee. _Jon Bon Jovi_ (Venus) got their name from John Bongiovi (Capricorn) who received a contract with Polygram (Neptune, promoting) which stipulated that John Bongiovi would become _Jon Bon Jovi_ and only he would be given a contract. The other four members of the band would be employed by him. The name "Bon Jovi," (Neptune); known as a "rocker" (Pisces word; Neptune rules Pisces)

The Rolling Stones (Virgo) consists of Mick Jagger (Capricorn; born Michael Philip Jagger, Mars) lead singer with the group. The other members are all Neptune name vibrations; Keith Richards, Charlie Watts, Ron Wood; the exception is Bill Wyman (Capricorn). They got their name from the song _Rollin Stone_, (Gemini), sung by Muddy Waters (Scorpio, a water sign--Scorpio rules stagnant, dirty and muddy water), a blues singer.

Diana Ross (Aquarius) of _The Supremes_ (Jupiter, lucky planet) and the other original members of the group were Mary Wilson (Venus) and Florence Ballard (Capricorn) picked their name when Berry Gordy (Sagittarius name and Sun sign who is very compatible with Diana Ross's name-Aquarius-and her Sun sign, Aries) gave them a list of titles to choose from for his Motown (Saturn) label. Formerly they were called _The Primettes,_ (Jupiter). Diana Ross's parents had intended to name her Diana but a clerical error on her birth certificate called her Diane Ross(Scorpio). Their name as "Diana Ross and the Supremes," vibrates to Saturn. Her name is Aquarius, the sign of independence; thus, she broke (Aquarius traits) from the group and went out as a single. She wants people to call her "Miss Ross, (Capricorn, reserved, ambitious and status-seeking zodiac sign).

The Spice Girls (Aquarius, sign of being original and overnight sensation) was chosen by Geri "Ginger" Halliwell (also Aquarius). She first called the group "Spice" (Uranus, rules Aquarius), but another rapper had that name so it was changed to _The Spice Girls._ The name "Ginger" is a Uranus vibration; the planet of the unpredictable and breaking up; she (Ginger) broke with the group. The other members of the group are: Victoria "Posh Spice" Adams (Uranus; Posh Spice

(Aquarius). Melanie B. "Scary" Spice (Cancer); also goes by Mel B. "Scary" Spice (Saturn) or Mel B. (Jupiter). Melanie Jayne "Sporty Spice" Chisholm (Taurus) goes by "Sporty Spice," (Capricorn, same sign as her Sun sign).. Scary Spice named her daughter Phoenix Chi; Phoenix means "fire," and Chi means "aura"---a Taurus name vibration. The other girls are calling themselves (to Phoenix Chi) Auntie Spices (Capricorn), Aunt Sporty Spice (Scorpio) and Aunt Posh Spice (Taurus). The words "Spice Girls" vibrate to Scorpio, a sexy sign; they all have sex appeal with their sexy costumes mannerisms.

CHAPTER TWELVE

WHAT THEY ARE KNOWN FOR

HOW THEY USED THEIR NAME VIBRATION

Lillian Russell (Saturn) was practical (Saturn) and had down-to-earth (Saturn) good humor (Sun sign Sagittarius). Florenz Ziegfield (Uranus has a name that is synonymous with *Ziegfield Follies* (an Aries title and was the first (Aries and/or Uranus) to introduce the Parisian type of showgirls to the U.S.A.. Billy Rose (Aquarius) produced the first (Aquarius) *Aquacade* first Broadway show (*Jumbo*) with live animals on stage and the first theater-restaurant. He wrote original (Aquarius) popular songs and was the world's fastest shorthand (Aquarius) writer. Walter E. Disney (Aquarius) was the first (Aquarius) to use the improved 3-strip technicolor process. His animated cartoons were different (Aquarius). Disneyland (Taurus title) was a unique (Aquarius) idea of his. He inspired originality (Aquarius) in all he did.

Elizabeth Arden (Taurus name and Sun sign) was involved with beauty salons and cosmetics (Taurus). Her salons carry expensive (Taurus) accessories and clothes (Taurus).

Laurie Walters (Venus) spends most of her money on Persian rugs (Venus); however, she also buys artwork (Venus)--these are areas she calls her savings account. Ralph Nader (Aries) is a crusader (Aries) for the consumer. George Westinghouse (Cancer) is famous for household (Cancer) products; it's interesting that his name is on refrigerators which are mainly found in the home (Cancer) and contain food (ruled by Cancer). Alexander Graham Bell (Uranus) invented (Uranus) the telephone.

Frank Lloyd Wright (Saturn) was raised on a farm (Saturn) and always respected the land (Saturn). He termed his architecture (Saturn) "organic" to imply that each building grew out of its site (Saturn) as a natural (Saturn) thing. He encountered economic (Saturn) depression (Saturn) during different phases of his career. Margaret Mead (Aquarius) contributed largely toward the enlarging scope of anthropology (Aquarius) which is the past and present study of human beings from their physical, social, material and cultural developments. Gloria Steinem (Capricorn) is the conservative (Capricorn) element in the women's movement. David Frost (Capricorn) is known for his shrewdness (Capricorn) and ambition (Capricorn). His deal with Richard Nixon (Sun sign Capricorn) for a TV interview was smart and clever (Capricorn).

James Dean (Neptune) died in a car crash; his death caused a wave of worshiping (Neptune) hysteria (Neptune). His acting in films (Neptune) was considered superb. Amelia Earhart (Neptune), aviatrix (Neptune) was the first woman to fly (Neptune) the Atlantic. She was lost (Neptune) in the Pacific during a round-the-world flight attempt. To this day her disappearance (Neptune) has remained a mystery (Neptune). Various sections of the public wondered whether she was a spy, or involved in some sort of intrigue (Neptune).

James Hoffa (Pisces; born James Riddle Hoffa, Neptune---planet that rules Pisces, thus, similar traits). His nickname Jimmy also Neptune; however, Jimmy Hoffa is a Sagittarius name. He was a labor leader convicted of misdealings (Neptune). It is alleged he was involved with corruption, bribery, dishonesty, mysterious activities, wheeling and dealing---these traits are typical of the negative side of Neptune. He was abducted from a Detroit restaurant and presumably was murdered and his body was never found. He was the head of the Teamsters Union and involved with the mob. His disappearance (Neptune) is an unsolved (Neptune) riddle (no puns intended with his middle name.)

Mary Pickford (Venus, sweetheart; born Gladys Mary Smith, Aries name and Aries Sun sign), star of silent screen films was known as America's Sweetheart (Taurus; sign ruled by Venus, thus similar traits). During the early part of their, marriage, Debbie Reynolds (Capricorn) and Eddie Fisher (Gemini) were called "Eddie and Debbie" (Pisces); they were also dubbed, "America's Sweethearts," (Gemini, the sign represents a duo).

Jerry Springer (Aries) is independent and has the guts to put on shows that cause people to argue (Aries) or fight (Aries). Richard Simmons (Aquarius) is known as the "diet guru." His knowledge (Aquarius) has helped many. Often, his humanitarian (Aquarius) traits surface, when he helps extremely obese people lose weight. Florence Nightingale (Scorpio, hardworking) is founder of _The Red Cross_ (Aquarius, a humanitarian sign).

Neil Armstrong (Aquarius; born Neil Alden Armstrong, also Aquarius) was the first (Aquarius) man to walk on the Moon. Julia Child (Uranus) was the first (Uranus) person to teach gourmet cooking on television; her recipes were different (Uranus) and she gave her viewers shortcuts (Uranus). Wolfgang Puck (Aquarius) uses originality in his recipes at his various restaurants. Charles Monroe (Sagittarius; born Charles Monroe Schultz also Sagittarius) gained fame as a cartoonist (Sagittarius) for _Peanuts_ (Sagittarius), _Snoopy_ (Aries) and _Charlie Brown_ (Venus). He brought laughter (Sagittarius) to the world.

Vanessa Williams (Uranus, controversial), singer, actress. She was the first (Uranus) black Miss America. She was forced to resign (Uranus) after _Penthouse_ magazine printed nude photos of her in leather bondage gear in penthouse magazine with another woman (Uranus). Photos were taken several years before the Miss America (Neptune) contest.

Bill Gates (Mars; aggressive, pioneer, enterprising) boasted (when he was in the 11th grade) that he would be a millionaire by the time he was thirty years old. By the time he was thirty-one years old, he was a billionaire. He has a high I.Q., brilliant at math (Mars and his Sun sign Scorpio trait). By the age of nine, he had read the entire World Book Encyclopedia. His company _Microsoft_ (Neptune) is associated with his name. He promotes (Neptune) the products he manufactures.(Mars).

Robin Leach (Mars) is identified with the TV show, *Lifestyles of The Rich And Famous,* (Sagittarius; sign of wealth). Athina Onassis (Aquarius name and Sun Sign) is known as *The Richest Girl In The World* (Taurus, sign of money). Joseph P. Kennedy (Taurus) was a financier (Taurus). Norton Simon (Taurus name and Sun sign) is a multimillionaire art (Taurus) collector.

Aristotle Onasis (Capricorn) was a very ambitious (Capricorn) man who could wait patiently (Capricorn) for whatever he planned (Capricorn). This was shown by his business success and his private campaign to win Jackie Kennedy. Whenever he was called Ari Onassis(Aquarius) he would attract the unusual (Aquarius) be interested in new methods of business and modernization (Aquarius) and do as he pleased (Aquarius). His life would be unpredictable (Aquarius). He showered surprise (Aquarius) gifts on the woman he loved.

Saint Peter (Neptune) called "Simon Peter" (Capricorn) was the chief of the Apostles. Traditionally, he was regarded as the first bishop of Rome. When spelled St. Peter, he vibrates to Scorpio; otherwise, he vibrates to Neptune. (People idolizing and worshiping him). Judas (Venus; born Judas Iscariot, Scorpio) betrayed Jesus Christ. When someone is called a "Judas," that means he/she betrays. However, Venus is a planet which represents love and friendship--Is it that one appears charming (Venus), so others are fooled?

Pope John Paul II (Venus; born Karol Cardinal Wojtyla, Libra, ruled by Venus, thus, same traits). He expressed Venus traits: kindness, affection, warmth, friendliness and an interest in others. Brigham Young (Sagittarius) was a Mormon Leader: Sagittarius is the sign of religion. Mary Baker Eddy (Sagittarius) was the discoverer of the principles of Christian Science and founder of the same Church (Sagittarius).

Marco Polo (Jupiter, selling, confident, optimistic) was a Venetian traveler and adventurer. He was the first person to bring spices from the East to the West. Genghis Khan (Gemini) built a great empire; he was interested in variety (Gemini). Charlemagne (Uranus) was also called ""Charles The Great,," (Venus) and "King of Franks," (Mars, the conquering planet). He was the founder (Mars, Uranus) of the first (Uranus) empire in Western Europe since the fate of Rome. Alexander The Great (Sagittarius) was King of Macedonia (Neptune, grandiose) and was often referred to as "Alexander The Great, King of Macedonia (Cancer). He was the conqueror of a vast empire. Alexandria (Neptune), Egypt is named after him.

Nero(Uranus) was known to be "crazy," (Uranus) and weird (Uranus). He was born Lucius Domitrius Ahenobarbus (Taurus), he was called Claudius Caesar (Capricorn, ambition) and was Emperor Nero (lucky Sagittarius). He murdered his mother and wife. Also he used the name Claudius Caesar Nero (Taurus, sign of art and ear for music). It's alleged that he was playing the fiddle (Taurus) while Rome burned. If you add these words, "fiddled while Rome burned, "it will add to Libra, sign of music, peace and contentment. The name Nero as a Uranus vibration, on the negative side, is erratic and unpredictable.

Ludwig II, King of Bavaria (Neptune, grandiose thoughts, love of drama, the arts, music) was known as *Mad King Ludwig* (Mars). As *The Mad King,* he vibrates to Sagittarius, the sign of opulence and spending lots of money. His palaces were extravagantly furnished and at Linderhof he had a fake (Neptune) cave built in a mass of stone and within was a small lake with a stage---very Neptunian. He had a melancholy temperament, smoked (Neptune) Opium (Neptune), was a loner (Neptune, he withdrew, daydreamed and lived in a world of fantasyland) and in love with Richard Wagner, the composer. He was gay and was killed by drowning (Neptune) because the people did not like his lavish spending of money on his three palaces. (Sagittarius, Neptune, Mars)

Hippocrates (Aries, pioneer) called *The Father of Medicine,* (Capricorn) or *Father of Medicine,* (Pisces). Ptolemy (Taurus; born Claudius Ptolemaeus, Cancer). He was a mathematician and geographer who had the earth at the center of the universe, with the Moon and planets and stars revolving around it. It was known as the *Ptolemaic System,* (Leo title). His Earth sign (Taurus) name, perhaps, influenced him toward earthly destinations. Sir Isaac Newton (Aquarius; Isaac Newton, Scorpio; Newton, Taurus) was a mathematician (Scorpio, Aquarius) and physicist (Scorpio). He devised calculous and made important discoveries (Scorpio, Aquarius) about light. His greatest work is his treatise on gravitation (Taurus, Earth), which is known as *Newton's Law of Gravitation* and *Newton's Law of Motion.*

Darwin (Uranus; born Charles Robert Darwin, Aquarius). He was a naturalist (Uranus) who revolutionized (Uranus, Aquarius) theory (Aquarius)by putting forth his theory (Aquarius) of evolution based on natural (Aquarius) selection. His conclusions conflicted (Uranus) with traditional Christian opinion on the creation of the world and caused much controversy (Uranus). It's called *Darwinism.*(Cancer)

Albert Einstein (Uranus) was known for his work in photo-electric (Uranus) effect and his special theory (Uranus) of relativity (Uranus) on electrodynamics (Uranus) of moving bodies, and equivalence of mass and mechanical energy. He was a great mathematician and physicist (Uranus). Luther Burbank (Aquarius) was known as a biologist and plant breeder and developed (Aquarius) the Burbank potato, Shasta daisy, and numerous other new (Aquarius) plant varieties.

Louis Pasteur (Aries) pioneered (Aries) in his development (Aries of the process of "pasteurization," (named after him; the word vibrates to Uranus, planet of new discoveries and processes). He also developed (Aries) vaccines for rabies and chicken cholera. Admiral Richard E. Byrd (Pisces) or Richard E. Byrd (Jupiter; born Richard Evelyn Byrd, Sagittarius) was a U.S. Aviator and polar explorer who made the first flight over the North Pole.

Madam Marie Curie (Sagittarius: born Maria Sklodowska, Neptune and, often, called Marie Curie (Virgo). She was a chemist who discovered radium, used detail and analysis (Virgo) was visionary (Neptune) and confident (Sagittarius). She was married to Pierre Curie (Scorpio), professor of physics (Scorpio). Together (Marie and Pierre Curie---Cancer names together) they investigated (Scorpio, Virgo names) and laid the foundations of nuclear physics (Scorpio, Virgo).

Charles Lindbergh (Uranus) was unpredictable (Uranus) and an individualist (Uranus). His home life was disrupted (Uranus) because of his desire to take off (Uranus) whenever the urge came. Charles Lindbergh (a Pisces name) was a world-renowned aviator (Pisces). He achieved sudden (Uranus) fame from a solo (Uranus) trans-Atlantic flight (Pisces). Dr Alexis Carrel(Aries), French surgeon and biologist, pioneered (Aries) and won a Nobel Prize for his development (Aries) of suturing blood vessels. When he used his name Alexis Carrel, he was confident (Sagittarius name). Charles Lindbergh, together with Dr. Alexis carrel, invented (Uranus, Aries) the mechanical (Aries) heart. Later Lindbergh resigned (Uranus) from the army reserve after criticism of his anti-war, (Uranus action)speeches. Later he became involved in the Space program (Uranus) and Ecology (humanitarian pursuit, Uranus).

Albert Schweitzer (Neptune; Dr. Albert Schweitzer, Gemini) wrote (Gemini) books and donated (Neptune) royalties to finance the hospital he ran in Africa. He wanted better conditions for mankind (a Neptune trait). Another person who made the world a better place to live in (Neptune action) and alleviated the suffering of mankind (Neptune) is Jane Adams (Neptune) who opened Hull House in Chicago(It was in a slum neighborhood, and was to help and educate the poor).

Dr. Linus Pauling (Venus; born Linus Carl Pauling, Cancer), a biochemist, famous for the value of using Vitamin C. He enjoys helping (a Cancer trait) the world which he has through his work on the nature of chemical bonding and for his views in a book against nuclear weapons.

Carl Gustav Jung (Uranus), often he was called, "Jung," (Venus). His system is called, *Jungian,* (Aries). He was a psychiatrist (Uranus), a pioneer (Aries) of psychoanalysis (Uranus). He worked with Freud but developed (Uranus, Aries) his own (Uranus, Aries) approach to psychoanalysis. Jung coined the term "introvert," (Aquarius word when added,; Aquarius ruled by Uranus, thus similar traits) and "extrovert, " (Jupiter word when added and also, Jupiter is the planet of being an extrovert) to define psychological types.

Mack Sennett (Aries) , who started (Aries trait) Aries-born Chaplin in the cinema and used the Aries traits in founding a company to develop stars. He was considered to be a pioneer (Aries) in his field. Charlie Chaplin(Uranus; born Charles Spencer Chaplin, Venus; Sir Charles Spencer Chaplin, Pisces) was known for his comedy, also he was an actor, producer, director and choreographer (Venus). His wild (Uranus) partying (Venus) and sexcapades (Venus on the negative side) caused a lot of scandal in Hollywood. He left the United States suddenly (Uranus) due to being a victim of the McCarthy anticommunist witch hunt. Often he was called, "Charlie,"(Neptune, acting and movies).

Cecil B. DeMille (Scorpio) in his movie *Ten Commandments*: combined sex (Scorpio with moralizing (Scorpio); he also produced sex comedies. Roberto Rosellini (Capricorn) produced films that made him famous; they were shot in natural (Capricorn) settings with minimal resources (Capricorn for economic (Capricorn) reasons. George Lucas (Scorpio), screenwriter and producer is famous for *Star Wars*,: (Scorpio title). Alfred Hitchcock (Uranus,; born Alfred Joseph Hitchcock, (Aquarius). He is known for his thriller (Uranus) movies which employed shock (Uranus tactics) and created suspense (Uranus) not only from the audience's growing awareness of the situation, but also from positive identification with a character. He portrays a world of uncertainty (Uranus) in which life can be disrupted (Uranus) at any moment (Uranus) by chance disaster (Uranus).

Bela Lugosi (Mars, violence) famous for his role *Dracula* (Uranus title) on stage and later on screen. He played a variety of sinister characters (Uranus) and fanciful monsters. Boris Karloff (Uranus; born William Henry Pratt, Jupiter. He often used Wm. Henry Pratt, (Taurus) or William Pratt (Neptune, acting, movies), and was famous for his role as *Frankenstein* (Uranus title). He starred in many horror films.

Clara Bow (Saturn) was known as *The It Girl* (Uranus, title planet of fads) in silent films. Saturn traits are serious, thus, did being called, *The It Girl*, bring out her flamboyant nature? Betty Grable (Jupiter; born Ruth Elizabeth Grable, Jupiter) was famous for her legs (part of anatomy ruled by Sagittarius, her Sun Sign and Jupiter rules Sagittarius). She loved going to the horse (Sagittarius) races and betting lots of money (Jupiter trait) at the race track.

Lana Turner (Venus; born Julia Jean Turner, Pisces). She was beautiful (Venus) and acted (Pisces) in movies. She was known as *The Sweater Girl*, (Aries title) and made sweaters popular. Veronica Lake (Scorpio; born Constance Ockleman, Cancer) was known for her one-sided hairdo with the peek-a-boo (sexy Scorpio) bang. It gave her allure (Scorpio) and made her appear mysterious (Scorpio). She left Hollywood, after starring in many successful films, and went into hiding (Scorpio). Martha Raye (Capricorn; born Margie Yvonne Reed, Pisces) was known in films as *The Mouth*. (Aries title; ironically Aries rules the face area in astrology).

Sarah Bernhardt (Pisces) was born, Henriette-Rosine-Bernard. (Neptune) and was a French tragedienne who was called *The Divine Sarah*. (Venus title) She was idolized (Neptune-Pisces) for her voice and personality.

Shelley Winters (Sagittarius; born Shirley Schrift, Neptune, movies, acting.) She is known for her candidness (Sagittarius) on talk shows and her book, *Shelly* (Neptune title) In her book, she tells about how her name was Shelly Winter but when an "s" was added to her name for her role in the movie, *A Double Life*, (Aquarius title) her film career zoomed--no wonder her name without the "s" vibrated to Aries, whereas, her Sagittarius name (with the "s") vibrates to Sagittarius, the luckiest sign in astrology; however, her weight isn't helped by this name vibration--because Sagittarius is a sign that overindulges and gains weight easily.

Cary Grant (Libra; born Archibald Leach, Pisces) was handsome (Libra) and debonaire (Libra). Once in an interview, he stated, "The secrets of good health are just to relax,"---a Libra, Pisces trait.

Glenn Close (Jupiter), the actress came to me for a reading, before she was famous. I told her that I didn't like her name because it sounded like a boys name. However I informed her that it was a lucky name for her (Jupiter is her luckiest planet according to her Astrodynes). She said she wasn't about to change it (confidence of Jupiter that she would do well with her name as is---and she has!).

John Travolta (Aries) likes excitement (Aries) and enjoys flying an airplane because it's his idea of total freedom (Aries and his Sun sign Aquarius trait). However, this is not a lucky name for him, according to his Astrodynes. It is discordant in his horoscope, thus, he has to be careful of accidents (Aries).

Robert Mitchum (Aries) is a film actor often seen in war (Aries) films and in criminal (Aries) parts. Lindsy Wagner (Scorpio) has had her share of studio battles (Scorpio)--she doesn't let people walk over her (a Scorpio trait) like some stars do. She's known to be demanding (Scorpio) on the set. She has a temper and can get infuriated (a Scorpio trait) over how the TV and movie business is run, especially with people who just want to sell tickets and get good ratings. She has said that she's a sucker for morality (a Scorpio trait) plays.

Larry Hagman (Scorpio) played the role of J.R. in *Dallas* and villainy (Scorpio) has paid off handsomely for him. He enjoys playing the role of a person who is considered a no-good s.o.b. (Scorpio trait). He went on weekly 24-hour periods of enforced silence (a typical Scorpio trait).

Pam Dawber (Saturn) admits on interviews that she's a manic-depressive (Saturn). She searches for security (Saturn) even though she's been a success. (She was in *Mork & Mindy*:--she was Mindy, on TV). When she first went to Hollywood, she had a perfection (Saturn) problem and wanted everything to be perfect in her personal and professional life. She has held on (a Saturn trait) to a cabin in upstate New York. She wished that she had lived in the early 1900's (living in the past is Saturn's influence) when people used to do handwork (Saturn--doing it the hard way) themselves. She enjoys visiting antique (Saturn) stores.

Dianne Kay (Sagittarius) who was in *Eight is Enough* on TV started early in life using the Sagittarius traits when she sold (Sagittarius occupation) honey to health food stores dressed as a bee. She was lucky with getting parts on TV from the time she first landed in Hollywood--another bit of Sagittarian luck.

John Ritter (Pisces) as an actor (Pisces), was in the TV show, *Three's Company*. (Sagittarius title, comedy). On the set they considered him to be lovable John who kept the morale high. His philosophy is Piscean in nature, "take each day as it comes." He has empathy for his brother, and others, who suffer from Cerebral Palsy; therefore he contributes his free time to support the United Cerebral Palsy group by doing a telethon for the cause--a typical Pisces action.

Eric Estrada (Libra) was the star of *CHIPS* (Neptune title) on TV. He considers himself a lucky person (Libra is the second luckiest sign in astrology). His mother had told him when he was a child that he had the "gift of luck." He is known to be considerate of others because he prefers to be treated with kindness himself--all Libra traits. He's popular and everybody likes him (typical of Libra's way of working.

Jaclyn Smith (Libra) says, "The way to my heart is flowers and poetry," which is a typical Libra remark. She was a ballet dancer (Libra) and model (Libra)...likes to decorate (Libra) and to design fashions (Libra), and wants to produce beautiful love (Libra) stories. And she is gorgeous (Libra).

Linda Evans (Mars) was a co-star in *Dynasty* on television. In *TV Guide's* June 27, 1981 issue, they said that a key part of her battle (Mars) plan is to present an almost aggressively (Mars) cheerful face to the world. But her remark at the end of the interview is typical of Mars--when asked if she'd ever again toss her career away to go off with a man--she replied, "Of course I would. If the right man came along, he'd just have to snap his fingers and I'd be gone in a minute." And she did years later but with "Yanni" and it didn't last.

The beautiful (Libra) Lynda Carter (Libra) didn't get away from the vibration she was born with because her middle name "Jean" when added to her first and last name vibrates to Venus, the Goddess of beauty. Her role of *Wonder Woman* (Sagittarius title) skyrocketed her to fame. She will always be associated with Wonder Woman; it's Sagittarius title vibrates harmoniously to her name vibration Libra. And what's more, she resembled the comic strip character!

Jane Withers (Virgo) played *Josephine, The Plumber* (Mars title) in a long-running series of commercials for a leading cleanser. It's ironic that the traits of her name vibration (Virgo) represents cleaning and the Mars title vibration represents plumbing work! William Boyd (Saturn) is famous for his role as *Hopalong Cassidy*) (Pisces) in movies. He stayed (Saturn trait) with the part for years. Janet Leigh (Aquarius; born Jeannette Helen Morrison, Neptune) always will be remembered for her part of the victim in the shower of the film *Psycho* (Aquarius: title; also her screen name vibrates to Aquarius; thus, did her name vibration attract a part in this movie?)

Lucy Lawless (Aquarius) and the TV show she stars in, *(Xena: The Warrior Princess,)*: both vibrate to Aquarius. The show skyrocketed her to fame. She has received fan letters,, according to publicity reports, from Lesbians (ruled by Aquarius, the unconventional sign). Peta Wilson (Sagittarius) stars on TV as Nikita (Taurus) in *La Femme Nikita* (Capricorn title). A serious (Capricorn) show where very few people smile. The role has been lucky (Sagittarius) for her.

James Garner (Jupiter; born James Baumgartner, Aries--same as his Sun sign) dropped the "t" in the "Gartner" part of his name and, also, dropped the first four letters of his last name "Baum" and became "Garner" for a last name. James Garner is a Jupiter name, the luckiest planet in astrology. He played the part of "Rockford" (Capricorn) on TV's *Rockford Files* (Aquarius title) for years; thus is strongly associated with this role. It was full of action (Aries) and yet he had a way of portraying some comedic (Jupiter) lines in an original (Aquarius) way.

The title of the leading character in the James Bond movies: *James Bond 007* (Pisces title) or James Bond (Taurus, sign of romance). Roger Moore (Capricorn name) played James Bond which vibrated harmoniously to his own name (Taurus-Capricorn). Sean Connery (Jupiter) had luck playing the role. Pierce Brosnan (Pisces name and Taurus Sun sign) vibrates with both James Bond and James Bond 007 (Pisces and Taurus). No wonder he yearned for the part!

Judge Judy (Aries) as she is called is outspoken (Aries). As Judge Judy Sheindlin she vibrates to Uranus which traits are abrupt, erratic, liking to shock others and is unpredictable. Sally Jessie Raphael vibrates to Gemini, the sign of talking. No wonder she's a talk-show host! Orson Welles (Aries) frightened everyone through the radio with his realistic version of *War* (Aries) *of the Worlds*. (Aquarius title, shock).

Missy Gold (Virgo) appeared on the TV show *Benson*, (Aquarius title) when she was nine years old. It was said that she has a brain that never stops going, click, click, click (a Virgo trait) and at that time she had read *Macbeth*. She was known to be able to pick up a script, read and understand it--at just nine years of age. The character she played in *Benson* was a typical Virgo role---a girl who wears plain dresses, glasses and acts somewhat like a bookworm.

What do Milton Berle, Fanny Brice, Art Carney, Dick Gregory, and Lily Tomlin have in common? They all have names that vibrate to Jupiter, the planet of comedy. Carol Burnett, George Burns, Carol Channing, Richard Pryor and Danny Kaye all have names that vibrate to Sagittarius, the sign ruling comedy.

Rodney Dangerfield (Gemini) is one comic who is witty (Gemini) and can talk (Gemini) up a storm. He's not content with just being a performer, he had a nightclub in New York City named after him. It's typical of a Gemini name vibration to be actively involved in more than one occupation. When he first started in show business as a comedian, he used the name Jack Roy (Mars). However, his success came with the Gemini name vibration--no wonder, since it rules communication and is more involved in the area he works in than a Mars vibration would be. By having the Gemini vibration, he gave additional energy to his professional talents and thus, made it easier to become identified as a comic-- this was a smart move on his part.

He was born Benjamin Kubelsky (Pisces) and took the name Jack Benny (Saturn name; was a master of timing), and a gentle observer (Saturn) of mankind's common foibles, virtuoso of the long pause (Saturn) and the lengthy stare (Saturn). He used Saturn on the negative side when he got in his low states which those close to him said, "were the lowest anybody could get in." He was an acclaimed worrier (Saturn) and was overly concerned (Saturn) about every little thing--even in a small town, at 80 years of age, he worried about the critics, the curtains, etc. His career came first. He was a perfectionist (Saturn), such a stickler for detail (Saturn), that when he did an imitation of Gracie Allen, he not only dressed up in women's clothes (Aquarius Sun sign, the unconventional))but shaved his legs, just like she did. He knew she did, so he did too. Also Saturn was used in other ways: he was a lonely man and was a loner in spite of being married. He built up a myth which is synonymous with his name vibration--he was stingy ; however, this was only a myth--he was known by those close to him as a giver (Aquarius Sun sign). This Saturn name vibration, gave additional energy to bring out the Saturn traits which helped make him famous.

Redd Foxx (Saturn; born John Sanford, (Venus was ambitious (Saturn) and worked hard (Saturn). He never gave up his goals (Saturn). His TV show *Sanford and Son* was taken from his real last name and involved a junk(Saturn) store. Flip Wilson (Aquarius) was a great comedian whose most famous role was as "Geraldine" (Neptune) in which he played (masqueraded-Neptune) as a female. Did his Aquarius (unconventional) name vibration, help make him famous with this part?

Neptune and/or Pisces rule designing, creative imagination and promoting; traits necessary to be a successful fashion designer. Some famous fashion designers who vibrate to Neptune are: Pierre Cardin, Christian Dior, Georgio Armani, Vera Wang. Those who have Pisces name vibrations are: Bill Blass, Givenchy, Yves St. Laurent and Donna Karan when she uses the initials "DKNY." She was born Donna Faske Jupiter and uses Donna Karan (Saturn, hard-working and ambitious.) It is interesting that Yves St. Laurent introduced a perfume that is popular, expensive and dramatically (Pisces) promoted (Pisces) --it's named after the drug (Pisces) "Opium."

Supermodels Cheryl Tiegs, Claudia Schiffer and Cindy Crawford vibrate to the ambitious sign of Capricorn which also gives stability and reliability. Naomi Campbell vibrates to Uranus. (Charisma, outrageous acts, unpredictable and unexpected publicity. Tyra Banks is gorgeous (Libra, sign of beauty and modeling. Ingrid Casaris vibrates to Venus (planet of beauty and modeling).

Peter Max (Gemini) keeps his hands (ruled by Gemini) busy with his artistic work. Leonardo da Vinci (Aquarius), the artist, had an unusual (Aquarius) way of writing: his handwriting runs from right to left across the page and its letters are reversed so that it can be read with the aid of a mirror. However, when he wrote directions for others, he wrote in the usual way.

Leonardo's lifelong interest in gadgets (Aquarius) and inventions (Aquarius) made him produce many: he invented a machine for grinding needles, one for making files, a rolling mill to produce sheet iron, a cloth-shearing machine, mechanical saw, water hoes, life preserver and numerous other inventions some of which were impractical. His alarm clock device was strictly of an Aquarian nature (it was before the invention of reliable timepieces with alarm attachments): it involved the slow drip of water from an upper into a lower vessel which, when full, operated a lever that jerked his feet upward. To magnify the force of lever he employed what is now known as a "mechanical relay," by which a small force is increased--and this force being doubled jerks violently upward the feet of the sleeper, who is thus wakened.

Salvador Dali (Aquarius) is known for his abstract, weird and unusual paintings--all typical of Aquarius. Andy Warhol (Neptune; born Andrew von Warhol, Taurus) is a pop artist (Neptune rules creative imaginations) who knows how to promote (Neptune) his work. James Browning Wyeth (Neptune; known as Jamie, Pisces) is another artist who has gained prominence through visualizing a creation and then executing it perfectly (a Neptune trait). The famous artist "El Greco," (Sagittarius, the Spanish words for "The Greek"). His birth name is Domenicos Theotocopoulos (Aries) and is compatible with the Sagittarian name he is known by.

Mikahil Baryshnikow (Neptune) is a world-renowned ballet (Neptune) dancer who took a cut in salary by joining a ballet company that would allow him to be more creative (Neptune). Alexander Godunov (Uranus) is the Russian ballet dancer who defected (Uranus) to the U.S.A. He danced with Martine Van Hamel (Uranus). She is known for her unconventional (Uranus) postures, angles and phasing--they are her trademark. Because she changed teachers so frequently, she developed a very personal (Uranus) style.

Margot Fonteyn (Pisces, sign of the feet; born Margaret Hookham, Taurus, an aesthetically artistic sign who perseveres) became Dame Margot Fonteyn (Mars; physical energy). As a ballerina (Taurus, ruled by Venus, dance planet) the beauty (Taurus) of her line, her musicality (Mars), and her dramatic (Pisces) interpretation of roles made her famous.

George Balanchine (dancer, choreographer), Isadora Duncan (dancer). Rudolf Nureyev (ballet dancer), and Ruth St. Denis (popularized modern dance in America). Their names vibrate to Venus, the planet which represent the dance, aesthetic and artistic expression. Note: Isadora Duncan (Venus) was the forerunner of modern dance (Venus). She was killed when her long scarf (Venus) caught the wheel of her car and strangled her). Martha Graham (Aquarius) was a leading figure in Modern (Aquarius) dance, which employs natural (Aquarius) movement and often enacts psychological (Aquarius) situations rather than the story-telling found in more conventional dancing.

Ray Bolger (Gemini) was known for his agility (Gemini) and ability to sing (Gemini) while dancing. Another performer who could sing and dance simultaneously was Cubby Checker (Mars, physical energy planet: born Ernest Evans, Capricorn). Rock and Roll (Mars title, planet of rhythm). The dance he made famous was *The Twist,* (Taurus title; Taurus ruled by Venus, planet of dance). Gypsy Rose Lee (Uranus) was original (Uranus) in the way she sang and danced while doing the strip tease (Uranus, controversial dance form). She defied convention (Uranus trait) and went to the top. Her life was portrayed on stage and in the cinema in the play/movie *Gypsy,* (Sagittarius title).

John Philip Sousa (Gemini) was a composer and band master. He wrote (Gemini) about 100 marches and several operettas and designed the Sousaphone (a form of tuba which coils around the player's body, the bell projecting over the shoulder). It is easier to carry (something a Gemini name vibration would think of -- hands, arms, and shoulders ruled by Gemini) when marching than the normal tuba.

Benny Goodman (Scorpio; born Benjamin David Goodman, Capricorn) was a famous jazz musician and band leader. He played the clarinet and was famous as *King of Swing,* (Taurus, title, artistic.) He could concentrate (Scorpio); thoroughly when he performed live, and practiced. Dick Clark (Uranus) has a cottage with a series of office rooms furnished in electi-eccentric (Uranus) and advanced (Uranus) whimsy. With his American Bandstand he introduced (Uranus) rock and roll years ago and made it popular.

Ruth Brown (Neptune;) was born Ruth Westin,(Libra). Neptune is her best planet, according to her Astrodynes. When she sings, she dramatizes (Neptune) her emotions (Neptune) and puts body and soul into a song. As an actress (Neptune) she excels. She is artistic (Venus) in private creative endeavors (hobbies). Ruth is known as : *Miss Rhythm,* (Sagittarius title, which rules the house of work in her horoscope). Billy Holiday (Scorpio; born Eleanor Holiday, Aquarius). As *Lady Day,* she vibrates to Venus and always wore a flower (Venus) in her hair while performing . Scorpio is a sign that can easily become addicted; she was a heroin addict.

Carol Channing (Sagittarius) is well known for her stage portrayal of "Dolly," (Aquarius) in the Broadway production of *Hello Dolly* (Capricorn title). She has an enchanting smile (Sagittarius). Al Jolson (Libra; born Asa Yoelson, Aquarius) was a famous singer who was the star of the first talkie (Sagittarius) movie, *The Jazz Singer,* (Scorpio). His artistic (Libra) talent brought success.

Hildegrade (Aquarius was an American who took a trip to France and returned to the U.S.A. as a French chanteuse, with her new (Aquarius) French name and repertoire. She dared to please herself (Aquarius) and be different (Aquarius) by changing her personality into a foreigner (Aquarius) that, as a result, brought her overnight (Aquarius) success. Dusty Springfield (Mars;) was born Mary Isabel Catherine O'Brien, (Pisces). She was a singing sensation in the 1960's---a pop (Mars) legend. Her trademark was a Beehive (Jupiter word; Jupiter also represents something big-i.e. her beehive hairdo) hairdo.

Cliff Richard (Jupiter) is a British pop star, who is quite religious (Jupiter). He tours at least once a year with a gospel band, has cut three devotional records (royalties go to Christian charities, a Jupiter trait to donate money to a Church) and appeared in two films for Billy Graham's Worldwide Pictures. Meat Loaf (Saturn) a top rock star who was rejected (Saturn's influence) in the early years of his career (it took eight years for him to make it--eight is a Capricorn number (Capricorn's ruled by Saturn). He was staunch and immovable (Saturn traits). Bruce Springsteen (Mars, aggressive, enterprising) is known as *The Boss*, (Neptune) he's active (Mars) and has a fighting spirit (Mars).

Robert Merrill (Saturn), the opera star, has had to rehearse (Saturn) long hours (Saturn), discipline (Saturn) himself rigidly (Saturn), make personal sacrifices (Saturn) and stick to his goal (Saturn)to reach the top (Saturn). Maria Callas (Scorpio), the Opera Singer who had a stormy (Scorpio) love affair with Ari Onassis was known to be temperamental (Scorpio), bitchy (Scorpio), sexy (Scorpio) and possessive (Scorpio).

These illustrious songwriters all have Aquarian name vibrations: Irving Berlin, Cole Porter, Stephen Collins and Andrew Lloyd Webber. They all used originality (Aquarius). Andrew Lloyd Webber for years has been a successful composer of musical shows. He used his Aries Sun sign pioneering traits with his Aquarian name sign to independently do something different. He had the courage (Aries) to march to the beat of a different drummer (Aquarius). *Cats*, (Libra title), *Starlight Express*, (Sagittarius title) and *Jesus Christ Superstar* (Sagittarius title) were unique (Aquarius) offbeat (Aquarius) and unusual (Aquarius). Isn't it ironic that *Jesus Christ Superstar* has the sign of religion---Sagittarius--as the name title it vibrates to ? Princess Di's favorite musical was *Phantom of the Opera* which vibrates to a Cancer name and her Sun sign was Cancer.

Bob Beattie (Saturn) was an Olympic ski coach who turned into a broadcaster. As a ski coach, he disciplined (Saturn) one of his top athletes by making him somersault the length of a football field. Bruce Jenner (Scorpio) is a Gold Medal Olympic winner. He's competitive (Scorpio) and enjoys racing cars. It takes a tremendous amount of guts, timing and right judgment--all Scorpio traits to be successful.

Cathy Rigby Aries) competed (Aries) in gymnastics and was a champion. "Flo-Jo," (Capricorn, ambition; was born Florence Delorez Griffith, Pisces. Her married name was Florence Griffith Joyner, Aquarius). She was a field and track star that broke (Aquarius) all records. She was known for her skin-tight running suits, flowing hair, glittering nails and stunning (Aquarius) speed. Tara Lipinski (Taurus) and Oksana Baiul (Taurus) both have won the Gold Medal in the Olympics for Figure Skating. Taurus gives the ability to persist until one is perfect. Peggy Fleming vibrates to Scorpio, another determined sign. Kristi Yamaguchi vibrates to the competitive sign of Aries. The tennis champion Pete Sampras has a name that vibrates to Sagittarius, sign of sports.

Billie Jean King (Neptune) has promoted (Neptune) herself and tennis on a grand scale (Neptune); she also spoke up for better conditions (Neptune) for women in tennis. Hulk Hogan (Mars) has been an all-time favorite and famous wrestler. He's muscular (Mars), energetic (Mars), gutsy (Mars) and competitive (Mars). He has performed in many action (Mars) films. Don King (Aquarius) known as a "fight promoter," (title vibrates to Pisces, sign of promoting) is recognizable by his "hair,"---it is like a "Lion's Mane," (His Sun sign is Leo, sign of the Lion).and stands high and gets center stage (Leo); this feature makes him appear different (Aquarius) and stand out in a crowd. (Leo)

Mike Tyson (Jupiter, luck and wealth planet;) was born Mike G. Tyson (Capricorn, ambition). He has always been confident (Jupiter) and his "I don't care" attitude (Jupiter on the negative side) has jeopardized his career due to many various legal (Jupiter) difficulties. No one will forget how he took a bite out of Evander Holyfield's (Taurus, sign ruling the ear) ear. The words, "Bite out of his ear," add up to Uranus, the planet that rules sudden and unrespected shocks! Evel Knievel (Uranus) was an original (Uranus) daredevil who did things his way (Uranus). He kept reaching out for more amazing (Uranus) stunts that were death-defying. His bones have been broken (Uranus) many times from his motorcycle (Uranus) stunts. The martial arts world champion is called Don "The Dragon" Wilson (Taurus; Don Wilson, Jupiter; The Dragon, Aquarius same as his Sun sign. He has Taurus charm, Jupiter good fortune and performs his own martial arts stunts using originality (Aquarius).

Lillian Carter (Venus), socialized (Venus) and represented her son (ex-President Jimmy Carter) at important national and international functions. She was known to be charming, sweet and kind (all Venus traits). Martha Mitchelle, like Betty Ford (both Uranus names), is outspoken, and controversial (Uranus). Paul Revere (Mars) was a patriot (Mars) and silversmith (Mars). He took part in the Boston Tea Party and is remembered for his ride (Mars) to warn the people that "The British are coming," (entire sentence of words in quotes add to the sign Cancer, patriot sign of the zodiac).

George Washington (Pisces Name and Sun Sign) was idealistic (Pisces) and had grandiose (Neptune) ideas and wanted better conditions for mankind (Neptune). His famous saying, "I never told a lie," is interesting. When a person lies it is because either Pisces or Neptune is afflicted in their horoscope. Benjamin Franklin (Saturn) was known for his common-sense (Saturn) philosophy, proposed plan (Saturn) of union for the colonies and as a diplomat (Saturn) and a scientist (Saturn). His works were written in plain (Saturn) style and exemplify 18th-century faith in reason (Saturn), humanity and deism (Saturn).

James Monroe (Capricorn) was known for his diplomatic (Capricorn) missions to France, Spain and England. There were many compromises (Capricorn) in his policies (Capricorn) when he served as President of the U.S.A." The historical (Capricorn, Saturn) *Monroe Doctrine* (Saturn title) was named after him. Hiram Ulysses Grant (Uranus) defied convention (Uranus trait) when he changed his name to Ulysses Simpson Grant (Mars). He was a military commander (Mars) and became President, at which time he signed important documents as

Ulysses S. Grant (Saturn, planet of stability, planning, negotiating, strategy and ambition.

Theodore Roosevelt (Cancer) was known to champion the rights of the "little man" (Cancer). His foreign policy exemplified his principle, "Speak softly and carry a big stick." Harry Truman (Pisces) believed (Pisces) in cat-naps (Pisces) to recharge energy. Benito Mussolini (Pisces) known as *Il Duce*, (Pisces) was a dictator who could promote (Pisces) and believe (Pisces) in his promises (Pisces). Ronald Reagan (Libra) was charming (Libra), courteous (Libra) and a gentleman (Libra), especially toward his wife. Earl Warren(Jupiter) was Chief Justice (Jupiter) of the United States Supreme Court (Jupiter).

Hedda Hopper (Venus) was known for her hats (Venus) and socializing (Venus). She spent her evenings at parties (Venus) gathering information (gossip). Miss Hopper established friendships (Venus) as a necessary part of her career. Earl Wilson (Aquarius) wrote about celebrities and in a book created controversy (Aquarius) over Frank Sinatra. Ann Landers (Sagittarius) has been a successful syndicated columnist for a long time. She is outspoken (Sagittarius) and a giver of advice that hits home (Sagittarius). Her encouragement and honesty (Sagittarius) has helped millions. Gertrude Stein (Aries) , author, is one of America's most influential expatriates (Aries) and linguistic experimentalists (Aries).

Emile Zola (Aquarius; born Emile Edouard Charles Antoine Zola, (Mars) was a genius (Aquarius) and controversial (Aquarius) novelist who had a typical negative side of Aquarius life: he had a wife, mistress, two illegitimate children, and played a prominent part in the Dreyful Affairs by writing the famous open (Aquarius) letter, *J'accus* (1898) condemning the government (Aquarius) institutions of France from conniving at injustices. As a result, he was forced to flee (Aquarius). He was an ardent social reformer (Aquarius) and leader of the naturalist (Aquarius) movement (Aquarius). His many powerful scenes, in his writing of sex and violence (Sun sigh Aries) shocked (Aquarius) contemporaries. *Nana* (Libra, sign of love, romance) was one of his most famous novels.

Earnest Hemingway (Aries) had been under fire (Aries) in three wars (Aries), fished (Aries) for marlin in the Caribbean, hunted(Aries) big game in Africa, followed the bulls (Aries sport) in Spain, be brought a new (Aries) style of writing to American literature. He shot (Aries) birds at his ranch in Idaho, swam (sports, Aries) played the races (Aries). He did just about everything. And yet he was known, by those who were really close to him, to be a shy man. However, his Aries name vibration helped offset his shyness a little. Hemingway began his career as an ambulance driver (Aries) in world War 1 (Aries) and he was severely wounded (Aries). His fictional world is typically a cruel (Aries), violent (Aries) and disordered one. His favorite theme was the struggle (Aries)of man mutilated (Aries) by environment. He wrote about bullfighters, soldiers and game-hunters, all of which are ruled by Aries. His reckless desire to live life to the fullest affected his health: however, he took his own life in the end.

Hans Christian Andersen (Aquarius) is famous for his fairy tales. He was extremely original (Aquarius) and had a great understanding of human nature (an Aquarian trait). Taylor Caldwell (Aquarius;) was born Erskine Preston Caldwell, (Pisces) and is famous for his book *Tobacco Road* (Libra title, lucky sign). His graphic novels about poverty and degeneration established him as a controversial (Aquarius) author.

Louisa May Alcott (Pisces) was a novelist famous for *Little Women*, (Neptune title which rules Pisces--- both represent creative imagination and drama). Zane Grey (Neptune) wrote Westerns and most of his works became movies (Neptune). Harold Robbins (Neptune), his books about love, ambition and power became blockbuster films (Neptune). Sir Arthur Conan Doyle (Libra) creator of *Sherlock Holmes*, (Pisces title) was very involved in spiritual realms. Dr. Deepak Chopra (Neptune) author of spiritual (Neptune) healing books that deal with transcendal meditation (Neptune) and positive thinking.

Karl Marx (Pisces), journalist and philosopher, who adapted a theory of social change, and believed (Pisces) violent revolutions theory of social change, and believed (Pisces) violent revolutions were necessary to create a classless society. His books greatly influenced socialism and communism. It's interesting that *Marxism* (Neptune title) and *Marxism* (Pisces title; Pisces ruled by Neptune, thus similar traits) represents an ideal world (Neptune) according to Karl Marx's views.

Kit Williams (Neptune) wrote a puzzling (Neptune) children's book that holds the key to underground treasure (Neptune). By the light of the full Moon, somewhere in Britain, he buried a terra-cotta casket containing an 18-karat gold pendant which he had made in the shape of a hare. Adorned with mother -of pearl, rubies, and other precious stones, the bejeweled hare will be worth $25,000 to the person who finds it. The one essential tool is a copy of his book, *Masquerade* (Neptune) which gives clues, riddles and anagrams that will lead their decipher to the hare. He says his thinking is closer to that of a child so if you find the key to his mind, you may find the hare (all of the preceding are Neptune actions and traits).

Kit is an artist (Neptune) and when he wrote this book during the winter, he wrapped himself in a cocoon-like polyethylene tent (Neptune). An opera is being planned around this book, he's sold 16 color paintings that illustrate the book so it's being well promoted (Neptune). With his fertile imagination (Neptune), kit wants his ashes (upon his death) made into a glaze and applied to a beer mug (Neptune). He has tattoos (Neptune) on his body; a dragon's head on his left arm, a skull and crossbones on his right and a snake's tail on his right calf.

Jules Verne (Jupiter), author and founder of modern science-fiction, he foresaw submarines and space travel years before they were thought about. He's famous for his book-turned-movie, *Around The World in 80 Days*, (Aries title) The title of this book is harmonious with his Jupiter name vibration. The author of *The*

Exorcist, (Capricorn title), William Peter Blattey (Scorpio; often called Bill Blatty, Venus) wrote about an exorcist which is a Scorpio action. Blatty admits that he is compulsive (Scorpio) and will write until he's tired (Scorpio trait). Mystery (Scorpio) tales are big among his writings.

Judith Krantz (Scorpio) had a huge success with her book *Scruples*, (Jupiter, title good fortune). It was her first novel and was turned into a TV movie. She has a great power of concentration (Scorpio) and the subject matter is thoroughly researched (Scorpio) by her.

Alex Haley (Saturn) was able to persevere (Saturn) for years in spite of what must have been obstacles and hardships (Saturn) to research and write *Roots*, (Sagittarius title, lucky sign). He sacrificed (Saturn) a large part of his personal life to accomplish this tremendous task (Saturn). Ironically, she was able to stick with a schedule due to the Saturn name; Saturn rules Capricorn which was his Sun sign, thus similar traits of ambition and not giving up until he accomplished his goal.

Mary Higgins Clark (Saturn) has written many best-selling books. She has great perseverance (Saturn) and can stick with the writing until it is completed (Saturn trait). Judith Viorst (Capricorn) has written many books which have sold more than a million copies. It's interesting that her book, *Love & Guilt & the Meaning of Life*, has the word "Guilt " in it and that she writes about that subject-- guilt is ruled by Capricorn. She also wrote, "Sometimes I hate my husband, " although that could be a Capricorn statement (on the negative side), it wasn't really meant. She's organized (Capricorn), and leads a productive life with little time to waste (typical of Capricorn's influence). Both her prose and poetry seem increasingly concerned (Capricorn) about growing old (Capricorn). Earlier in her career her writings were rejected (Capricorn) and there was a time when she was incapable of sending anything out until her husband said it was ready (again Capricorn's influence).

A poet, playwright and dramatist are all ruled by Neptune and Pisces. Among the famous ones are Paddy Chayefsky (Neptune), Alfred de Musset (Pisces; born Louis Charles Musset, Aquarius) and Sir Noel Coward (Pisces; Noel Coward, Venus, artistic sign) who began his career as an actor (Pisces) and is also famous as a composer and entertainer. All of these authors used their dramatic talent and creative imagination (Neptune, Pisces) in their works.

There were two novelists and dramatists by the same name (father and son): Alexander Dumas (Jupiter). One was called "Dumas Pere," (Neptune)which means father; he's famous for *The Three Musketeers*, (Neptune title) and *The Count of Monte Cristo*, (Mars title, The other one is called "Dumas fils," (Venus) which means son; he's famous for his play *La Dame aux Camelias*, (Venus title) which is the same story used in Verdi's (Pisces) opera *La Traviata*,(Aquarius title). .

The dramatist and writer, George Bernard Shaw (Capricorn) was a heavy research (Capricorn), as well as a serious (Capricorn) and historical (Capricorn) writer. Carl Sandburg (Neptune) was a novelist, poet (Neptune) and biographer.

Sir Walter Scott (Neptune) was a novelist, poet (Neptune) and famous for his romantic (Neptune) ballads.

Alfred Lord Tennyson (Neptune) was a revered (Neptune) and famous poet (Neptune). His birth name, Alfred, 1st Baron. Tennyson vibrated to Aries. Ogden Nash (Pisces) was a humorist who was best known for his single-thought short poems (Pisces) and observations which contains terseness and wit.

Omarr Khayyam (Sagittarius) was famous for his nearly 500 stanzas of verse (four lines to each stanza) with his poem the *Rubaiyat*, (Aquarius) which was original and unique (Aquarius traits). Also he was a mathematician. His astronomical (Aquarius) observations were instrumental in the reform of the Islamic Calender.

Henry David Thoreau (Aries) was a poet and essayist (Aries) who wrote short literary compositions expressing his personal (Aries) views. He made excursions (Aries) and practiced his doctrines of self-sufficiency (Aries). He believed in living simply, without ties (Aries). He spent a night in jail for refusing to pay his taxes because he opposed the Mexican War--all typical Aries traits.

Ralph Waldo Emerson (Pisces) poet (Pisces) and essayist disliked being called Ralph (a Jupiter vibration by itself), instead he wanted to be called Waldo (A Pisces name by itself). He was known to be a daydreamer (Pisces). From his 18th birthday, for about a dozen years, he was frustrated, and had false beginnings (Pisces) and confusion (Pisces). He dreamed (Pisces) of all the travels he never had a chance to take. He loved to walk and would lose his own sense of personality (Pisces) and become one (Pisces) with nature. Often he'd look into himself and report his own perceptions, reveal as far as he could the possibilities that lay in the soul of man (Pisces trait). He lectured about the soul being divine (Pisces thinking) and that divinity flowed more in some people than it did in others. He believed that the individual can only find redemption in his own soul (Pisces belief). Principles of Transcendentalism (Pisces) were set forth in his writings. The writing *Nature*, by him, was an early manifesto of transcendalist (Pisces) belief (Pisces) in the mystical (Pisces) unity of nature.

The name *Casanova*, (Capricorn) is synonymous with romance. It is interesting that if you split the word Casanova into Spanish you have "casa" "nova" which means "house" "love", house of love or love house. There are several spellings for his birth name due to transliteration: Giovanni Jacopo de Seingalt, Capricorn; Giovanni Giacomo Chevalier de Seingalt, Neptune; Giovanni Casanova (Uranus). He was an Italian amorous-adventurer-philanderer and legendary lover. He was known for his many sexual conquests. His Uranus name vibration was the way he signed his name, thus, he thought of himself in this light. It was the Uranus negative traits that would attract the wild life, and love-them-and leave-them attitude he had towards women. The Capricorn name vibration, which is as the world thinks of him, would give him the traits of a man who was insecure and feared impotency; thus, he compensated for this by making women fall in love with him. Whenever anyone thinks of another person as a Casanova the same thoughts are sent in that person's direction. And modern day psychologists say that a man who behaves like a Casanova does lack confidence in himself and compensates by playing the field. Casanova was expelled (Uranus) from a seminary for immoral (Neptune and/or Uranus expressed on the negative side) conduct. He lived in many cities and worked as a violinist (Capricorn ambition, seriousness and ability to practice perseveringly), spy (Neptune), writer, (Uranus) librarian (Capricorn).

Julio Iglesias (Neptune) sings romantic (Neptune) songs. He boasted that he has bedded thousands of women. Is this a Neptune exaggeration? Errol Flynn (Jupiter) expressed these Jupiter traits on the negative side: He played pranks on others, didn't care what others thought of him, engaged in indoor sports (Sagittarius), especially overindulging in sex to the point of exhibitionism and drank enormous amounts of alcohol. He took drugs, was in court (ruled by Jupiter) often for paternity suits and rape accusations. He got off each time--was that the luck of his Jupiter name vibration? He had a abundance (Jupiter) of love affairs, the women he chased, usually gave in to his advances, thus, the saying *In Like Flynn*, is derived from his luck (Jupiter) with seducing women. He abused Jupiter's beneficence once too often--and died at an early age from so much self-abuse.

Numerous tabloid reports have said that Michael Douglas(Scorpio) is oversexed (Scorpio) and going for treatment for sex addiction (Scorpio). Havelock Ellis (Scorpio; born Henry Havelock Ellis, Gemini, sign of writing). This psychologist wrote a monumental book published in seven volumes, *Studies in the Psychology of Sex*, (Scorpio title). This power of concentration (Scorpio trait) on one subject was thoroughly researched (Scorpio trait)

Dr. Alfred Kinsey (Uranus; born Alfred Charles Kinsey, Gemini, writing), did research (Uranus) which revealed (Uranus) startling (Uranus) sex information (Gemini); it was published in *The Kinsey Report*, (Aquarius title; Aquarius ruled by Uranus, thus similar traits).

Dr. Sigmund Freud (Pisces; Sigmund Freud, Venus) psychiatrist. The word *Freudian*, (Taurus, love sign) pertains to some of Freud's theories. He was known for his work with love relationships (Venus); and his description of the unconscious mind and psychoanalysis was used by the surrealists and action painters (Venus). His work is said to have had a major influence on art (Venus).

The infamous Marquise de Sade (Scorpio) was born Comte Donatien Alphonse Francoise de Sade (Moon). Often he was called Donatien Alphonse negative side) Francois (Pisces). He was a novelist who was known for the licentiousness of his life and writing. His novels contained sexual excesses (Scorpio) and cruelty (Scorpio on the negative side) portrayed in his works. He had a peculiar philosophy which elevated evil (Scorpio) into a Universal principle. His obsession with the corrupt (Pisces on the negative side) and cruel (Scorpio on the negative side) was dramatized (Pisces) by him. He was imprisoned for prohibited sexual (Scorpio practices. In prison he wrote several pornographic (Scorpio) fantasies (Pisces) whose preoccupation (Scorpio with sexual violence (Scorpio on negative side) led to the term, *Sadism*.

Heidi Fleiss (Venus, love socializing) is known as *The Hollywood Madam*, (Neptune title; Neptune involves prostitution). Xaviera Hollander (a Venus name), author of *The Happy Hooker* and other books, had been a prostitute and took the easy way out with making money (Venus expressed on the negative side).

Linda Lovelace (Uranus) made porno movies which are controversial (Uranus) and shocking (Uranus). Hugh Hefner (Pisces) has success with the dreams (Pisces) and imaginative (Pisces) yearnings (Pisces) of the average male, when he promoted (Pisces) a fantasy (Pisces) world with his *Playboy* magazine, nightclub and hotel empire. Rudolph Valentino (Aries) was known for his sex appeal (Aries) and as a Latin-lover (Aries). Ironically, his real name Rodolpho d' Antonguolla, vibrated to Venus the planet of love.

Is it simply coincidence that Elizabeth Taylor portrayed the role of Cleopatra on the screen? Both names vibrate to Venus, the planet of beauty and love. No wonder her love affair with Burton during the shooting of *Antony and Cleopatra* got such publicity! This same vibration just enhanced everything that Venus signifies. Ironically her 6th husband, Senator John Warner, has a Venus name vibration also!

Susan Anton (Scorpio) has sex appeal (Scorpio) that is evident to anyone who has ever watched her sing a song--there's that look in her eyes that gives away the Scorpio influence. Sophie Tucker (Aquarius) shocked (Aquarius) people with her risque songs. Mae West (Uranus) was notorious for her vulgar, but very amusing sexy innuendos. Her wisecracks startled (Uranus) sections of the public. She used astrology (Uranus) before making important engagements.

Alan Bates (Mars), the actor, made a typical Mars statement in an interview in *Photoplay* magazine. They asked him why he appeared completely nude on the big screen in the movie, *Women In Love*, which shocked the 60's audiences. He said, "I like being appreciated for my looks and my body. I'm as vain as the next man."---typical of Mars outspokenness and interest in the physical anatomy.

Christine Jorgensen (Neptune) became a real woman after her sex change, which satisfied her dreams (Neptune). As a young boy, he used the name George Jorgensen, Jr. (Uranus). He was unconventional (Uranus) in his views, desirous of changing his identity (Uranus) and being his real self (Uranus); thus he dared to do the new (Uranus) and different (Uranus) and made the sex switch (Uranus). Thus , overnight (Uranus) fame was attracted and a new trend (Uranus) was begun for everyone who wanted to change their sex.

Years ago, the singer, Anita Bryant (Aquarius) publicly spoke against homosexuals (Aquarius; the word "gay" adds to Taurus, love). She lost commercial endorsements as a result of her revolt (Aquarius) against the gay community. It is interesting that her name vibration is Aquarius, the sign that rules homosexuality. There are numerous celebrities that have come out of the closet: The following Lesbians have Aquarian name vibrations: Sandra Bernhard, K.D. Lang, Madonna (she's supposedly, bi-sexual). Martina Navratilova (Uranus, ruler of Aquarius, thus, same traits.)

Melissa Ethridge (Aries, sexy sign); her Sun sign Gemini has a dual nature. Ellen De Generes (Scorpio, sex sign; Aquarian Sun sign) and lives with Anne Heche (Venus, love ; Gemini Sun sign). Their Sun signs are compatible. Isn't it ironic that their name as a couple: "Anne Heche and Ellen De Generes" vibrates to Scorpio. They can't seem to keep their hands off of each other (Scorpio) and flaunted their relationship publicly.

Richard Pryor (Neptune) set his house on fire when he was spaced out (Neptune) from hard-drugs (Neptune). Timothy Leary (Neptune) has been a proponent of drugs (Neptune) for self-realization (Neptune) and spiritual (Neptune) development. He is interested in space (Neptune) migration. His dream (Neptune) is to get away from earth and live in a space station between the Earth and the Moon.

Freddie Prinze (Pisces) was on drugs (Pisces), alcohol (Pisces) and shot himself; he was depressed over his wife whom he needed (Sun sign Cancer)--they were separated.

Charles Manson(Neptune) was behind the murder of numerous victims in a one-night rampage. A famous victim , Sharon Tate (Neptune), the actress (Neptune) was pregnant when she was murdered. Charles Manson used the Neptune traits on the negative side: drugs, escapism, conning others to do his bidding and keeping them in bondage, bizarre sex practices and letting his slaves do the dirty work. He had grandiose illusions (Neptune) and lived in his own mind-created (Neptune) world.

Richard Speck (Neptune) had grandiose dreams (Neptune) of fame, they came true when he shot and killed the nurses in a dormitory. At the time he was under the influence of drugs (Neptune). One of his mental problems was paranoia (Neptune); he lived in a foggy (Neptune) world. Perhaps, if he had a name that vibrated to another planet, he would have come out of his fog and seen reality! He used Neptune energy on the negative side.

During World War 11, Tokyo Rose (Neptune; born Iva Toguir, Aries; Iva D'Aquino, Saturn married name; Iva Toguir D'Aquino (Pisces). She was known to the G.I.'s in the South Pacific for her broadcasts of lies, intrigue, propaganda, distortions, dramatizing of the emotions, illusions and vaguely concealing the facts (Neptune traits on the negative side). She was apprehended and convicted of treason (Neptune).

Mata Hari (Aries stage name; born Margaretha Geertruida Zelle, Libra) was a Dutch spy (Aries, love of adventure), married to a Dutch army officer and became a professional dancer in Paris (that's when she adopted her stage name).

During World War I (Aries) she worked for both the French and Germans. She was shot (Aries) by the French for espionage.

The Rat Pack, (Mars were known to be mischievous (Mars on the negative side), hard-drinking (Mars), fast-living (Mars) and had untiring energy (Mars) to stay up all night playing pranks. If they cut off (Mars) a person's necktie, the next day that individual received ten neckties as a replacement. Property that was damaged (Mars) was paid for the moment they left the restaurant they had turned upside down. Frank Sinatra (Capricorn name, Sagittarius Sun sign) was the leader of the group which consisted of Dean Martin (Jupiter name and Gemini Sun sign), Joey Bishop (Jupiter name and Aquarius Sun sign), Sammy Davis, Jr. (Scorpio name, Sagittarius Sun sign) and Peter Lawford (Uranus name). With their combined Jupiter, Sagittarius and Uranus name signs; anything could occur. They were compatible.

The Rat Pack, were frequently seen with the mob. Sam Giancana (Aquarius) and Carlo Gambino (Neptune) were pals with them. Isn't it odd that the word "Mafia", when added is a Venus vibration? Venus represents the social scene, partying, wining and dining; a pleasure the Mafia members enjoy indulging (Venus) in--it's the planet of "ready cash" and love of ease. "Mafioso" when added vibrates to Aries. Aries (on the negative side) represents fighting, anger, violence, murder, guns and taking thrilling risks. John Gotti vibrates to Scorpio; Scorpio on the negative side represents murder, violet crimes, illegal activities. Carlo Gambino vibrates to Neptune; Neptune on the negative side represents drugs, prostitution, cons, deception, wheeling and dealing. Sam Giancana vibrates to Aquarius; Aquarius on the negative side represents anything goes; however he was interested in legal business deals--a new order to crime).

In conclusion, in this chapter you have learned how famous, and infamous, people are identified (associated with) by a sign or planet which their name vibrates to. Also, you can see whether they were fortunate, or unfortunate, with their name vibration. Therefore, the name you choose is extremely important, and how you utilize that name vibration (for good or evil) is equally vital. Your Astrodynes will be the best aid you can have when you select a name that is lucky for you.

CHAPTER THIRTEEN

WOULD THEY HAVE BEEN FAMOUS,
IF THEY HAD USED THEIR REAL NAMES?

The importance of changing your name is evident when you see the names these celebrities had when they were born. How many stars would have gone as far as they had, if they had not changed their real names?

Alan Alda (Uranus; born Alphonso D'Abruzzo, Sagittarius).

Jason Alexander (Aries; born Jay Scott Greenspan, Venus).

June Allyson (Scorpio; born Ella Geisman, Sagittarius).

Eve Arden (Venus; born Eunice Quedens, Sagittarius).

Bea Arthur (Uranus; Beatric Arthur, Venus; born Bernice Frankel, Pisces)

Jean Arthur (Taurus; born Gladys Georgianna Greene, Uranus).

Mary Astor (Sagittarius; born Lucille Vasconcells Langhanke, Saturn).

Lauren Bacall (Mars; born Betty Jane Perske, Capricorn).

Alec Baldwin (Saturn; born Alexander Rae Baldwin III, Capricorn).

Anne Bancroft (Neptune; born Anna Maria Luise, Uranus).

Brigitte Bardot (Aries; born Camille Javal, Aries)

Janet Blair (Mars; born Martha Jane Lafferly, Saturn).

Amanda Blake (Neptune; born Beverly Louise Neill, Pisces)

Robert Blake (Capricorn; born Michael Gubitosi, Aries)

Morgan Brittany (Saturn; born Suzanne Cupito, Venus).

George Burns (Sagittarius; born Nathan Burnbaum, Scorpio).

Yul Brynner (Jupiter; born Tadji Khan, Aquarius).

Rory Calhoun (Capricorn; Note: 2 sources born (1) Francis Timothy Durgin, Venus) OR born (2) Francis Timothy McCown, Neptune)

Vicki Carr (Cancer; Note: 2 sources born (1) Florence Bisentade Casillas, Cancer OR born (2) Florence Cardona, Taurus)

Tia Carrere (Sagittarius; born Althea Janairo, Mercury)

Jackie Chan (Capricorn; born Chan Kwong-Sang, Scorpio)

Cyd Charisse (Aries; born Tula Elice Finklea, Uranus)

Mae Clarke (Mars; born Mary Klotz, Taurus)

Mike Connors (Scorpio; born Krekor Ohanian, Pisces)

Buster Crabbe (Aquarius; born Clarence Linden, Pisces)

Joan Crawford (Uranus; born Lucille Le Sueur, Capricorn)

Tony Curtis (Capricorn; born Bernard Schwartz, Jupiter)

Rodney Dangerfield (Neptune; born Jacob Cohen, Aries)

Bobby Darin (Aquarius; born Walden Waldo Cassotto, Scorpio)

Linda Darnell (Uranus; born Monetta Eloyse Dannell, Capricorn)

Sandra Dee (Pisces; born Alexandra Zack, Aries)

Marlene Dietrich (Taurus; born Maria Magdalena Dietrich, Mars)

Troy Donahue (Jupiter; born Merle Johnson, Uranus)

Fifi D'Orsay (Aquarius; born Yvonne Lussier, Sagittarius)

Kirk Douglas (Sagittarius; born Issur Danielovitch Demsky, Sagittarius)

Marie Dressler (Aries; born Lelia von Koerber, Neptune)

Barbara Eden (Pisces; born Barbara Hoffman, Sagittarius)

Chad Everett (Gemini; born Raymond Crampton, Uranus)

Alice Faye (Aquarius; born Ann Leppert, Uranus)

Peter Finch (Pisces; born William Mitchell, Neptune)

Barry Fitzgerald (Capricorn; born William Shields, Capricorn)

Rhonda Fleming (Neptune; born Marilyn Louis, Uranus)

John Garfield (Libra; born Julius Garankle, Venus)

Boy George (Capricorn; born George Alan O'Dowd, Sagittarius)

Paulette Goddard (Sagittarius; born Marion Pauline Levy, Uranus)

Whoopi Goldberg (Pisces; born Caryn Johnson, Neptune)

Colleen Grey (Uranus; born Doris Jensen (Jupiter)

Ann Harding (Gemini; born Dorothy Walton Galley, Cancer)

Rex Harrison (Venus; born Reginald Carey, Capricorn)

Laurence Harvey (Sagittarius; born Laruska Mischa Skikne, Gemini)

Sterling Hayden (Taurus; born John Hamilton, Aquarius)

Susan Hayward (Jupiter; born Edythe Marriner, Uranus)

Peewee Herman (Jupiter; born Paul Reubens, Aquarius)

Englebert Humperdink (Aquarius; born Arnold Dorsey, Capricorn)

Kim Hunter (Uranus; born Janet Cole, Taurus)

Tab Hunter (Mercury; Note: 2 sources born (1) Arthur Kelm, Mars OR born (2) Art
        Gelian, Mars)

Ice Cube (Jupiter; born O'Shea Jackson, Sagittarius)

Buck Jones (Mars; born Charles Frederick Gebhart, Venus)

Jennifer Jones (Capricorn; born Phyllis Isley, Jupiter)

Danny Kaye (Sagittarius; born David Daniel Kaminsky, Aquarius)

Patsy Kelly (Saturn; born Briget Veronica, Uranus)

Larry King (Virgo; born Laurence Harvy Zieger, Pisces)

Ted Knight (Cancer; born Tadeus Wladyslaw Konopka, Uranus)

Dorothy Lamour (Capricorn; Note: 2 sources born (1) Mary Dorothy Stanton, Aries
        OR born Dorothy Kaumeyer, Neptune)

Mario Lanza (Taurus; born Alfred Arnold Cocozza, Saturn)

Jack La Rue (Taurus; born Gaspar Biondolillo, Mars)

Queen Latifah (Libra; born Dana Owens, Uranus)

Piper Laurie (Venus; born Rosetta Jacobs, Saturn)

Bruce Lee (Pisces; born Lee Yeun Kam, Uranus)

Peggy Lee (Venus; born Deloris Egstrom, Aquarius)

Hal Linden (Capricorn; born Harold Lipshitz, Neptune)

Jack Lord (Aries; Note: 2 sources born John J.P. Ryan, Libra OR born John Joseph
        Ryan (Aquarius)

Guy Madison (Gemini; born Robert Moseley, Taurus)

Jayne Mansfield (Venus; born Vera Jane Palmer, Scorpio)

Frederic March (Capricorn; born Ernest Prederick McIntyre Becket, (Capricorn)

Margo (Capricorn; born Maria Marguerita Guadalupe Boldaoy-Castilla, Uranus)

Dina Merrill (Scorpio; born Nedinia Hutton, Sagittarius)

Ray Milland (Mars; born Reginald Truscott Jones, Saturn)

Yves Montand (Aquarius; born Ivo Levi, Neptune)

Demi Moore (Libra; born Demetria Guynes, Aries)

Rita Moreno (Neptune; born Rosito Alverio, Sagittarius)

Michelle Morgan (Capricorn; born Simone Roussel, Aquarius)

Mike Nichols (Libra; born Michael Igor Peschowsky, Venus)

Chuck Norris (Neptune; born Charles Ray Norris, Venus)

Sheree North (Scorpio; born Dawn Bethel, Aries)

Tony Randall (Aquarius; born Leonard Rosenberg, Mars)

Edward G. Robinson (Pisces; born Emmaunuel Goldenberg, Aquarius)

Sugar Ray Robinson (Saturn; born Walker Smith, Aquarius)

Ginger Rogers (Jupiter; born Virginia Katherine McMath, Mars)

Meg Ryan (Pisces; born Margaret Hyra, Sagittarius)

John Saxon (Sagittarius; born Carmen Orrico, Aries)

Lizabeth Scott (Pisces; born Emma Matzo, Uranus)

Jane Seymour (Scorpio; born Joyce Frankenberg, Neptune)

Omar Sharif (Capricorn; born Michael Omar Shaloub, Uranus)

Ann Sheridan (Virgo; born Clara Lou, Mars)

Simone Signoret (Uranus; born Simon-Henriette Charolette Kaminker, Pisces)

Ann Southern (Libra; born Harriet Lake, Sagittarius)

Sissy Spacek (Taurus; born Mary Elizabeth, Taurus)

Connie Stevens (Neptune; born Concetta Ann Ingolia, Gemini)

Martha Stewart (Venus; born Martha Kostyra Stewart, Virgo)

Gloria Swanson (Neptune; born Josephine May Swenson, Pisces)

Robert Taylor (Aries; born Spangler Arlington Brugh, Uranus)

Danny Thomas (Scorpio, born Amos Jacobs, Scorpio)

Tiny Tim (Virgo; born Herbert Khaury, Pisces)

Rip Torn (Neptune; born Elmore Raul Torn, Jr., Jupiter)

Steven Tyler (Sagittarius; born Steven Tallarico, Gemini)

Mamie Van Doren (Jupiter; born Joan Lucille Alander, Aries)

Stevie Wonder (Capricorn; born Stevland Morris, Taurus)

Keenan Wynn (Aries; born Francis Xavier Aloysius James-Jeremiah Leopold, Neptune)

Gig Young (Neptune; born Byron Barr, Venus)

CHAPTER FOURTEEN

MIXED VIBRATIONS,
SAME NAME AS SUN SIGN,
CAN'T GET AWAY FROM NAME VIBRATION,
LIST (FAMOUS PEOPLE)

An example of how one person can have many name vibration and <u>use them all</u> is the following: Richard Milhous Nixon vibrates to Neptune (promoting, idealism, lies, deception, corruption). Richard M. Nixon (Uranus) and President Richard Nixon (Aquarius) have the same vibration (Aquarius is ruled by Uranus); thus, attracting the unexpected, new ideals, reform, resignation (all Aquarius and Uranus traits). The name Nixon vibrates to Saturn (ambition, diplomacy, evasiveness, shrewdness, secretiveness, selfishness and a desire to use others to gain one's own advantage). His Sun sign is Capricorn and since Capricorn is ruled by Saturn, this reinforces the preceding Saturn traits. Richard Nixon vibrates to Venus (peace, contentment, charm, kindness, love, social affairs); which is the mental remedy that should be used when Saturn's negative side is expressed.

Jackie was christened Jacqueline Lee Bouvier (Aquarius) and when this name was used she would be magnetic (Aquarius), freedom-loving (Aquarius) and desirous of doing her own thing (Aquarius). As a photographer/reporter, she used the name Jacqueline Bouvier (Taurus) and met John F. Kennedy. Some typical Taurus and Libra traits are good manners, a desire to socialize, entertain and an attraction to art, beauty, jewelry, clothes and expensive items. (Note: Taurus is practical, whereas Libra is not.)

As Jackie Kennedy (Libra) she was lucky, spoiled (Libra) and lived in the lap of luxury (Libra). She was known for her wardrobe (Libra), hairdo (Libra), and extravagance with money (Libra). When she is called "Jackie" or Jacqueline Kennedy (both Pisces names) she tends to be pleasant, emotional, timid, lazy and could be an actress with the status of a star. She received top billing as "Jackie" on the headlines of newspapers all over the world.

The name Jacqueline Bouvier Kennedy vibrates to Jupiter; some typical traits of Jupiter are opulence, wealth, big spending sprees, high aspirations, an interest in religion, and friendliness. As Jackie Onassis and Jackie Kennedy she vibrated to the sign Capricorn. Some typical Capricorn traits are: ambition, covetousness, greed, shrewdness, indifference, coldness, responsibility, practicality and dependable. If she used Jacqueline Kennedy Onassis she vibrated to Taurus, the same as when she used Jacqueline Bouvier.

When she used Jacqueline Onassis she vibrated to Gemini, the sign which represents change, uncertainty, communication, variety and multiple personalities. With all of these names, Jackie had many sides to her nature, and this can be confusing; but at least she didn't get bored with all of these many names.

As Jamie Lee or Jamie Lee Curtis, she vibrates to Sagittarius, the same sign as her Sun sign. It's the lucky sign that keeps one optimistic, confident, happy and contented. If she uses Jamie Leigh, a Taurus vibration, she is charming and quiet and not as outgoing as with the Sagittarian vibration. However, Taurus gives stability and makes one stubborn, whereas, Sagittarius is adaptable and restless.

She was Roseanne Barr, an Aries vibration; temperamental, aggressive, gutsy, energetic and enterprising. When she uses Roseanne, a Saturn vibration, she is stable, ambitious and practical. As Roseanne Arnold, a Uranus vibration, she was unpredictable, erratic, high strung, inventive, talkative and her world was always turned upside down. No wonder! Her ex-husband, Tom Arnold's name vibration is also Uranus!

Dr. Ruth, vibrates to Taurus, a quiet and sensual sign interested in love and romance. Also, Taurus tends to influence one to be stubborn, persevering and practical. Her birth name, Karola Ruth Siegal vibrates to the ambitious sign of Capricorn. If she uses Karola Ruth Siegal Westheimer, she vibrates to sensitive Pisces. Most of the time she uses Dr. Ruth Westheimer which vibrates to Aquarius, the sign which rules psychology, intuition, independence, unconventional behavior, such as kinky sex (she believes couples should do what both consent to) and the unpredictable. Radical changes can take place, disruptions and cancellations occur, and she can talk openly and shock people with her words and unusual voice.

Dr. Benjamin Spock, (Mars; aggressive, courageous, fast action, and pioneering), was born Benjamin Mc Lane Spock, (Libra; the sign of socializing, love, taking the easy way out and charming everyone). Benjamin Spock, (Uranus; controversial, interested in the new and different and dares to do things his way. Reform can come about when one uses this planet's energy). He is known as Dr. Spock, (Mercury; change, ideas, writing and communication). The books (Mercury) he wrote (Mercury) on child care revolutionized (Uranus) the raising of children. He gave freedom (Uranus) to the child and took away spanking (Mars).

Dr. Jonas Edward Salk, is an Aquarian vibration and "Salk", also, is an Aquarian vibration. As a microbiologist, he developed (Aquarius) a vaccine against polio (Aquarius; all types of paralysis are ruled by either Aquarius or Uranus). His name, Dr. Salk, vibrates to serious, ambitious, persevering and hard-working Saturn. The words, "salk vaccine," add to Mercury, planet of change and news.

Jesse, "The Body" Ventura, a former wrestler, vibrates to Neptune, planet of promoting, and wanting ideal and better conditions for mankind. "The Body," and "Jesse Ventura," vibrate to Uranus, the planet of reform, independence, and being interested in changing the laws and setting new precedents. Now that he is known as Governor Jesse Ventura, he vibrates to the same name vibrations as he used as a wrestler---Neptune. Promises can be made under the influence of Neptune...promises to make this a better world. His Sun sign is Cancer so, most likely, he'll keep his word.

Henry Kissinger, a Uranus vibration, is a U.S. foreign policy adviser.

Under the Uranus influence, he could be magnetic, a genius, unpredictable, intuitive, independent and have an innate understanding of human nature. When he is called, "Kissinger," he vibrates to confident, optimistic, honest and outgoing Sagittarius. His birth name, Henry Alfred Kissinger, vibrates to Venus the planet of charm, socializing and good manners.

When he used John Fitzgerald Kennedy, Sr., he vibrated to the ambitious sign of Capricorn. As John F. Kennedy, he vibrated to Neptune, the planet of idealism, wanting peace for mankind, believing in his ideas, promises, also Neptune can be excesses such as with romance, infidelity and attracting schemes. President John F. Kennedy vibrated to Uranus, the planet of reform, freedom, having ideas that are ahead of the times, and daring to march to the beat of a different drummer. Uranus is the planet of the unpredictable, doing things on the spur of the moment, cancellations, changes of plans, it and charisma. His assassination occurred suddenly (Uranus) and unexpectedly (Uranus).

Abraham Lincoln (an Aquarius name and Sun sign) was known for his revolts (Aquarius), freedom-loving beliefs (Aquarius), reform (Aquarius) and humanitarianism (Aquarius). He had been a lawyer and opposed (Aquarius) slavery. He freed (Aquarius) the slaves. When he was called, "Lincoln," he vibrated to Gemini, the sign of communication, ideas, changes, education and adaptability. As Abe Lincoln, he vibrated to Mars which can make one gutsy, impatient, enterprising--the planet that rules war and leadership. It, also, on the negative side is involved in assassination. John Wilkes Booth (Pisces; acting, imaginative, idealistic, unrealistic and emoting dramatically--visions of grandeur can occur) came from a family of actors (Pisces) and assassinated Lincoln in a theatre (Pisces).

He was born Winston Leonard Spencer Churchill (Neptune) which could make him idealistic. As Sir Winston Leonard Spencer Churchill he vibrated to Gemini, and was quite an intellectual (Gemini). However, as Sir Winston Churchill, he vibrated to Jupiter, the planet of wealth, excess (he drank and smoked well into his 90's), confidence and optimism. He was an author (Gemini), statesman (Jupiter), Prime Minister (Jupiter) and was knighted (Jupiter)---Jupiter rules pomp and ceremony.

Anwar Sadat, (Uranus; an interest in the new, reform, and humanitarism.) He was born Muhammad Anwar el-Sadat (Taurus, quiet and charming). As President Anwar Sadat, he vibrated to Neptune, and was a visionary. He made a dramatic (Neptune) visit to Israel to promote (Neptune) peace with Egypt and Israel. Under Neptune's influence, one can be a dreamer. He was assassinated.

As Mohandes K. Gandhi, he vibrated to Pisces, the sign ruled by Neptune; thus, similar traits. He was an Indian politician (the promoting side of politics is Neptune). He was a spiritual (Neptune, Pisces) leader of the home rule movement (Uranus). Mohandas Gandhi (Uranus) was known for being a major figure in gaining India's freedom (Uranus). As Mahatma Gandhi (Cancer--food) he had a vegetarian diet and received publicity for his fasting. Under the name Mohandes Karamchand Gandi (Neptune) he wanted better conditions (Neptune) for his people. He was murdered by a fanatic (Neptune).

Her name Indira Gandi and the combination of her title and birth name, i.e., "Prime Minister Indira Gandi," vibrated to Cancer. She was known for her interest in aiding (Cancer, Aquarius) the needy (Cancer) and getting help for her fellowman (Aquarius, Cancer; Note: Cancer is the sign that wants to mother and protect its people). When she was called Prime Minister of India or Prime Minister of India, Indira Gandhi, she vibrated to Aquarius. Under this sign's influence one is interested in reform new ideas, humanitarism, crusades and setting precedents. On the negative side of Aquarius, one needs to be ready for the unexpected, sudden events, radical people and assassination. Unfortunately, she was killed.

He was born Rafael Leonidas Trujillo Molina (Sagittarius) which could make him confident, optimistic and attract wealth. As Molina Trujillo, a Pisces vibration, he was idealistic and had great dreams of grandeur. When he used Rafael L. Trujillo, he vibrated to Taurus, the sign of being stubborn, persevering, making the social scene and charming others. He was known as "Trujillo," (Aquarius, the sign of independence, reform, revolutions, abruptness, rebellion and being unpredictable, erratic or contrary and opinionated. His policies (Aquarius) brought (Aquarius) some social (Taurus) and economic (Taurus, Sagittarius) progress (Aquarius), but his tyranny led to his assassination.

THE NAME SIGN IS THE SAME AS YOUR SUN SIGN

If you wish to stimulate and emphasize your Sun sign traits, you will reinforce them with additional energy by having your name and Sun sign vibrate to the same sign. An example of this is the case of Elizabeth Barrett Browning, the poetess: among other things, the sign Pisces rules poetry; thus, with her name sign vibrating to Pisces the energy to write poetry inspired by her Sun sign was reinforced.

FAMOUS PEOPLE WHOSE SUN SIGNS IS THE
SAME AS THEIR NAME SIGN

Aries Sun and Aries name: Hugh Hefner, David Letterman, Loretta Lynn,
Williard Scott, Spencer Tracy
Taurus Sun and Taurus name: Jay Leno, Shirley Temple, Pia Zadora
Gemini Sun and Gemini name: Richard Loeb, Duchess of Windsor
Cancer Sun and Cancer name: None known at this time
Leo Sun and Leo name: Carroll O'Connor
Virgo Sun and Virgo name: Peter Falk
Libra Sun and Libra name: Catherine Deneuve, Lillian Gish, Mickey Rooney
Scorpio Sun and Scorpio name: Dick Cavett, Mahalia Jackson, Roy Rogers,
Martin Scorsese

Sagittarius Sun and Sagittarius name: Ludvig von Beethoven, Benjamin
Disraeli, Kirk Douglas, Don Johnson,
Emperor Nero, Anna Nicole Smith, David
Suskind, Keifer Sutherland, Cicily Tyson,
Walter Winchell
Capricorn Sun and Capricorn name: Thomas Becket, Dr. Thoms Dooley, John
Edgar Hoover, Margaret O'Brien
Aquarius Sun and Aquarius name: Ernest Borgnine, Princess Caroline, Darwin
and Charles Robert Darwin, King Forouk,
Eva Gabor, Hildegarde, Abraham Lincoln,
Douglas MacArthur, Norman Rockwell,
Babe Ruth, Cybill Shepherd, Oprah Winfrey
Pisces Sun and Pisces name: Elizabeth Barrett Browning, Chopin, Jean Harlow,
Neil Sedaka, Sharon Stone, George Washington

SOME PEOPLE CAN'T SEEM TO GET AWAY
FROM THEIR NAME VIBRATION

It seems like some people, regardless of what they are called, can't seem
to get away from their name vibration. For example: Goethe, Wolfgang von
Goethe and Johann Wolfgang von Goethe all vibrate to Neptune--poetry, drama;
Andrew Wyeth and Andrew Newell Wyeth--Capricorn (ambition and hard work,
which certainly was typical of his life as an artist).

Billy Graham (a Neptune name) was born William Granklin Graham (a
Neptune name) and promoted (Neptune) his evangelistic beliefs (Neptune). Anne
Ford (a Uranus name) married Deane Johnson, but uses Anne Ford Johnson (a
Uranus name)' however, she could escape to another vibration if she used Anne
Johnson (a Sagittarius name).

Two women who are well known, but can't seem to get away from their
Aquarius name vibrations are Lady Bird, also known as Lady Bird Johnson and
Mrs Lyndon B. Johnson; Angie Dickinson, an Aquarian name, who was married
to Burt Bacharach (a Uranus name; she was born Angeline Brown, a Uranus name)
still couldn't escape from the Aquarian/Uranus vibration (Uranus rules Aquarius;
thus, similar traits).

The famous fashion designer Ralph Lauren vibrates to an Aquarian name.
He was born Ralph Lifshitz, also an Aquarian name. Thus, he can use these
Aquarius traits to be original in his designs.

Leopold Stokowski (an Aquarius name) was born Stanislaw Antoni
Boleslowowicz (no wonder he changed his name) which vibrates to Uranus, the
planet which rules Aquarius; thus, giving similar traits of genius.

Prince Philip (a Capricorn name) uses Prince Philip, Duke of Edinburgh
(a Saturn name and title); thus, his ambitions (Capricorn ruled by Saturn) are
satisfied and he attends to his duties (Capricorn, Saturn).

Cat Stevens (a Neptune name) can't escape the name he was born with, Steven Georgio (also, a Neptune name), and in some of his performances (like one at Madison Square Garden in New York City) he sings by candlelight which is representative of romantic and spiritual Neptune traits.

Regardless of the name he uses, they all vibrate to the same sign of Taurus: J. F. K. Jr., John F. Kennedy, Jr. and John Fitzgerald Kennedy, Jr. Taurus is a steady, preserving sign, that plods along and doesn't give up easily. His Sun sign is Sagittarius and can make him restless, adaptable and a jet setter or playboy, he thrives on fun in his personal life. The Taurus name keeps him from "goofing off."

FAMOUS PEOPLE
(WHOSE NAME VIBRATES TO #1--MERCURY)
Jimmy Cagney, Mariah Carey, Jim Carrey, Madame Du Barry, King Edward VIII, Zsa Zsa Gabor, Bishop Pike, Liv Ullman, George Wallace.

FAMOUS PEOPLE
(WHOSE NAME VIBRATES TO #2--VIRGO

Marty Allen, Celine Dion, Peter Falk, Bryant Gumbel, Hirohito, Alger Hiss, Martin Luther King, Jr., Eartha Kitt, Cyndi Lauper, George Michael, Kate Moss, Norman Vincent Peale, Rembrandt, Red Skelton, Steinbeck, Dylan Thomas, Tiny Tim.

FAMOUS PEOPLE
(WHOSE NAME VIBRATES TO #3--LIBRA)
Clara Barton, Lynda Carter, Johnny Cash, Agatha Christie, Jean Costeau, Catherine Deneuve, John Denver, Mike Douglas, Sir Arthur Conan Doyle, Queen Elizabeth II. Erik Estrada, Douglas Fairbanks, Sr., Gerald Ford, Lillian Gish, Jackie Gleason, Cary Grant, John Hancock, Henrik Ibsen, Al Jolson, Jackie Kennedy, Ernie Kovacs, John Lindsay, Lucky Luciano, Harpo Marx, Louis B. Meyer, Bette Midler, Liza Minnelli, Dudley Moore, Mike Nichols, Edgar Allen Poe, Rasputin, Ronald Reagan, Jaclyn Smith, Harriet Beecher Stowe, Dennis Weaver.

FAMOUS PEOPLE
(WHOSE NAME VIBRATES TO #4--SCORPIO)
Steve Allen, Herb Alpert, Susan Anton, Angela Bassett, Bernard Baruch, Maria Callas, James Cameron, Amy Carter, Dick Cavett, Confucius, Pablo Cruise, Cecil B. DeMille, Marion Davies, Sammy Davis, Jr, Marquis de Sade, Neil Diamond, Havelock Ellis, Peter Fonda, Joe Franklin, Robin Givens, Larry Hagman, Valerie Harper, Billie Holiday, Oliver Wendell Hollmes, Rachel Hunter, Chet Huntley, Mahalia Jackson, Jesse James, Bruce Jenner, Diane Keaton, Shari Lewis, Guy Lonbardo, Melba Moore, Isaac Newton, Florence Nightingale, Gregory Peck,

Juan Peron, Jon Peters, Charley Pride, Victoria Principal, Emilio Pucci, Rachmaninov, Oliver Reed, Roy Rogers, George Romney, Jane Seymour, Casey Stengel, Danny Thomas, Leslie Uggams, Lindsay Wagner.

FAMOUS PEOPLE
(WHOSE NAME VIBRATES TO #5--JUPITER)

Anastasia, Grand Duchess of Russia, Spiro Agnew, Marc Antony, Desi Arnaz, Jr., Benedict Arnold, Annette Bening, Benji, Milton Berle, Fanny Brice, Yul Brynner, Sandra Bullock, Richard E. Byrd, Art Carney, Nell Carter, Sir Winston Churchill, Sean Connery, Robert Culp, Honore De Balzac, Thomas Dooley, Thomas A. Edison, Mia Farrow, Sally Field, Bobby Fisher, Errol Flynn, Elliot Gould, Betty Grable, Rocky Graziano, Dick Gregory, Dorothy Hamill, David Hartman, Susan Hayward, Hussein, King of Jordan, Joan Kennedy, Francis Scott Key, Stephen King, Anne Morrow Lindberg, Franz Liszt, Sandra Locke, Lyle Lovett, Susan Lucct, Ann-Margret, Dean Martin, Mark McGuire, Yehudi Menuhin, Walter Mondale, Philip Mountbatten, Wayne Newton, Marco Polo, Basil Rathbone, Cliff Richard, Ginger Rogers, Brooke Shields, Marlo Thomas, Lily Tomlin, Jules Verne, Earl Warren, Whistler, Walter Whitman ,The Duchess of Windsor, Katarina Witt, James Woods.

FAMOUS PEOPLE
(WHOSE NAME VIBRATES #6--VENUS)

Bella Abzug, Julie Andrews, Beatrice Arthur, George Balenchine, Candice Bergen, Bill Blatty, Dixie Carter, Lillian Carter, Cervantes, Charles the Great, Cher, Cleopatra, Imogene Coca, Nicholas Copernicus, Howard Cosell, Noel Coward, Walt Disney, Tommy Dorsey, Isadora Duncan, Britt Ekland, Glenn Ford, Henry Ford, Sigmund Freud, Garbo, Samuel Goldwyn, Steffi Graff, Alec Guinness, Oscar Hammerstein II, Julie Harris, Rex Harrison, Rita Hayworth, Xaviera Hollander, J. Edgar Hoover, Hedda Hopper, Glenda Jackson, Kate Jackson, Jung, Ernie Kovacs, John Lennon, John L. Lewis, Mayor Lindsay, Sophia Loren, Carol Lynley, Princess Margaret, William Somerset, Maughan, Steve McQueen, Carmen McRae, Lorrie Morgan, Grandma Moses, Gamel Abdul Nasser, Richard Nixon, Rudolf Nureyev, Sir Laurence Oliver, Dr. Linus Pauling, Gearge Peppard, Mary Pickford, Bishop James Pike, Pope John Paul 11, Priscilla Presley, Claude Rains, Lynn Redgrave, Geraldo Rivera, Joan Rivers, Mickey Rooney, Baruch Spinoza, Ruth St. Denis, Isaac Stern, Elizabeth Taylor, Arturo Toscanini, Mao Tse-Tung, Laurie Walters, Senator John Warner, Orville Wright, Daryl F. Zanuck.

FAMOUS PEOPLE
(WHOSE NAME VIBRATES TO #7 — SAGITTARIUS)

Alexander the Great, Benedict Arnold, Mary Astor, Robert Blake, Marlon Brando, Pearl S. Buck, Carol Burnett, George Burns, Julius Caesar, Alexis Carrel,

Tia Carrere, Enrico Caruso, Oleg Cassini, Carol Channing, Maurice Chevalier, George M. Cohan, Gary Coleman, Betty Comden, Courteney Cox, Madam Marie Curie, Charles de Gaulle, Johnny Depp, Benjamin Disreali, Shannen Doherty, Kirk Douglas, Bob Dylan, Clint Eastwood, Mary Baker Eddy, Edison, Duke Ellington, Freud, Dizzy Gillespie, Barry Goldwater, Andy Griffith, David Hasselhoff, Margeaux Hemingway, Angelica Houston, Howard Hughes, Peter Jennings, Joan of Arc, Van Johnson, Grace Jones, Dianne Kay, Danny Kaye, Rudyard Kipling, Kissinger,̈ Calvin Klein, Ann Landers, Lassie, Steve Lawrence, Jack Lemmon, Carole Lombard, Peter Loree, Shirley MacLaine, Barry Manilow, James Mason, Roddy Mc Dowell, David Merrick, Monet, Robert Morse, Wolgang Mozart, Joe Namath, Ramon Navarro, Emperor Nero, Donny Osmond, Marie Osmond, George Pompidou, Sylvia Porter, Mary Quant, Vanessa Redgrave, Le Ann Rimes, Molly Ringwald, Carl Sandburg, Telly Savalas, Steven Seagal, Norma Shearer, Robert Stack, Johann Strauss, Jr., David Susskind, Joan Sutherland, Lana Turner, Cicely Tyson, Ludvig van Beethoven, Vincent Van Gogh, Virgil, Diane Von Furstenberg, Clint Walker, Denzel Washington, Ethel Waters, Walt Whitman, Oscar Wilde, Walter Winchell, Shelley Winters, Joanne Woodward, Brigham Young.

FAMOUS PEOPLE
(WHOSE NAME VIBRATES TO #8--CAPRICORN)

Paula Abdul, Antonio Banderas, Rona Barrett, Thomas Becket, Beethoven, Yasmine Bleeth, Humphrey Bogart, Toni Baxton, Tom Brokaw, Robert Browning, Richard Burton, Glen Campbell, Billy Carter, Butch Cassidy, Jacques Yves Cousteau, Edgar Cayce, Billy Crystal, Pam Dawber, Charles Dickens, Emily Dickinson, Henry Ford II, Michael J. Fox, David Frost, John H. Glenn Jr., Charles Grodin, Emperor Hirohito, John Edgar Hoover, Aldous Huxley, Caroline Kennedy, Edward M. Kennedy, Rose Kennedy, Nancy Kerrigan, The Aga Khan, Ayatollah Khomeini, Martin Luther King, Sandy Koufax, Lisa Kudrow, Alan Jay Lerner, Chico Marx, Victor Mature, Paul McCartney, Aimee Semple Mcpherson, James Michener, Marilyn Miller, James Monroe, Anthony Newley, Aristotle Onassis, Jackie Kennedy Onassis, Eugene O'Neill, Eugene Ormandy, Mohammed Rexa Pahlavi, Andre Previn, Burt Reynolds, Debbie Reynolds, Jackie Robinson, Richard Rodgers, Will Rogers, Linda Ronstadt, Lillian Roth, Vidal Sassoon, Franz Schubert, Omar Sharif, George Bernard Shaw, Frank Sinatra, Tom Snyder, Mickey Spillane, Barbara Stanwyck, Gloria Steinem, Adlai Stevenson, Jacqueline Susann, Tchaikovsky, Cheryl Tiegs, Leo Tolstoy, Margaret Truman, Ike Turner, Tina Turner, Judith Viorst, Robert Wagner, Jimmie Walker, Barbara Walters, Stevie Wonder, Natalie Wood, Wilbur Wright, Andrew Wyeth, Tammy Wynette, Robert Young.

FAMOUS PEOPLE
(WHOSE NAME VIBRATES TO #9--AQUARIUS)

Hans Christian Anderson, Princess Anne, Marie Antoinette, Neil

Armstrong, Eddy Arnold, Fred Astaire, Johann Sebastian Back, Count Basie. Harry Belafonte, Irving Berlin, Pat Boone, Ernest Borgnine, Anita Bryant, Georges Braque, Luther Burbank, Raymond Burr, Michael Caine, Taylor Caldwell, Diahann Carroll, Jimmy Carter, Prince Charles, Jesus Christ, Jackie Collins, Stephen Collins, Buster Crabbe, Cindy Crawford, Salvador Dali, Darwin, Leonardo da Vinci, John Dean, Claude Debussy, Jack Dempsey, Bo Derek, Thomas E. Dewey, Angie Dickinson, Dillinger, Walter E. Disney Fran Drescher, George Eliot, Christ Everett, Fabian, Alice Faye, Totie Fields, Aretha Franklin, J. Paul Getty, Martha Graham, Edvard Greig, George Harrison, William Randolph Hearst, Hildegarde, Engelbert Humperdink, Hubert H. Humphrey, Jr., Jeremy Irons, Bianca Jagger, Jesus, Elton John, Lyndon B Johnson, Tom Jones, Janis Joplin, Henry J. Kaiser, John Keats, Grace Kelly, Val Kilmer, Coretta King, Nikita S. Khrushchev, Hope Lange, Abraham Lincoln, John V. Lindsay, Liszt, Clare Booth Luce, Douglas Mac Arthur, Louis Malle, Margaret Mead, Edna St. Vincent Millay, Arthur Miller, Moliere, Yves Montand, Sir Isaac Newton, Jack Nicholson, Laurence Olivier, Ari Onassis, Ovid, Dolly Parton, George Patton, Pablo Picasso, Cole Porter, Elvis Presley, Deborah Raffin, Tony Randall, Robert Redford, Christopher Reeves, Nelson Rockefeller, Billy Rose, Norman Rockwell, Diana Ross, Babe Ruth, Jerry Seinfeld, Willie Shoemaker, Neil Simon, Wally Simpson, Bessie Smith, Socrates, Sylvester Stallone, Rod Steiger, Isaac Stern, Jimmy Stewart, Jill St. John, Buffy St. Marie, Leopold Stokowski, Johann Strauss, Sr., Sally Struthers, Sophie Tucker, Kathleen Turner, Jean Claude Van Danme, Verdi, Lawrence Welk, Earl Wilson, Henry Winkler, Emile Zola.

FAMOUS PEOPLE
(WHOSE NAME VIBRATES TO #10--URANUS)

Muhammad Ali, Marian Anderson, Brigette Bardot, Bee Gees, Alexander Graham Bell, Bizet, Johannes Brahms, Eva Braun, David Brinkley, Augustus Caesar, Drew Carey, Dale Carnegie, Princess Caroline, Castro, Miguel De Cervantes, Charlie Chaplin, Charlemagne, Julia Child, Cicero, Dick Clark, George Clooney, Natalie Cole, Christopher Columbus, Joan Crawford, Bing Crosby, Billy Ray Cyrus, Dante, Darwin, Robert De Niro, Sandy Dennis, Phyllis Diller, Joe Di Maggio, Fats Domino, The Duke of Edinburgh, Albert Einstein, Douglas Fairbanks, Jr., King Farouk, Henry Fonda, Jane Fonda, Anne Ford, Betty Ford, Charlotte Ford, Dennis Franz, Mohandas Gandhi, Edyie Gorme, Edith Head, O. Henry, Alfred Hitchcock, Adolph Hitler, Dustin Hoffman, Harry Houdini, Rock Hudson, Victor Hugo, Burl Ives, Harry James, James Earl Jones, Boris Karloff, Bob Keesham, Helen Keller, John F. Kennedy, Dr. Alfred Kinsey, Henry Kissinger, Ted Koppel, Gene Krupa, Kruschev, Ricky Lake, Gypsy Rose Lee, Charles Lindbergh, Jack London, Huey P. Long, Henry Wadsworth Longfellow, Linda Lovelace, Norman Mailer, Groucho Marx, Walter Matthau, Margaret Mead, Martha Mitchell, Claude Monet, Marilyn Monroe, Lola Montez, Nero, Richard M.

Nixon, Tony Orlando, Al Pacino, Edith Piaf, Pucci, Nelson A Rockerfeller, Rodin, Franklin D. Roosevelt, Dean Rusk, Anwar Sadat, Tito Schipa, Jimmy Smits, Benjamin Spock, Josef Strauss, Stravinsky, Mary Stuart, Ed Sullivan, Donna Summer, Tutankhamun, Dick Van Patten, Queen Victoria, Daniel Webster, Mae West, James Whistler, Martine Van Hamel, Florenz Ziegfield.

FAMOUS PEOPLE
(WHOSE NAME VIBRATES TO #11--NEPTUNE)

Bella Abzug, Jane Addams, Anastasia, Anne Bancroft, Tallulah Bankhead, Charles Barkley, John Barrymore, Mikhail Baryshnikov, Warren Beatty, Ingmar Bergman, Ingrid Bergman, Georges Bizet, Brian Boitano, Carrie Jacobs Bond, Brahms, Pierre Cardin, Hoagy Carmichael, Andrew Carnegie, Lewis Carroll, Johnny Carson, Paddy Chayefsky, Chopin, Nat King Cole, Perry Como, Gary Cooper, Kevin Costner, Emile Coue, Patrick Duffy, Oliver Cromwell, Macaulay Culkin, James Dean, Christian Dior, Placido Domingo, Sam Donaldson, John Foster Dulles, Jimmy Durante, Amelia Earhart, Blake Edwards, King Farouk I, Stephen Collins Foster, James Franciscus, George Gershwin, Vince Gill, Goethe, Princes Grace of Monaco, Billy Graham, Sheila Graham, Erin Gray, Zane Grey, Melanie Griffith, James R. Hoffa, Jenny Jones, Christine Jorgensen, Franz Joseph, Chiang Kai-shek, Jerome Kern, Billie Jean King, Gladys Knight, Kris Kristofferson, Jack La Lanne, Timothy Leary, Jerry Lewis, Little Richard, Huey Long, Traci Lords, James Madison, Charles Manson, Marcel Marceau, Jenny McCarthy, Reba McEntire, Marilyn Monroe, Zero Mostel, Jack Nicklaus, Brigitte Nielson, David Niven, Jennifer O'Neill, Bert Parks, Michelle Pfeiffer, Sidney Poitier, Dan Rather, Rex Reed, Harold Robbins, Oral Roberts, Auguste Rodin, Tokyo Rose, President Anwar Sadat, George Sand, Carl Sandburg, Albert Schweitzer, George C. Scott, Sir Walter Scott, Tom Selleck, Carly Simon, Suzanne Somers, Richard Speck, Cat Stevens, Barbara Streisand, Gloria Swanson, Alfred Lord Tennyson, Peter Ustinov, Pancho Villa, Voltaire, Cornelia Wallace, Andy Warhol, Richard Widmark, Hank Williams, Kit Williams, The Duke of Windsor, Jane Wyman.

FAMOUS PEOPLE
(WHOSE NAME VIBRATES TO #12--PISCES)

Louisa May Alcott, Susan B. Anthony, Aristotle, Bach, Francis Bacon Ethel Barrymore, Sarah Bernhardt, Bill Blass, John Wilkes Booth, Pat Boone, Elizabeth Barrett Browning, Admiral Richard E. Byrd, Caruso, Cezanne, Paul Cezanne, Colette, Sir Noel Coward, John Derek, John Dillinger, Phil Donahue, Dr. Thomas Dooley, Faye Dunaway, Ralph Waldo Emerson, Gloria Estefan, Roberta Flack, Mohandas K. Gandhi, Greta Garbo, Ava Gardner, Uri Geller, Givenchy, Al Gore, Amy Grant, Dag Hammarskjold, Daryl Hannah, Jean Harlow, Katherine Hepburn, John W. Hinckley, Jr., Bob Hope, Harry Karl, Jacqueline Kennedy, Robert F. Kennedy, Aga Khan, Liberace, Charles A. Lindbergh, Lorenzo Lamas,

Charles Luciano, Malcolm X, Barbara Mandrell, Karl Marx, Matisse, Willy Mays, Clayton Moore, Mary Tyler Moore, Benito Mussolini, Emperor Napoleon I, Ogden Nash, Vaslav Nijinsky, Kim Novack, Rosie O'Donnell, Ryan O'Neal, Peter O'Toole, Estelle Parsons, Louella Parsons, Freddie Prinze, Otto Preminger, Prince Rainer, Diana Rigg, John Ritter, Edward G. Robinson, Kenny Rogers, Steve Rossi, Dr. Laura Schlessinger, Ricky Schroder, Neil Sedaka, Monica Seles, Peter Sellers, Beverly Sills, Jean Simmons, Wesley Snipes, Ringo Starr, James Stewart, Yves St. Laurent, Mary Stuart, Queen of Scotts, Harry S. Truman, Robert Urich, Giuseppe Verdi, George Washington, John Wayne, Robin Williams, Kate Winslet, Loretta Young.

FAMOUS PEOPLE
(WHOSE NAME VIBRATES TO #13— ARIES)

Kristie Alley, Billie the Kid, Napoleon Bonaparte, Debby Boone, Sid Caesar, James Cagney, Truman Capote, Fidel Castro, Coco Chanel, Frederic Chopin, Julie Christie, Davy Crockett, Walter Cronkite, Jeane Dixon, Madam du Pompadour, Cristina Ford, Judy Garland, Kelsey Grammer, Halston, Mata Hari, Averell Harriman, Hugh Hefner, Ernest Hemingway, Hippocrates, Hitler, Hussein, Ethel, Robert and Ted Kennedy, Cheryl Ladd, Hedy Lamarr, Burt Lancaster, Vivian Leigh, Loretta Lynn, Norman Mailer, Edgar Dean Mitchell, Robert Mitchum, Moses, Bess Myerson, Ralph Nader, Nostradamus, Lois Pasteur, Eva Peron, Carlo Ponti, Giacomo Puccini, Renoir, Franklin Delano Roosevelt, Arthur Rubinstein, George Segal, Mack Sennett, Sirhan Sirhan, Stephen Sondheim, Gertrude Stein, Robert Taylor, Henry David Thoreau, Henri de Toulouse-Lautrec, Spencer Tracy, John Travolta, Rudolph Valentino, Shirley Verrett, Raquel Welch, H. G. Wells, Orson Welles, Tammy Wynnette.

FAMOUS PEOPLE
(WHOSE NAMES VIBRATE TO #14— TAURUS)

Bud Abbott, Elizabeth Arden, Pearl Bailey, Faith Baldwin, Lucille Ball, P.T. Barnum, Leonard Bernstein, Halle Berry, Caesar, Al Capone, Richard Chamberlain, Lou Costello, Doris Day, Marlene Dietrich, Dwight D. Eisenhower, Lola Falana, W. C. Fields, Harrison Ford, Clark Gable, Galileo, Patty Hearst, Victor Herbert, Lena Horne, Houdini, Betty Hutton, Thomas Jefferson, Franz Joseph, Emperor of Austria, Carl Jung, Joseph P. Kennedy, Napoleon, Jacqueline Kennedy Onasis, Bob Newhart, Newton, Luciano Pavarotti, Roberta Peters, Plato, Ptolemy, Sergei Rachmaninov, Sir Walter Raleigh, Rubens, Rosalind Russell, Salome, Norton Simon, Spinoza, Joseph Stalin, John Steinbeck, Igor Stravinsky, Shirley Temple, Rafael L. Trujillo, Rembrant Van Rijn, Ben Vereen, Vergil, Trisha Yearwood.

FAMOUS PEOPLE
(WHOSE NAME VIBRATES TO #15--SATURN)

Woody Allen, Maxwell Anderson, Louis Armstrong, Jack Benny, Bob Beattie, Van Cliburn, Jimmy Connors, Bill Cosby, Joseph Cotten, Adelle Davis Angela Davis, Arthur Conan Doyle, Federico Fellini, Jennifer Flavin, Redd Foxx, Benjamin Franklin, Annette Funicello, Richard Gere, Mel Gibson, Princess Grace, Ulysses S. Grant, D. W. Griffith, Mick Jagger, Paul Klee, Evel Knieval, Ali Mac Graw, Meat 'Loaf, Philip Mountbatten, the Duke of Edinburgh, 'Joe Namath, Napoleon I, Nixon, Helen Reddy, Lillian Russell, Dinah Shore, William Shakespeare, Steven Spielberg, Benedict Spinoza, Dick Van Dyke, Vanna White, Thornton Wilder, Frank Lloyd Wright.

FAMOUS PERSONALITIES
(WHOSE NAME VIBRATES TO #16--MARS)

F. Lee Bailey, Alan Bates, Dr. Joyce Brothers, Nigel Bruce, Delta Burke, Rosalynn Carter, Frank Costello, Criswell, Elizabeth Dole, James Doolittle, Linda Evans, Gunther Gebel-Williams, Louis Gossett, Adolph Green, Goldie Hawn, Patricia Hearst, Abe Lincoln, Julia Louis-Dreyfus, Charles 'Lucky" Luciano, Kristy McNichol, Zubin Mehta, Mozart, Picasso, Puccini, Paul Revere, Rimsky-Korsakov, Elizabeth Bayley Seton (Mother Seton), Dr. Benjamin Spock, Leon Trotsky, Liv Tyler.

FAMOUS PEOPLE
(WHOSE NAME VIBRATES TO #17--GEMINI)

Ray Bolger, Patsy Cline, Winston Churchill, Rodney Dangerfield, Bette Davis, Patty Duke, Eddie Fisher, Helen Hayes, Charleton Heston, Genghis Kan, Lincoln, Richard Loeb, Peter Max, Paul Newman, Jacqueline Onassis, Shah Mohammed Reza Pahlavi, Floyd Peterson, Jason Priestly, Dr. Albert Schweitzer, John Philip Sousa, Tolstoy, Mark Twain, Tennessee Williams, Ephrem Zimbalist, Jr.

FAMOUS PEOPLE
(WHOSE NAME VIBRATES TO #18— CANCER)

Daniel Boone, Indira Gandhi, Mahatma Gandhi, Jack Jones, Rush Limbaugh, Michelangelo, Ann Miller, Yoko Ono, Claudius Ptolemaeus, Theodore Roosevelt, George Westinghouse.

FAMOUS PEOPLE
(WHOSE NAME VIBRATES TO #19 --LEO)

Carroll O'Connor, F. Scott Fitzgerald, Larry Fortensky

FAMOUS PEOPLE
(WHOSE NAME VIBRATES TO #20--THE MOON)

Comte Donatien Alphonse Francoise de Sade

FAMOUS PEOPLE
(WHOSE NAME VIBRATES TO #21--THE SUN)

At this time, there are none known to the author. Refer to Chapter Three as to why this number (21) is difficult to obtain. Possibly due to this , there aren't any celebrities with a Sun name vibration.

FAMOUS PEOPLE
(WHOSE NAME VIBRATES TO #22--PLUTO)

At this time, there are none known to the author.

www.ingramcontent.com/pod-product-compliance
Lightning Source LLC
Chambersburg PA
CBHW080516090426
42734CB00015B/3079